IBN KHALDŪN
AN ESSAY IN REINTERPRETATION

IBN KHALDŪN
AN ESSAY IN REINTERPRETATION

Aziz Al-Azmeh

CEU PRESS

Central European University Press

First published as
Ibn Khaldūn, An Essay in Reinterpretation
in 1982 by *Frank Cass*

This edition published in 2003 by
Central European University Press

An imprint of the
Central European University Share Company
Nádor utca 11, H-1051 Budapest, Hungary
Tel: +36-1-327-3138 or 327-3000
Fax: +36-1-327-3183
E-mail: ceupress@ceu.hu
Website: www.ceupress.com

400 West 59th Street, New York NY 10019, USA
Tel: +1-212-547-6932
Fax: +1-212-548-4607
E-mail: mgreenwald@sorosny.org

ISBN 963 9241 58 X
ISSN 1587-6470
CEU Medievalia Volume 4

Library of Congress Cataloging-in-Publication Data
Al-Azmeh, Aziz.
Ibn Khaldun : an essay in reinterpretation / Aziz Al-Azmeh.
p. cm.
Originally published: London : Cass, 1982.
Includes bibliographical references and index.
ISBN
1. Ibn Khaldūn, 1332-1406. 2. History--Philosophy. I. Title.
D116.7.I3 A95 2003
907'.202--dc21

2002152316

Printed in Hungary by
Akaprint Kft.

CONTENTS

PREFACE

That the absolute difference introduced by the passage of time between us and past authors is a fact of paramount importance to our evaluation of past discourse is one of the foremost scholarly commonplaces of our epoch. The two great strands of historical conception that prevail in our epoch–history as a continuous evolutive process, and history as the succession in time of abiding structures–disagree on everything but that history labours to produce difference. Yet despite explicit general assent, the past is often detemporalized in actual historical practice. This was noted by Arnaldo Momigliano in a lecture on *Polybius between the English and the Turks* (J. L. Myers Memorial Lecture, Oxford [1974], p. 13): 'We must be free to ask our own questions, to build our own models of the past and make our own evaluation of it. This means that we can no longer accept Herodotus, Thucydides, Xenophon, Polybius, Tacitus and Ammianus as guides to their respective periods. We must measure the exact size of even the greatest of our predecessors; we must understand from what point of view and with what limitations he wrote; and we must ultimately subordinate him to us ...'

Ibn Khaldūn has proved to be what is perhaps the great predecessor most resistant to this act of subordination. Not only is he considered the true historical source of his time; he is also taken as the unchallenged sociological and cultural interpreter of medieval North Africa and much of medieval and modern Arab-Islamic culture as well. The validity of his discourse is considered to be so universal as to confer upon his ideas the status of progenitor–or, at the very least, anticipator–of a great variety of modern ideas. So unassailable has this position occupied by Ibn Khaldūn's thought been that the general accepted description of his thought has gone unchallenged even by scholars who took to criticizing the undue modernization of his writings. Even these scholars have accepted what is in fact an ahistorical description of Ibn Khaldūn's historical and 'sociological' methods and conceptions.

I have studied this Ibn Khaldūn vulgate in detail in another book. And it was in my *Ibn Khaldūn in Modern Scholarship* that I addressed topics which have so far been considered paradigmatic in Ibn Khaldūn scholarship. I showed that such topics, dictated by the manifest content of Ibn Khaldūn's text and by the orientalist, evolutionist, and positivist myths of our time, are not truly germane to the study of Ibn Khaldūn or of his culture. What has hitherto been considered axial to the study of Ibn Khaldūn–his supposed sociology, the 'incompatibility' between reason and belief as the animating centre of the *Muqaddima*, the scientificity of his historiography, and cognate topics of the imagination–are only touched upon in this book in so far as such topical proximity is justified by our attempt to subordinate Ibn Khaldūn to history: to historical study as the study of difference rather than of similarity. One specification in the realm of difference is, however, called for. The difference of Ibn Khaldūn is the real determinate difference of his bygone culture, not the difference of a spurious orient from an occidental touchstone. The subordination of Ibn Khaldūn is a subordination to the real requirements of history as articulated by and specified in the parameters of his culture.

The historical approach which we might broadly call anthropological and which is adopted in the present essay makes no claims to novelty in method. What is thoroughly novel is the consistent application of the common patrimony of modern historical sciences to oriental material without the intrusion of the mythological patrimony of orientalist categories. As such, this book claims membership of an emergent class of writings which seek to reconstitute all aspects of the Arab-Islamic past in a manner unfettered by the dead weight of received orientalist (or fundamentalist) scholarship.

It is precisely given the situation of this book that it is not conceived in monographic terms. It is considered imperative for the more general enterprise within which this book is embedded that principles for the direction of monographic work should be formulated in order to avoid their implicit direction by implicit ideologies and mythologies. This applies not only to the work of Ibn Khaldūn. The *tabula rasa* presented by the reconsideration of the 'state of the field' of Ibn Khalduniana extends to–and is informed by–the 'state of the field' of Arab-Islamic cultural history, with its perspectives limited in scope as well as in orientation by considerations of the type just mentioned. Thus interpretations had to be made of exegetical logic, of the common conceptual patrimony of astrology, alchemy, medicine, and other natural sciences, as well as of notions of historical significance, of temporality, of historical criticism, and of much else, without the benefit of monographic illumination from previous work except to the most limited degree. And such interpretations were vital for the reconstitution of Ibn Khaldūn's discourse and of the historicity of this discourse.

Thus the present work is an essay. But its status as essay does not imply that it is tentative; though it might not be quite definitive, it is yet very definite in its interpretive orientations. It starts with a biographical note which does not aspire to more than contribute to the didactic aspect of this book's task by providing the reader with some spatial and temporal orientations, without pretending to dabble into the uselessnesses of psychohistory or of the biographical interpretation of ideas. The book then opens with a chapter which analyzes the structure of Ibn Khaldūn's historical discourse in terms of its implicit notions of historical significance, of historical units, and of historical succession, and then demonstrates that it is the conception of the state in its historiographic (and not sociological) physiognomy that dictates the locus around which the *Muqaddima* revolves. The book then goes on to study the structure of the *Muqaddima* in terms of the principles of order that govern the succession of its topics, and analyzes the logic according to which, in real terms, the project of the New Science validates its status as an historical *Organon.*

Throughout, an attempt is made to relate ideas that emerge through the analysis to the semantic fields and the paradigmatic contexts within which their cultural incidence is embedded. And it should be stressed at the outset that the term 'science' is used in the general sense of *Wissenschaft* and denotes every self-consistent system of statements and complementary concepts which cohere under a rubric ('astrology', for instance) which acts as the repository for scientific legitimacy: a science is also a paradigm to which scientific statements have to conform and which is manned by a specialized body of practitioners who conserve its paradigmatic integrity. It is this sense of science that informs the analysis of Ibn Khaldūn's relation to his culture. The presence of Ibn Khaldūn's culture in his work is not conceived in terms of the moribund notion of 'influence' which tries to track the presence of the discrete ideas of discrete individuals in those of others, although one could probably cite such precedents for all Ibn Khaldūn's statements. Rather, this presence is studied in terms of the semantic fields that ideas and terms acquire in the paradigmatic formations where they occur and where they are elaborated.

In this way, the historicity of Ibn Khaldūn's discourse is analyzed in the only real terms available for the inscription of such historicity: the organized structure of high culture which consists of paradigms, and the floating notions of vernacular vision. In this context, the last chapter of this book locates the eclecticism of Ibn Khaldūn and the impossibility of his entire enterprise as illustrated by the immediate impact he made on his contemporaries and others who shared his culture. The consistent utilization of a rational anthropological approach which discounts nothing in the Khaldunic discourse–such as the rational status of irrationality–and which does our great author the courtesy of taking seriously every one of his statements without taking the unfounded liberty of differentiating 'science' from 'fiction', is one which is best designed to historicize not only the discourse of Ibn Khaldūn. It is hoped that it will help indicate perspectives from which scholars could approach, at very long last, the real units that compose Arab–Islamic sciences and Arab–Islamic culture, and the points at which they cohere as an integrated historical unit.

*

I should like to thank all those who suggested I write this book. It is my pleasure to acknowledge 'Ajāj al-Ḥakīm's prompt and faultless drawing of the Diagram.

A. Al-Azmeh

PREFACE TO THE 2003 IMPRESSION

Since this book was published almost exactly twenty years ago, it has gone through one original hardback edition and two paperback editions, and still appears to be in demand at an easy but sure pace. This was itself sufficient ground for a publisher to wish to bring out a new impression. As a new impression rather than a new edition, I have changed very little in the text as originally published, and have not tampered with it, but made only slight emendations here and there, mainly by way of correcting typographical errors and making very slight additions to the endnotes. I have also appended an addendum to the Bibliographical Orientations at the end of the book in which I take note of some work published since.

A number of considerations justified to my eyes bringing out the book yet again as it originally stood. Scholarship on Ibn Khaldūn has not in the intervening years seen significant analytical or historical advances whose cumulative harvest may have caused me to embark upon a labour of revision. I continue for my part to stand by the theses I propounded and the historical and conceptual analyses I presented. The book has with time acquired a certain presence and credibility, and had attracted when originally published both praise and some criticism. I chose not to take this opportunity to answer the latter, as it was of a rather generic and complacent character, and occasionally fretful or peevish, which did not address the book, in general or in matters of detail, in a substantive way that might justify discussion. I was not convinced by the main line of criticism expressed that the rigour and technical nature of analytical distinctions and discussions made within it, 'difficulty' so-called, were in fact a drawback. If the difficulty ascribed to this and to some of my other writings, like difficulty overall, were to be considered as caused by a certain interference between intention and utterance, I am not persuaded that the source of such interference can be sought apart from certain lax and conservative institutional habits of mind. The complexity of the medieval Ibn Khaldūn, and the complexity of his historical and intellectual world, required a commensurate treatment informed by the standard equipement of the social and historical sciences. That these might not tally with formulaic expectations was not my concern.

As a scholar, I have over the past two decades become not only older and hopefully wiser, but also more intensively and extensively read in fields of study that are of relevance to the study and interpretation of Ibn Khaldūn. This has not compelled me to wish to revise the main theses I propounded here as a budding scholar, though it might have enhanced certain detailed discussions. Yet I feel the book stands as it did originally, and I have not seen the vital necessity of attempting the *aggiornamento* of the endnotes by referring to my (and other scholars') work that would have further supported points of detail there sustained. I would now with the lapse of time have written the book somewhat differently. But the main points made will have remained unaltered.

Aziz Al-Azmeh
29 September, 2002

SYMBOLS AND ABBREVIATIONS

Ibn Khaldūn's works

BB *Muqaddimat al-'allāma Ibn Khaldūn* (vocalized edition, Beirut, 1900)

BD *Tarīkh al-'allāma Ibn Khaldūn*, ed. Y. A. Dāghir, 7 vols., Beirut, 1956 ff

L *Lubāb al -muḥaṣṣal fī uṣūl ad-dīn*, ed. L. Rubio, Tetouan, 1952

Q *Les prolegomènes d'Ebn Khaldoun*, ed. E. Quatremère, 3 vols., Paris, 1858

S *Shifā' as-sā'il li-tahdhīb al-masā'il*, ed. M. b. Tāwīt al-Ṭanjī, Istanbul, 1958

T *At-Ta'rīf bi-Ibn Khaldūn wa riḥlatuhu gharban wa sharqan*, ed. M. b. Tawīt al-Ṭanjī, Cairo, 1951

Reference works

EI^2 *Encyclopedia of Islam*, new ed., Leiden-London, 1960 ff

GL A.-M. Goichon, *Lexique de langue philosophique d'Ibn Sīnā*, Paris, 1938

JL F. Jabre, *Essai sur le lexique de Chazali. Contribution à l'étude de la terminologie de Ghazali dans ses principaux ouvrages à l'exception du Tahāfut*, Beirut, 1970

JT Jurjānī, *Kitāb al-Ta'rifāt* (Liber Definitiones), ed. G. Flügel, Leipzig, 1845

LA Ibn Manẓūr, *Lisān al-'Arab*, 20 vols., Būlāq, A. H., 1300 ff

TK Tahānawī, *Kashshāf iṣṭilāḥāt al-funūn*, ed. M. Wajīh, A. Sprenger, and W. Nassau Lees, 2 vols., Calcutta, 1854 ff

ANATOMY OF THE MUQADDIMA: SYSTEMS OF ORDER, CONCEPTUALIZATION, AND RELATION

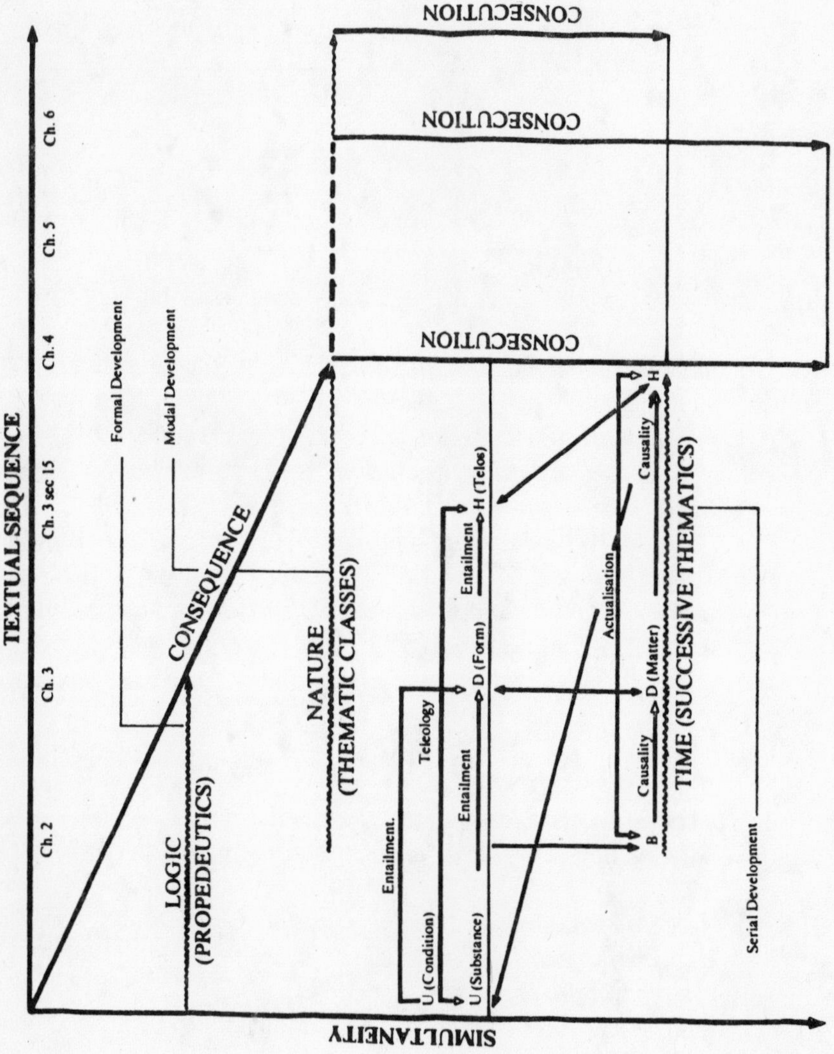

Key:

Axes of textual order:

Principles of conceptual order:

Types of relation:

Transformation of thematic units:

B: *Badāwa*
D: *Daula*
H: *Ḥaḍāra*
U: *ʿUmrān*

BIOGRAPHICAL NOTE

Walī ad-Dīn Abū Zaid ʻAbd ar-Raḥmān b. Muḥammad Ibn Khaldūn al-Ḥaḍramī al-Ishbīlī was born in Tunis in 723/1332 and died in Cairo in 808/1406.[1] He was the scion of a family that claimed descent from a certain Khaldūn, who is supposed to have been a Ḥaḍramī who settled in Seville in the eighth century, a family which in the ninth century formed part of a short-lived patrician despotism in Seville. The family emigrated to Ceuta and shortly thereafter to Tunis, just before the fall of Seville to the Crusaders in 1248, and in North Africa it enjoyed a very warm welcome and joined the established Andalusian expatriate patriciate which was engaged in the higher affairs of state.[2] The Banū Khaldūn themselves had already established close contacts with the Ḥafṣid masters of Tunis ever since Abū Ḥafṣ and his sons ʻAbd al-Wāḥid and Abū Zakarīya were Almohad governors of Seville. The family bond was sealed just over a century before the birth of ʻAbd ar-Raḥmān, when Abū Zakarīya, who was later to proclaim himself sovereign in Tunis, was presented by the Banū Khaldūn with a slave girl who bore him three sons all of whom were to become Ḥafṣid caliphs, Abū Yaḥyā Zakarīya, ʻUmar, and Abū Bakr.

It is little wonder, therefore, that Ibn Khaldūn's grandfathers should have held the chamberlaincy, the finance ministry, and senior military positions. Ibn Khaldūn himself married the daughter of Muḥammad b. al-Ḥakīm, commander of the Ḥafṣid armies. But politics played havoc with the fortunes of the Banū Khaldūn and other Andalusian expatriates in Tunis and, by the time Ibn Khaldūn was born, they no longer seemed to enjoy power, but still had wealth and status, and had recently started acquiring a taste for scholarship.

But by the time Ibn Khaldūn had started growing, the Black Death of 1347/48 had carried away his parents, many of his teachers, and a large proportion of the inhabitants of Tunis. At almost the same point in time, the long established Ḥafṣid order was receiving sustained blows from the upstart Merinids of Fez, and the power of the Zayyānid (ʻAbd al-Wādid) court in Tlemcen was precariously filling in the crevices left by the Ḥafṣid quest for territorial integrity, the Merinid imperialist bid for the unification of the whole of North Africa, the fragmentation of Ḥafṣid territories under different claimants to the throne, and the shifting alliances of the masters of the plains and of the trade routes (the nomadic and semi-nomadic clans of the Banū Hilāl, Banū Sulaim, Banū Tūjīn, and many others). When the Merinid Abul-Ḥasan took Constantine and Tunis almost unopposed and at the invitation of the Ḥafṣid chamberlain and king-maker Ibn Tāfrāghīn in 1347, the whole trend of events in favour of Merinid power was compromised by the battle of Qairawān, in which the armies of Abūl-Ḥasan were routed by the Banū Hilāl in 1348. The result was that Abūl-Ḥasan's son, the great Abū 'Inān, proclaimed himself king in Fez, and Tlemcen, which had fallen to the Merinids shortly before this, reverted to Zayyānid suzerainty, while the Ḥafṣids, now less a dynasty than a family of warring princes, took back control of Tunis, of Bone, of Constantine, and of other cities. Ḥafṣid cities were to fall repeatedly to the Merinids and to others until about 1370, when the internal affairs of the Ḥafṣid clan had achieved a renewed centralized equilibrium.

It was in the midst of this inter-dynastic and intra-dynastic turmoil that Ibn Khaldūn served his political apprenticeship and continued his studies. The political situation was a *force majeure* in more than one sense: it reversed the trend towards an imperial Maghrib,[3] and it simultaneously brought to the fore the contours of 'a new world' about which Ibn Khaldūn was to speak in the *Muqaddima*. And perhaps one manifestation of the rise of upstarts is the decline in the status of patrician individuals. The first public position that Ibn Khaldūn filled was under Ibn Tāfrāghīn's Ḥafṣid regime as *kātib al-'alāma*: he was charged with writing the mark of royal ratification on official correspondence. It was a position that made him privy to secrets of state (for which his status prepared him), but one which he considered too lowly for a person of his background. He therefore made his way westwards, closer to the abode of the upstart Merinids, first to the nearby Merinid Bougie, and then, at royal invitation, to the court of Abū 'Inān in Fez, where he stayed between 1354 and 1362.

His stay in Fez was very eventful. Abū 'Inān threw him into prison in early 1357, having suspected him of courtly treachery, and he was released only upon the king's death 21 months later. Abū 'Inān's successor Abū Sālim appointed Ibn Khaldūn to various senior positions (including supervision over civil law, *maẓālim*) and, upon Abū Sālim's murder in late 1361, Ibn Khaldūn was given safe passage out of Fez on condition he leave the Maghrib altogether. He was welcomed at the Naṣrid court in Granada by the king, Muḥammad V, and his powerful, urbane, and scholarly *wazīr*, Ibn al-Khaṭīb (both of whom Ibn Khaldūn had welcomed as political fugitives from a Granadan *coup d'état* in 1360–1361). He was given sundry duties, including an embassy to Pedro El Cruel in Seville in 1364, but had to leave Granada soon afterwards because of obscure disagreements with Ibn al-Khaṭīb.[4]

In March 1365 Ibn Khaldūn became Chamberlain to the Ḥafṣid prince of Bougie, Abū 'Abd Allāh, who had taken refuge in Fez when our author was still there. Just over a year afterwards, Abū 'Abd Allāh was killed by rebels, and Ibn Khaldūn, to safeguard his life, promptly handed over the city to them. And for the next nine years, he wandered around the central and western Maghrib, recruiting tribal levies and otherwise arranging tribal relations, first on behalf of the Merinids (this period included another spate of residence in Fez), and then, after an unsuccessful flight to Spain (from whence the Merinids sought to extradite him), briefly on behalf of Abū Ḥammū of Tlemcen.

It was in the course of an expedition into Dawāwida tribal territory in the central Maghreb on behalf of the Zayyānids that Ibn Khaldūn first retired to a sūfī shrine, then liberated himself from royal connections and installed himself at Qal'at Ibn Salāma (near the contemporary Tawghzut, close to Mascara, in Algeria) and wrote the *Muqaddima*, which he completed in November 1377. The peregrinations, which one contemporary Merinid courtier attributed to the curse of excessive ambition,[5] were at an end, for a short while at least–long enough for the first yield of his long intellectual gestation to come to fruition.

Ibn Khaldūn unceasingly followed intellectual endeavours. In Tunis he followed a standard, yet very rigorous, educational programme, which included Arabic, the Koran, Tradition, poetry, and law. Much of his teaching seems to have been done privately, some by his own father. His education was to become rather more public when he went to Fez, but it was no less privileged. For there it became a courtly education, Abū 'Inān having gathered at his court the most illustrious scholars of the Maghrib in his age. The king himself taught Ibn Khaldūn the *Ṣaḥīḥ*, of Bukhārī.[6] In Fez Ibn Khaldūn was taught logic, *uṣūl al-fiqh*, theology, philosophy, and the occult sciences (*ta'ālīm, al-funūn al-ḥikmīya wat-ta'allumīya*)–(T, 22, 37). Chief among his teachers was Al-Ābilī, considered an unequalled exponent of the rational sciences and the occult arts.[7] It was as a student of Ābilī's that he composed his epitome of Rāzī's theological compendium, the *Muḥaṣṣal*, and it was on the basis of his learning from Ābilī that, when in Granada, he composed a small logical treatise for the use of the king, an epitome of Ibn al-Khaṭīb's didactic poem on *uṣūl al-fiqh*, a tract on arithmetic, and epitomes of Averroes. It also seems to have been in Granada and through Ibn al-Zayyāt as well as Ibn al-Khaṭīb that he acquired the thorough knowledge of mysticism which he used in composing his polemic, *Shifā' as-sā'il*, which attacks in no uncertain terms the immanationist gnosticism of Ibn 'Arabī and others.[8] There is no reason to disbelieve Ibn Khaldūn's assertion that he was engaged in scholarly activity even when he was Chamberlain of Bougie, where, he says, he received students every afternoon as well as delivering the Friday sermon every week.

It was ostensibly because of his need for library resources that Ibn Khaldūn left Qal'at Ibn Salāma for Tunis at the end of 1378. The four years he was there were spent teaching, as well as fending off political attacks by his older contemporary and rival in scholarship since his early days, Ibn 'Arafa, the Imam of the Zaitūna mosque, and guarding himself against suspicion of intrigue. Indeed, when the Ḥafṣid monarch Abūl-'Abbas left Tunis on an expedition, it was felt expedient not to leave Ibn Khaldūn alone in town but to have him accompany the court. The situation therefore became intolerable, and Ibn Khaldūn had to use the excuse of pilgrimage to Mecca for obtaining royal permission to take to sea and travel eastwards to Alexandria. He was never to return to the Maghrib, but throughout the remaining 24 years of his life, he was never to shed Maghribi dress and don oriental costume.

His arrival in Alexandria coincided with festivities throughout Egypt on the occasion of the accession to the Mamlūk sultanate of Abū Sa'īd Barqūq. It was not long before Ibn Khaldūn established contact with the Mamlūk court and he received his first appointment as grand Mālikī judge in the summer of 1384 an appointment that scandalized Ibn 'Arafa. He was soon relieved, but was reappointed three times subsequently; he died soon after his fourth appointment to the post. He received other appointments in Egypt in the juridico-religious hierarchy, as a professor of Mālikī law and as Superior at the Baibarsīya sūfī lodge (*khanqā*). When out of office, he was ceaselessly active as a teacher of a variety of subjects from the *Muqaddima* to Arabic grammar, and he spent much time completing his main work, the universal history entitled *Kitāb al-'Ibar wa dīwān al-mubtada' wal-khabar fī ayyām al-'Arab wal-'Ajam wal-Barbar was man 'āṣārahum min dhawī as-sulṭān al-akbar* or the Book of Exemplaries and the Record of Narrative and its Principles concerning Arabs, Persians, and Berbers, and those Nations of Great Might contemporary with them, to which the *Muqaddima* is the prolegomenon.[9]

Needless to say, he came into conflict with a variety of people. His activities among the Maghribi community (with whom he was connected in legal and other capacities) produced situations of acute tension (T, 257-8). He was very severe as a judge and this occasioned conflicts, clashes, intrigues, and dismissals. For inevitably, he became party, if not in any major way, to the courtly intrigues of the Mamlūk capital.[10] His legal conduct was the subject of severe criticism by other judges–and, inevitably, rivals.[11] He was once gleefully lampooned by a popular poet when dismissed from office.[12] He was not, in short, an altogether popular person in Cairo although, as one hostile witness admits, he was accused of much that was not true[13]–he was said to have associated with the colourful and flourishing sexual underworld of Cairo, among other things. One particular episode could have compromised him mortally. When in 1389 the Mamlūk prince Minṭāsh proclaimed himself Sultan, Ibn Khaldūn joined other persons from the legal and religious hierarchy in producing a *fatwa* proclaiming the legality of this act. However, Barqūq soon restored himself to power and Ibn Khaldūn was out of favour for a while. His rivals naturally took heart, and especially Rakrākī, another incumbent of the grand Mālikī judgeship.[14] Ibn Khaldūn took this rival so seriously that he forged a *fatwa* attacking Barqūq and attributed it to Rakrākī. This bit of intrigue proved unsuccessful and he was dismissed from the judgeship as a result.[15] It may be worth noting that Rakrākī refused to sign the *fatwa* that Minṭāsh had demanded.

Ibn Khaldūn was to travel three times during his stay in Cairo, twice on pilgrimages to Mecca and Jerusalem, and once to Damascus where he had an historic meeting with Tamerlane.[16] He had to accompany the Sultan Faraj, Barqūq's son and successor, along with the Mamlūk armies to Damascus in late 1399–probably for the same reason that he had to accompany the Ḥafṣid Abūl-'Abbas–and, when the Sultan and his retinue along with much of the army had to hasten back to Cairo as soon as they heard of a conspiracy, he was left alone in Damascus. When the Mongols laid siege, his position with regard to the ways and means of dealing with Tamerlane was the subject for controversy. Ibn Khaldūn says at one point that he feared for his life. The city was finally surrendered against safeguards by Tamerlane for life and property, but no sooner were the gates of the city opened than the population received the treatment for which the Mongols are famous–it may be worth mentioning that Damascenes are to this day sometimes popularly called 'Tamerlane's bastards'. While Damascus burnt, Ibn Khaldūn was comfortably settled in Tamerlane's camp, where he composed for the conqueror a geography of the Maghrib, entered into historical and other conversations with him. and otherwise used his consummate courtliness, spirited grace, and inspired flattery to set himself back on the road to Cairo rather than join the trail of scholars and artisans to Samarqand. On his death six years later, Ibn Khaldūn was buried at the sūfī cemetery which is no longer in evidence.

NOTES

1 The main sources for Ibn Khaldūn's life are, primarily, his autobiography (T), supplemented by the following: (1) the account of Ibn al-Khaṭīb in his Iḥāṭa, reproduced with additions in Maqqarī, *Nafḥ aṭ-Ṭīb min ghuṣn al-Andalus ar-raṭīb*, ed. I. 'Abbās (Beirut, 1968). vol. 6, pp. 171–73, 180–192. This volume also contains the texts of correspondence between Ibn al-Khaṭīb and Ibn Khaldūn, on pp. 173–180 and 389–96; (2) the accounts of Ibn Ḥajar: *Raf' al-'iṣr 'an quḍāt Miṣr* (ed. H. 'Abdul Majīd *et al.*, Cairo, 1957 ff., vol. 2, pp. 343–48), *Inbā' al-ghumr bi abnā' al-'umr* (ed. H. Ḥabashī, Cairo. 1971. vol. 2, pp. 339–40), and *Ad-Durar al-kāmina fī a'yān al-mi' a al-thāmia*, (Hyderabad, 1929 f., 4 vols., *passim*).

2 On the Andalusian patriciate in Tunis. see Q, 2:19–20; R. Brunschvig, *La Berbérie orientale sous les Hafsides* (Paris, 1940 ff.), vol. 1, pp. 50–51; vol. 2, pp. 56–57. 155 ff; D. Latham. 'Towards a Study of Andalusian Immigration and its Place in Tunisian History'. in *Cahiers de Tunisie*. 5 (1957), p. 216 and *passim*.

3 This is the interpretation of A. Laroui, *History of the Maghreb* (Princeton, 1977), pp. 216 ff.

4 Ibn Khaldūn claims that he was getting too powerful and coming too close to the Naṣrid monarch, while Ibn al-Khaṭīb is silent on this matter.

5 Ibn al-Aḥmar, *Mustauda' al-'alāma wa mustabdi' al-'allāma*, ed. M. Turkī Tūnisī and M. Tiṭwānī (Tetouan and Rabat, 1964), pp 64–65.

6 M. B. A. Benchekroun, *La vie intellectuelle marocaine sous les Merinides et les Waṭṭasides* (Rabat, 1974), p 347, citing the *fahrasa* of a certain Majīrī. Ibn Khaldūn makes no mention of this.

7 On Ābilī, see N. Nassar. 'Le maître d'Ibn Khaldūn: Al-Ābilī', in *Studia Islamica*, 20 (1964). pp. 103 ff.

8 Direct borrowing by Ibn Khaldūn in his book on mysticism from Ibn al- Khaṭīb's *Rauḍat at-ta'rif bil-ḥubb al-sharīf* is extensive and very clear; parallels have been pointed out by Tanjī in his introduction to S, pp. 'mr' ff. Ibn Khaldūn's views of mysticism have been the subject of some conflicting opinion which has generally posed the wrong questions on the matter. Ibn Ḥajar contended that Ibn Khaldūn was very hostile to Shī'ism (Sakhāwī, *Aḍ-Ḍau' al-lāmi' li-a'yān al-qarn at-tāsi'*, Cairo, A. H. 1353, vol. 2, pp. 147–48), and this may provide us with a clue. Ibn Khaldūn directs his wrath at the eschatological, messianic, and metaphysical (and their ancillary epistemological) aspects of mysticism, which he sees to be connected with Shī'ism and with the passions of the mob, and it is not far fetched to suggest that it is in this that is grounded Ibn Khaldūn's hostility to the mysticism prevalent in his day in the Maghreb. It should never be forgotten that the issue which prompted the composition of *Shifā' as-sā'il*, the issue of the necessity for a teacher, is closely connected

with issues of mystical education (and hence organization) and with the modalities of control over mystical doctrine and activity, and that this is not far from issues relevant for Ibn Khaldūn in an age rife with messianic movements and expectations. Our author obviously had before him the example of Ibn Qasī who in the twelfth century, proclaimed himself Mahdī and ruled Algarve for some time (see BD, 6:390, 449, 680). On the connections between Shīʿism and ṣūfism, see K. M. Shībī, *Aṣ-ṣila bayn at-taṣawwuf wat-tashayyuʿ*. 2nd ed. (Cairo, 1969).

9 Ibn Khaldūn's activities in Egypt are the topic of a special study: W. J. Fischel, *Ibn Khaldūn in Egypt* (Berkeley and Los Angeles, 1967).

10 The close examination of one episode, in which Ibn Khaldūn hid 20,000 *dīnārs* for a Mamlūk grandee who was being persecuted, may unravel the arcana of Ibn Khaldūn's political affiliations in Cairo. The episode is described in Ibn al-Furāt, *Tārīkh*, ed. Q. Zuraiq and N. ʿIzz ad-Dīn (Beirut, 1936), vol. 9, pp. 435–36, and Ibn Iyās, *Badāʾiʿ az-zuhūr* (Būlāq, A. H. 1311), vol. 1, p. 305.

11 Sakhāwī, *Dau'*, vol. 2, p. 138.

12 *Ibid.*, vol. 2, p. 47

13 *Ibid.*, vol. 4, p. 146.

14 See the notes on Rakrākī in K. Salibi, 'Listes chronologiques des grands cadis de l'Egypte sous les Mameloukes', in *Rev. d'Etudes Islamiques*, 25 (1957), no. 19, p. 113.

15 Ibn Ḥajar, *Raf' al-iṣr*, vol. 2, p. 345.

16 Ibn Khaldūn's description of this meeting has been translated into English with detailed commentary by W. J. Fischel as *Ibn Khaldūn and Tamerlane* (Berkeley and Los Angeles, 1952). See also the eyewitness account of Ibn ʿArabshāh, *ʿAjāʾib al-maqdūr fī akhbār Timūr* (Calcutta. 1881), pp. 210 ff., 439 ff.

CHAPTER ONE

THE PRIMACY OF THE HISTORICAL

Ibn Khaldūn's *Books of Exemplaries (Kitāb al-'Ibar)* is a dissertation on the history of the world. As its subtitle indicates, it treats of historical narrative (*khabar*) concerning Arabs and Berbers, in addition to those people contemporary with them who merit historical significance by their assumption of power. These contemporaries, in effect, amount to all peoples of the world known at the time of our author, with the exception of the Indians and the Chinese, knowledge of whom was, curiously, largely confined to the lore of mythogeography and of fantastic ethnology.[1] The subtitle of the *Book of Exemplaries* (henceforth referred to as the *History*) further informs the reader that the book will also treat of that constituent (*mubtada'*) of which historical narrative is forged. The use of the term *mubtada'* is of course figurative; it denotes generally the grammatical inchoative, and is used by Ibn Khaldūn to indicate a relationship of multiple priorities, logical and ontological, between it and historical narrative, the term for which (*khabar*) also refers to the grammatical predicate. In other words, the *History* is composed of a prolegomenon (*muqaddima*) and of historical narrative proper (*tārīkh*).

The relationship between these two textual units of the *History* is very complex and will be encountered at more than one juncture during the course of this book. In terms of textual content, it must be emphasized here that there is, to the mind of Ibn Khaldūn, an unbroken continuum along which both the prolegomenon to history and history itself are ranged, and this is what we shall for the moment call the subject-matter of historical writing.

The *History*, we are told, is divided into a prolegomenon (*muqaddima*) and three books (Q, 1: 6). This prolegomenon is not the book known as the *Muqaddima*, on the strength of which Ibn Khaldūn established his international reputation. It is a disquisition on the failures of historians, which forms a small section at the very beginning of the *History* and is easy to take for a prolegomenon to the book known as the *Muqaddima* because it is invariably printed along with this book. This prolegomenon is a statement of intent with which the whole of the *History* is prefaced. It is the statement with which the *History* opens and states the aim of rectifying historical knowledge and erecting historical writing as a veracious discipline rather than one weighed down by gullibility, sectarian mendacity, sycophancy, and other such impediments to the veracious transmission and rendition of historical narrative. The substance of Ibn Khaldūn's criticism of historians is of no importance in this context and will be taken up later. What is of direct concern to us here is that historical narrative and its prolegomenon together constitute one unit, preceded by a general prolegomenon which pronounces them as belonging to the same type of content: that of history.

The fact that what has come to be known as the *Muqaddima* proper textually precedes the historical narrative does not therefore necessarily mean that they are concerned with two distinct substances. They both treat of history; only they address it in two different ways. The *Muqaddima* does so discursively, while what follows it does so narratively. History, Ibn Khaldūn tells his readers, is 'a narrative of human aggregation which is the organized habitation (*'umrān*) of the world' (Q, 1: 56), and it is as narrative that history enters historical writing, while it is as organized habitation that it figures in the *Muqaddima*. The identity of content between the two major textual components of the *History* is located precisely here: that they possess the same subject-matter, this being organized habitation, in two distinct modes. And since the *Muqaddima*, as we will have occasion to see, stands in a thematically subordinate position with respect to historical narrative, in that it serves to sharpen the investigative capacities of the historian by providing a gauge against which historical reports are measured–in view of this, the prolegomenon to history is really its instrument. In terms of the tripartite division of the *History* therefore, the first book (the *Muqaddima*) must conform, in a specific manner, to the exigencies of books two and three which respectively narrate the histories of the Arabs and the Berbers, along with peoples contemporary with them. It must conform thematically–that is, it must construct its object of investigation in terms of the properties of the object of historical narrative. It is a major thesis of this chapter–and, indeed, of this book as a whole–that the basic object of study in the *History* (*'umrān*) is constituted and structured by the science of history as Ibn Khaldūn and his age understood it, and not, as commentators almost invariably claim, by some spurious sociology which they are wont to dream up. The object of the prolegomenon is eminently historical, in that it corresponds to, and consciously takes as its model, the conception which historical writing in Arab-Islamic culture has of the object of historical study, a conception that, immanently, devolves upon the category of the historically significant unit: the state. It is the state in its historiographic physiognomy that is carried over from this field and elaborated in the *Muqaddima.* The question which the *Muqaddima* sets itself and the problem which it addresses is thus set within history, i.e., in terms of what historical writing as a constituted science in Arab-Islamic culture provided implicity as the subject matter of history. But before this point is developed further, one caveat is in order: the dominance that history exercises over the object of the *Muqaddima* is purely thematic. History, that is, provides the *Muqaddima* with a real object with which to concern itself. The manner of this concern, and the form in which this object is elaborated, is a distinct matter altogether.

The Criterion of Historical Significance

Not everything that happens in history is historically significant. Neither is there any question, in the real practice of historical writing, of 'pure' events. An event is selected in accordance with the relevance it has to what historical writing utilizes as its principal working unit. An event, in other words, is relevant only in so far as it pertains to that principal working unit of historical writing which is the category of the historically significant unit. It is this category that organizes historical material into historical narrative and endows it, not only with significance, but with its very veracity: it establishes a continuum of reality within which this event is embedded and lodges the event in the realm of the real. A Rankean raw reality exists only in the vestigial and retrograde positivism that still marks much of orientalist historiography.[2]

I have shown elsewhere that there is a case to be put for the contention that the category of an historically significant unit in Arab-Islamic historical writing is that of a people under the aegis of political organization and as manifested and (in the most literal sense) represented in the form of a state. It can also be argued that the state in question is not the 'form of political organization' or some other politologically defined entity, but is rather, and exclusively, the rule of a dynasty.[3] That dynasticism in historical writing is itself subject to a precise conceptual determination can be shown with reference to Ibn Khaldūn, who, as will become apparent, was a very orthodox historian, albeit under a different regime of orthodoxy than that proclaimed by commentators on his work and by orientalist conceptions of Arab-Islamic historiography.

History, according to Ibn Khaldūn, is a narrative of organized habitation, as we have seen. At the level of purely narrative practice, however, it takes the form of 'the register of those narratives proper to an age or people' (Q, 1: 50).[4] The study of organized habitation as such is relegated to the prolegomenon and, in the *History* itself, performs a prefatorial function, consisting of the mention of those general conditions which herald the particularities of historical narratives (Q, 1: 7). That which is subsumed under 'an age or people' is various, but fairly well defined: names and exploits of kings, their sons, their wives, descriptions of their insignia and seals, in addition to narratives about the men of rank who execute their powers and prerogatives such as chamberlains, judges, and *wazīrs.* Yet those topics subsumed under 'an age or people' that we have just encountered are a generous collection. They are not all equally essential, and some are not essential at all for the purposes of history. Ibn Khaldūn states very explicity the case with respect to history in the 'pure' historiographic state: in treating ancient states, it is absolutely essential, but adequate, to make mention of the kings as well as of other contemporary states, along with a register of the relative powers of these entities. Such constitute the skeletal essentials of the historical object. With respect to narratives about (the inessential) subaltern state authorities, Ibn Khaldūn makes exception for great *wazīrs* such as the Barmacids in Baghdad and Kāfūr in Cairo under the Abbasids: they are, he says, 'for all intents and purposes, kings' (Q, 1: 50).[5] A state is the succession of sovereigns in the form of a dynasty.

The prime title to historical worth is therefore, that form of rulership which is answerable to none other but itself. That which falls short of this and which is incapable of absolute and final arbitration is incomplete kingship whose reality and very nature remain unconsummated (Q, 1: 341-2). Kingship, however, is not merely a proper name attached to the royal title. It is, in historical writing, the appurtenance of a sovereign to a state, *daula,* and the state is the state of a people in which the ruling dynasty, as has been mentioned, stands for the people and represents it completely, embodying it within itself so completely that, should it chance to wane, the people itself would fall into historical desuetude which, from the point of view of historical writing, is tantamount to non-existence.

Thus the Jews, for example, do not figure as an historically significant unit subsequent to the destruction of the second temple–the fact that accounts for corruption of the Bible, for, without the presence of a vigilant power, the biblical text was left at the mercy of the ignorant who, with the absence of a controlling order, were capable of becoming on a par with the learned (BD, 2: 11).[6] Historical insignificance was also the lot of those Berber peoples that had already ruled and whose dynasties had waned: they became the subordinates of others and slaves to tax farmers, so much so, indeed, that they disintegrated as lineages and their members sought to disengage themselves from their own kin (BD, 6: 104 and *passim*). The Persians fared likewise, and not even the Arabs are immune from historical insignificance. They are all but extinct, historically though not physically, having been 'spent by the Arab–Islamic states ... and swallowed by faraway lands ... while Islam was upheld by others' (BD, 6: 6). Neither the Arabs nor the Persians, however, were subject to the same fate as the Copts who, although (to Ibn Khaldūn) the longest continuously historical (i.e., political and dynastic) people in history, were wiped out of existence by the Arab conquest of Egypt (BD, 2: 140). Perhaps nothing demonstrates the necessary correlation between statehood and historical significance more than this attitude towards the Copts. Ibn Khaldūn decrees the disappearance and extinction of an entire nation once its political power was overwhelmed by others. And this is all the more significant an indicator of the import of the notion of historical significance being argued here as, at the time of Ibn Khaldūn, and as he well knew, Coptic Christianity was still the religion of a very sizeable proportion of the population of Egypt. The extinction of the nation, therefore, is synonymous with the extinction of its sovereignty, and its historical significance is coterminous with the appurtenance to it of a power structure, i.e., a dynasty.

To qualify for historicity, therefore, a people has to take the form of a state, *daula*. The state and the sovereign are indistinguishable; states are designated by the names of their impropriators, whether these be persons or peoples. The difference does not amount to a typology of states, but rather strictly to a matter of nomenclature: such is the difference between the personal state of Hārūn al-Rashīd or of Anūshirwān and the oecumenical state (*daula kullīya*) of the Arabs, of the Persians, or of the Umayyads (Q, 2: 265). The difference is one of referents and not of types, and the state of Anūshirwān, for instance, would not have become historical had it not belonged to the Sassanian state, in which it figures as a chronological moment. The difference between the personal and the oecumenical states is, as some would say, one of 'degree'. And just as the state and the sovereign are one, so the identity between the oecumene and the oecumenical state is presupposed in the writing of history, the history of the former being that of the latter. Indeed, in its purest form, the history of a people, according to the consensus of Arab-Islamic historians, is the consecutive enumeration of their kings along with the length of time each spent in power and what unusual, solemn, or catastrophic events took place during their reigns.[7] The string of sovereigns which forms the oecumenical state is the mode of historicity taken by peoples, and it is of these peoples that the history of the world is made.

The chart of world history which Ibn Khaldūn used to organize his *History* is a slightly adapted version of what we may call the historical cosmography of medieval Arab-Islamic culture. It is a temporal universe inhabited by the progeny of Noah's three sons, Shem, Ham, and Japheth. The history of the world is that of the strings of kings which the proliferation of three progenies has produced. Ibn Khaldūn does not agree with the mainstream opinion that the differentiation of nations is a differentiation of lineages and that the three sons of Noah produced seven lineages that later pullulated the world.[8] Lineages, he says, are notoriously unreliable things, which accounts for the considerable differences of opinion that exist with regard to them (BD, 2: 4–5).[9] His own treatment of this matter in the prolegomenon to the second book of the *History* does not subscribe to the idea that the original lineages numbered seven, although he does not explicitly criticize this. He questions the contention that all of humanity was in fact solely descended from the three sons of Noah, and affirms that the ascription of exclusive apparentage to Shem, Ham and Japheth is no other than the register of the fact that there are three types of human beings, inhabiting what he took to be the three corners of the world: the south, the west, and the north or, alternatively, the south, the temperate zones, and north, inhabited respectively by those taken to be the descendants of Ham, Shem, and Japheth (Q, 1: 154; T, 354). Moreover, peoples are distinguishable from each other and classified according to criteria which override that of genealogy: there are some, such as the Arabs, the Israelites, and the Persians, who can be classified as such on the basis of their genealogies; but others, such as the Black Africans, Ethiopians, Slavs, and sub-Saharan Africans (Sūdān), who are classified as such according to their appearance and geographical location. There are yet others, such as the Arabs, who are distinguished by customs and habits in addition to genealogy (Q, 1: 154). Peoples are differentiated by a great number of things: genealogies, languages, colours, habits, creeds, habitats, and much more (BD, 2: 3–4).

Our author's contestation, however, remains within the bounds of his own personal scepticism and remains discursively inactive in the *History*.

At one point in a passage critical of genealogical ascription he declares that, although the monogenetic theory of human origins is not the product of a process of reasoning from certain premisses, it is a narrative about reality (Q, 1: 154). This does point to a most important historiographic constraint: historical writing is not a transcription of fact but the recension of a narrative. This is the principle of historical writing in medieval Arab–Islamic culture, and Ibn Khaldūn did not deviate from it in his capacity as a practising historian.[10] So real is this constraint that the claim to exclusive progeny made for Noah, undemonstrable as it may be, is a narrative about reality, and it is as a narrative that it is adopted and made into the principle of historical classification (T, 354–5). The discussion of the world-historical genealogical chart forms the prolegomenon to the entire historical narrative of the *History* (BD, 2: 3 ff.).

Shem, of course, is the fount of greatness. From him issued the Arabs, the Israelites, and the Persians.[11] His descendants not only inhabited the temperate centre of the world, but were the exclusive source of prophethood. No other line produced any prophets, except the antediluvian Adamic line (BD, 2: 8–9). From Japheth descended the Turks, the Chinese, the Slavs, the Franks, and Gog and Magog, while Ham produced the Indians, the Sindhis, the Copts, the black Africans and, last but by no means least, the Canaanites, for it is from this last people that the Berbers have their descent after a migration from Canaan to North Africa. Of the descent of other peoples, controversy rules. Some think the Nabateans and Syriacs, for instance, to be one people, while others believe them to be two peoples (BD, 2: 134). Each of the principal nations became historical, some more than once, and some even world-historical, like the Arabs. Like the Persians, their successive states are the testimonial of their continuing historicity, one that goes back to the very beginning of history: after the first state of the Arabs had opened the historical scene, their second state, which is extremely ancient, was contemporaneous with the first states of the Persians and the Israelites (BD, 2: 308). Each of these peoples is represented on the chart of world history by consecutive but unconnected strains of historicity, each in the form of a distinct dynasty which dramatizes a moment of historical apparition and survival, and each slicing off for itself a section of duration in which it embeds its sequence of kings.[12]

Such is the lot of the Arabs. They were dramatized on the historical arena in four chronological classes or layers (*ajyāl, ṭabaqāt*).[13] The Persians likewise ruled in four layers which together, give or take a year, lasted for 4,281 years (BD, 2: 310). But the Arabs had this advantage over the Persians and the Israelites, that their first feat of historicity preceded those of both other ancient peoples. The people of ʿĀd, Thamūd, Ṭasm, ʿAmāliqa, and others constitute this first layer of Arabs who succeeded Noah's immediate progeny (BD, 2: 28 ff.), and are called *al-ʿArab al-ʿĀriba*, denoting the fact of their being the most Arab of Arabs, they being the first Arabs. They reigned over the Arabian Peninsula, parts of the Levant, and elsewhere, where the line of ʿĀd, which was rendered numerous by the four thousand sons he begat during his excessively long life, built the city of Damascus (BD, 2: 35-6). Perhaps the most lasting mark they left on history was the fact that it was ʿĀd himself who was the first to use the Arabic script, a consideration that also affirms his quintessential Arabicity (BD, 2: 39). Like other layers of Arabs, this first chronological class possesses states, clans, tribes, and generations (BD, 2: 29). Like them also, it is unified by a common descent expressed in a dynastic sequence or a cluster of contemporary dynastic sequences. The Arabs were not, however, the sole inhabitants of the earliest historical periods. Peoples contemporary with the first Arabs did exist–the Babylonians being one–but present a confusing picture which is all the more wanting as it is genealogically imprecise and consequently lacking in the sequential continuity required for historicity. The history of these peoples is hence not narrated as that of historically self-sufficient units, but only in so far as they witnessed events contemporary with the prophetic line Abraham-Isaac-Ishmael-Lot (BD, 2: 58 ff.). The entirety of this first period of historicity is unclear in its details, however, and the veracity of narratives about it is dubious. Hence the attention paid to these peoples as well as to the first Arabs is relatively scant, in marked contrast to the second chronological class of Arabs, that contemporary with the Israelites and the earliest Persians.

The historicity of the Arabs was resumed by the second chronological class of this people, one whose Arabicity was assured by what one may call 'cultural borrowing' and not by descent: the first class of Arabs had become extinct, and the second class, the *ʿArab Mustaʿriba* (Arabized Arabs), conformed to their name and borrowed the Arabic language from their predecessors in Arabism. Their ancestors did not speak this language, and the ancestry, which goes back to Qaḥṭān, is uncertain because the ultimate ancestor's origin is the subject of considerable controversy (BD, 2: 55, 84-5). Regardless of the controversies about ultimate origin, Arabicity was embedded within this people by virtue of the language, and it took its historical course in its capacity of being Arab. Indeed, such is the extent of their Arabism that this people–which comprises the states of

Sheba, Ḥimyar, and others–is considered to be the origin of all southern Arabs until Ibn Khaldūn's time, including our author's own origin. From their base in Yemen, this class had dealings with the Sogdians in central Asia (where they destroyed Samarqand), with the Israelites (having become vassals of Solomon for a while) and, above all, with the original inhabitants of North Africa: the Arab king Ifrīqish, after whom Africa is named, conquered the Maghrib and transported thence the Berbers from Canaan, and also settled in that part of the world the Ḥimyarite tribal confederations of Ṣanhāja and Kutāma which were to play such important roles in the history of the Maghrib.[14]

Unlike those of 'Ād, the descendants of Qaḥṭān never ceased to be historically significant.[15] Along with the progenies of 'Adnān and Quḍā'a, they proliferated as the third class of the Arabs (BD, 2: 505 ff.). The historicity of this class was expressed in a number of states established by its members throughout Arabia, the Levant, and Mesopotamia: among these are the desert state of Kinda, one of whose kings is supposed to have been the great poet 'Umru' al-Qais (d. c. A.D. 540), as well as the client states of the Byzantines and Ṡassanians in the Golan and southern Iraq, not to mention the state of the Aus and Khazraj at Medina and the Quraish in Mecca. But this third class was to have an historical weight which by far outweighs its feeble manifestations: the Quraish produced the Prophet, the states of the Umayyads, the Abbasids, the Fatimids, and many more, and ruled alone as the sole state in the world for a long period of time.[16]

The contents of the history of the Arabs is thus organized according to the succession in time of four classes, each of which is definable in terms of a group of genealogies. This also holds true of the Israelites, the Berbers, and others. Other peoples are also treated in this manner: the state is transmitted from father to son: such is the lot of the Persians, the Macedonians, and others. The Romans, however, are among the small number of peoples where there is no explicit genealogical line holding together the continuity of the state. That this is true (with reservations, for the Julio-Claudians were a truly dynastic line, as Ibn Khaldūn registered, albeit inaccurately rendering the blood relations between the successors of Augustus–BD, 2: 408-12) is not as important as its very conceptual admissibility by Ibn Khaldūn. Genealogical continuity being the prevalent criterion of historical continuity (and hence of significance) in the *History*, state forms, whose diachronic structure is composed of elements (monarchs) related by a form of succession other than the genealogical, may seem anomalous. They may even seem unthinkable, for genealogy is a principle of continuity which, in historical writing, acts as a principle of coherence. But genealogy acts as a unit of nominal (literally) coherence, not of any 'real' coherence in the sociological or other senses of coherence. The formal structure is one of pure succession, and the articulation of this succession in terms of extra-serial coherence is accidental to succession. Being such, succession along lines other than strict genealogy are not anomalous, but represent a pure form, a limiting case, of the historiographic paradigm. Genealogy is a mode of presentation.

The fact of succession within the ambit of a state is the primary structure of historical writing according to the Arab-Islamic paradigm of this practice, as we have already had occasion to see. Genealogy provides a particularly cohesive conceptual glue in terms of which continuity in time can be expressed. It provides historical writing with narrative sustenance which is missing from the ultimate structure (and, historically, original structure) of historical writing. Most importantly, it provides a political form for the state which satisfies requirements of both the political and epistemological orders.[17] What is of relevance in the context of the present argument is that each of the classes of Arabs or of any other people is, in formal terms, a perfectly self-contained unit whose relation to its predecessors and contemporaries has absolutely no bearing on that state which is constituted by this class. A genealogy is active within the context of a single state as a principle of order. The fact that, for instance, the seed of Qaḥṭān held sway as the second class and as part of the third class of Arabs does not imply any continuity between the successive classes of the line of Qaḥṭān *sub specie historiae*, but only indicates physical, seminal continuity. Other than this biological, racial, continuity, no relation exists between the two appearances of Qaḥṭānism, for each belongs to that island of duration which forms it into a particular history. A history (*ta'rīkh*) is, ultimately, datation, the assignation of a temporal magnitude to an event on the basis of a base 'zero point' from which temporal reckoning started; this is the significance of the multiplicity of calendars that Arab-Islamic historians used with reference to the various histories of peoples they dealt with: Sassanian, Alexandrian, and other. I have explored this matter elsewhere[18] and will only emphasize what is of particular pertinence to the present argument: that historicity is the attribute of temporal embeddedness within the context of a state.

This is, of course, as true of the *History* as it is of all other historical works in Arab-Islamic culture without exception. While the chronologies of peoples and states which preceded the Hijra are sometimes uncertain and confused, a sort of chronological order still remains. The first class of Arabs, as well as the second, are made historical by means of dynastic succession, with the length of time of a sovereign's rule mentioned when reliably known. Others, such as the early Israelites, are synchronized with what must have looked to Ibn Khaldūn as firmer chronological ground: Moses, for instance, is dated in terms of Pharaonic chronology, which in turn consists, not of a continuously running calendar, but of sometimes episodic datation in terms of the durations of particular reigns (BD, 2: 152–3 and *passim*). Similarly, the birth of Jesus Christ is stated to have fallen during the forty-second year of the reign of Augustus (BD, 2: 407–8). Even the strict chronology of the Arabs of the third wave and prior to the Hijra suffers from the same problem.

Not so the history succeeding the Hijra of the Prophet from Mecca to Medina and the resultant calendar. This offered Ibn Khaldūn and, indeed, all other historians the felicitous opportunity to marry the certainty of successions with the exactitude of an all-embracing calendar, thus producing a history which, for all the intents and purposes of the Arab–Islamic historiographic paradigm, is at once perfect and exhaustive. The oecumenical states of the Arabs and the more humble states of their contemporaries and their successors (the Berbers, the Franks, and the Turkic peoples) can be historicized perfectly. An examination of the Arab state of the third class and its successor Arab states is very instructive and will reveal the workings in historical writing of the principle of succession within the state in its full extent, and will show how intelligibility in terms of history, and therefore pertinence, is relegated totally to appurtenance to a specific dynastic succession without any reference to anything that lies without the bounds of the succession.

Like all other peoples and classes of peoples that have entered history in truly historic form, the third class of the Arabs in Islam consisted of a main structure of succession succeeded by other structures of succession which constitute sub-structures of the main one with which they are, however, identical except for their temporal posteriority. This indeed conforms to Ibn Khaldūn's chosen graphic means of rendering genealogical charts in the form of a lineage tree (BD, 2: 24–5). If one were in a position to adopt a panoramic view of this historical chart of the third class of Arabs, one would see so many segments proliferating by division from a parent line, and one would, on the margin of these segments, observe similar structures of succession historicizing peoples contemporary with them. There is nothing that distinguishes any of these strains of historicity from another except for external factors: name and date. While these two elements are the very ones that define the specificity of an historical unit, the specificity in question is structurally and conceptually spurious. There is no difference of genus but only of sheer unspecific difference: the fact that a state is that of the Fatimids or of the Ḥamdānids, for instance, is not pertinent in any way to the constitution of the state. Both are structurally homologous in the strictest of senses: they consist of elements (sovereigns) in succession. In this structure, the name and date are contingent differences among structures that are, in essence, interchangeable.[19] The state is the succession of sections of duration, each designated by the name of a sovereign, without reference to structures of the social, geographical, or even genealogical orders which, in fact, the state integrates. In terms of Arab-Islamic historiography to which Ibn Khaldūn totally belongs, the state is the abstract sovereign as a slice of time.

Thus, the first state of the Islamic Arabs is that which finds its continuity between the first Caliph Abū Bakr and the fall of the Umayyad caliphate in 132/750. There is little by way of genealogy to connect the Medinese regime with that of Damascus except for the fact that all caliphal incumbents were of the Quraish. Ibn Khaldūn is absolutely unique among Arab-Islamic historians to postulate continuity between these two regimes. The Umayyads were generally considered to have been an iniquitous interregnum between the Medinese caliphate and the reign of the Abbasids ever since the latter commenced their anti-Umayyad propaganda, an attitude which became obligatory historiographic truth under the Abbasids and was subsequently solidified into historical traditional truth.[20] Ibn Khaldūn's contemporaries were never disabused of this. The position is repeated with classic forthrightness by the prodigious and authoritative Qalqashandī (d. 821/1418), for instance, a generation after our author.[21] Ibn Khaldūn's postulation of continuity is premissed on a distinction between a state attaching to a uniform fount of 'vertical pull' along which succession takes place–the Arabs of the Quraish-Mudar-'Adnān branch as such–and states where this pull bifurcated and was divided among the line of 'Abd Manāf into the clan of Banū Umayya and that of the Prophet, the Banū Hāshim (Ibn Khaldūn's summary narrative of the relations between these two clans in early Islam is in BD, 3: 3 ff.). With the fall of the Umayyad caliphate in Damascus, vertical pull in matters of succession which regulated this order dissolved into two, the Hāshimite Abbasids in Baghdad and the Umayyads again in Cordoba. In view of considerations which will be taken up later in this chapter, this appeared to be an eminently natural state of affairs. Indeed, the period during which the Prophet ruled and the period immediately succeeding him, especially the rule of Abū Bakr, was a time of miracles which distracted people from the normal course of affairs and entrusted political rule to a member of a minor Quraish clan (see especially the discussion in BD, 2: 1026-7 and cf. *ibid.*, vols. 2 and 3, *passim*).[22]

This initial bifurcation gave way to further divisions, each of which, in structural terms, duplicated its predecessor and its contemporaries. The initial and therefore major bifurcation is between the Sunna, identified with the Umayyads, and the Shī'a, whom Ibn Khaldūn, in an unusual conceptualization, identifies with the Abbasids, thus joining the Abbasids and their bitterest of enemies, the Fatimids, in one and the same historical line (BD, 3: 363 ff.). The Umayyad-Abbasid split came about as a result of a dispute over the legitimacy of the Umayyad caliphate, with the Shī'a claiming legitimacy only to the descendants of 'Alī. This is the origin of the State of the Shī'a (BD, 3: 363-4), the term Shī'a being understood in its generic sense and not in its various doctrinal acceptations. That the Abbasids are classified along with the Fatimids and the other 'Alid lines together in the same taxonomic category[23]–and in distinction from the category formed earlier by the Medinan and Umayyad caliphates–is a very curious position and utterly out of step with the paradigmatic classifications of Arab-Islamic historiography. There is a tendency to arrogate goodness to the Abbasids alone, and to categorize the Fatimids and Umayyads separately as historical manifestations of various kinds of evil. Ibn Khaldūn, however, does not only classify the Fatimids alongside the Abbasids in the same category.[24] This Shī'ite class also contains the Idrīsids of the Maghreb–who were, indeed, the first Shī'a of 'Alid descent–the Sulaiḥids in the Yemen, the Qaramiṭa of Bahrain, and other minor dynasties from central Asia to the Maghrib.

It is indeed curious that the 'Abbasids and the 'Alids are classified together in the same category. It seems as if Ibn Khaldūn thought an ideological split enough to warrant the postulation of a new regime of continuity and succession. Such a supposition, although it looks legitimate at first sight, cannot be held, and this for two reasons. It rests, first of all, on the misconception of Shī'ism: in the acceptation employed by the *History*, it does not, as already observed, denote doctrinal Twelvers or any other Imamist variety thereof, but refers to any category of political actors who, for any reason whatsoever, be it genealogical or ideological, favoured the delivery of the Islamic nation exclusively into the hands of the Prophet's own family as represented in the descendants of 'Alī. And of this category of people there were numerous groups. Under Sh'ism, the *History* includes minor 'Alid states that had no connection whatsoever with politico-theological arguments over legitimacy, such as the Hāshimids of Mecca who only at a late stage accepted the legitimacy of the Fatimids

(BD, 4: 219 ff.). And, moreover, the 'Abbasids are not the only dynasty classified by the *History* as Shī'ite regardless of their genealogy. The Qarāmiṭa join them in this category (BD, 4: 181).

More important than this consideration is one which is of more relevance to this argument. For instead of postulating a continuity in this classificatory scheme, it would be far more appropriate to posit a series of breaks. There is no reason to suppose that the Fatimids 'continued' the state of the Abbasids, or even that of their Idrisid kin. Succession and simultaneity there was; but continuity is only thinkable in terms of an individual state, and, within the context of a single state, it has to be safeguarded by all means at the disposal of the historian. When the Fatimids moved from Mahdīya and established themselves in Cairo, thus causing a total metamorphosis to befall what formations the state integrated, they are still Fatimids in the eyes of the *History*, constituting an identical state. When discussing Saladin and the Ayyūbid dynasty, Ibn Khaldūn very uncharacteristically reserves judgement on their ultimate origin: sketching the two conflicting opinions of their genealogy, the one provided by the very reliable Ibn al-Athīr (d. 630/1233) which purports their Kurdish descent, and that purveyed by the Ayyūbids' own genealogists and which derives them from Ḥimyar, Ibn Khaldūn does not state any preference. For the matter would be irrelevant: the Ayyūbids are a branch of the Turkic state, regardless of their real descent, and they started their historical career as the vassals of the Zanghids of Mosul and Damascus and never quite transcended the strict continuity of Turkic historical significance (BD, 5: 612; T, 279).[25]

This is the case in intra-state successions. In the case of the succession of states, the relation between posterior and anterior is one of mere consecution, not in any way of consequence. The Idrīsids of Morocco are described as that state which was 'crowding out' the Abbasids (BD, 2: 31).[26] And we have seen earlier in this chapter that the main units of historical writing, the units which are considered as historically significant and are therefore the main categories of historical order, are the people and the chronological class of people. These categories, as we have seen, organize and order history; they make material relating to the past into history, endowing it with significance, order, and historiographic relevance. They are adopted into historical writing by virtue of their being formal units of order composed of formal units of succession, and not in so far as they allow one to be derivable from another that precedes it or that is contemporary with it. The history of the Buwaihids, for instance, which is seen in the context of states coexisting with and deriving legitimacy from the moribund Abbasids, is sketched as a self-subsistent line of princes and kings who have their origin in the central Asian mountains and who proceed in time alongside the weakening authority of Baghdad, and their assumption of supreme power is seen not in terms of a vacuum, but as something that came about by virtue of some intrinsic power subsisting within their order of succession. It seems almost natural that, being who they are, they should have assumed supreme power. This does not, of course, make any sense today; it is tautological. But the tautology was not such in the *History:* history is the attribute of peoples represented by the succession of their sovereigns. When such a succession obtains, therefore, any attempt to look for the mechanics whereby this succession started in the first place is superfluous and almost unthinkable. The relation of the Buwaihids to the Abbasids is no more than an episode in the respective histories of these two dynasties which has virtually no effect on the inner structures of either. Similarly, when the very basis of Fatimid polity is transformed with the transfer of the dynasty (meaning capital, court, and army), *en masse*, from the Maghrib to Egypt, this is not perceived as a change but as a contingent event in a structure marked by a continuing succession.

For continuity to transcend the bounds of the single state, a mode of explanation is required which transcends the linear time of pure succession. One would require a real concatenation, not a sheer parataxis, which would conceptualize the differentiation of states. Indeed, the 'before' and the 'after' would need criteria of difference other than a dynastic rubric and a starting point in time. One would therefore require a criterion of continuity other than the genealogy in terms of which succession is articulated. Distinction between states in the *History*, however, is expressed in terms of difference, not of change. This is nowhere truer than in the case of the histories of different states belonging to the same people, like the Idrīsids and the Umayyads. Here, the transition between one and the other is straightforward, taking the form of the branching out of a line along the genealogical tree, a line that establishes its boundary with respect to a preceding one by the point at which it grows out as an independent unit. Such lines will keep on coming to their own in the context of a people as long as the people still exists as a constituted independent unit (Q, 1: 264 ff.).

The only type of historical succession that entails a major change is that which looks 'as if creation were altered by its root' (Q, 1: 52). Such situations involve the adoption of a new religion or the obliteration, however caused, of a society (Q, 1: 266). Or perhaps one could also include situations where a people as such, as a constituted independent unit, had waned, such as the lot of the Arabs described throughout the *History* (the most eloquent statement of this is in BD, 2: 3–5). But such changes do not relate the precedent and consequent. Historical writing represents such changes in the form of the succession of states. No religion establishes itself without the muscle of a state, and it establishes itself precisely because the conquered, according to the sagacity of the ages, adopt the habits and beliefs of the conqueror (Q, 1: 45, 266–8, 286 and *passim*). Change there certainly is. But it does not at all imply a transformation in continuity where one state generates another. It denotes only difference.

Perhaps nothing underlines the externality of states to one another and their intransitivity with respect to each other than the fact that grand historical happenings coincide with the conjunctions of Jupiter and Saturn: the Grand Conjunction, which occurs once every nine hundred and sixty years, denotes events such as the change of a religion or of oecumenical state or the transference of the power within a religion from one grand people to another, while more frequent conjunctions denote events of a lesser order (Q, 2: 187).[27] The advent of Tamerlane onto the world-historical arena was widely forecast in the Maghrib and the Andalus in 766/1365 and pretty accurately scheduled to take place in 784/1382 (T, 371).[28] While there is no matter here of adopting the hackneyed position of asserting that belief in the stars automatically excludes belief in the terrestrial causation of things, it must be pointed out that the fact that the agreement of terrestrial and extra-terrestrial events in matters of timing is not only a correspondence between the laws of two distinct orders of being.[29] It also entails conformity of the terrestrial order to the temporal pattern of the stars.[30] This pattern being the quintessential form of pure and abstract consecution in which the posterior repeats the anterior, the order in which states follow one another is, as we have seen, one of pure succession specified by name and date, bereft of an inner movement or of immanent necessity. A state comes to be at a time not set by itself, and all that causes it to come to be is a power which, as we have seen above, is inherent in its genealogy. Its coming to be at a particular time is therefore not due to some immanent factor: the immanent factor (genealogy) merely causes it to exist, and has no effect on the timing of its historical existence. It could therefore come before or after the time of its actual existence; and its anteriority or posteriority to other states is entirely contingent. This historical parataxis is inscribed in the very inner structure of the state, a structure which the *Muqaddima* unravelled for the sake of the rest of the *History* and in keeping with the conceptual exigencies of the *History:* it was the state that formed the object of historical writing which is the object of the *Muqaddima.*

The Structure of the Historical State

It is historical writing that provides the *Muqaddima* with its primary *denotatum*: the state as a self-sufficient unit of succession in time. The physiognomy of the state, *daula,* in the *Muqaddima* corresponds to that provided by historical writing and, contrary to the pseudo-axiomaticism professed by Ibn Khaldūn and by almost all his commentators and which will be discussed in great detail below, the state and organized habitation (*'umrān*) were not created by our author's mind *ex nihilo.* Indeed, in order to be meaningful, organized habitation has to be placed within the semantic field of the state; the latter, *daula,* is the primary object of study in the *Muqaddima.* Being such, it not only provides the *Muqaddima* with its main graphic concept of its object. It also sets limits for the concept, limits beyond which the *Muqaddima* could not venture in search of the supposedly green pastures of various modern sociological persuasions, as commentators of Ibn Khaldūn are so wont to claim. In other words, the *daula* of historical writing sets the *Muqaddima* a number of constraints of a paradigmatic nature, the transgression of which would have rendered *daula* absurd and unthinkable in the eyes of the *History.* But there is a very strict limit to the dominance of the historiographic state over the one in the *Muqaddima*: the historiographic state is imported into a text articulated by means of conceptual regimes which are distinct from that of historiography. The historiographic state provides the morphological aetiology of the state in the context of the science of organized habitation, which is the proper subject-matter of the *Muqaddima,* but it does not provide it with its conceptual profile, which is highly complex and which will form the bulk of chapter two below. Its dominance is thematic; it points out a 'real' object as the *denotatum* of the concept *'daula'*, and deems irrelevant that which falls beyond the bounds of this *denotatum* in historical writing as well as in 'real life': the self-sufficient unit in which monarchs succeed one another. We will now proceed to demonstrate this.

Throughout the *History,* prolegomena and narratives, the state is the embodiment of the power of an historical agent. It is the temporal extension of the power exercised in continuity by that historical agent. The agent could be, as we have seen (above, p. 13), either individual or oecumenical, but the former variety is a sub-structure in the continuity of the latter. True and consummate statehood accrues only to that agent which has exclusive control over its subjects, which collects taxes for its own benefit and on its own account, which has exclusive monopoly of all dealings, pacific or belligerent, with outside powers, and which, above all, is answerable only to itself (Q, 1: 341).[31] And it is precisely in terms of sovereignty–the qualification for historical significance, as we have seen–that this agency is treated in the *Muqaddima.* The state, *daula,* is this agency. It lies at the core of a semantic field which includes its ancillary concepts, such as the famous *badāwa, ḥadāra,* and *'aṣabīya.* This exclusive agency of power and of historical continuity–the temporal integrity of the former being coterminous with the latter–is that towards which the determination of these ancillary concepts is geared. In other words, without *daula,* the concept of *'aṣabīya* would be superfluous regardless of its 'real existence'. As a concept, it is subject to the exigencies of the concept of the state and cannot exist conceptually without it nor, indeed, except in its proximity. It exists only in so far as it relates to the state in the sense suggested above. From the optic of such a state, the internal constitution of the agency whose power it embodies is irrelevant and immaterial. All it requires for its determination are those elements of that internal constitution which are directly relevant to the temporal extension of power or, conversely, that which impedes such a continuity. It is not at all surprising, therefore, that Ibn Khaldūn developed what commentators like to see as a 'theory of the rise and decline of the state'; the primary motif for it is the historical state and not, as is almost always supposed, a political sociology. What in historical writing is referred to by genealogy is, in the theory of the historical state, designated by *'aṣabīya,* which, like genealogy, stands as a principle of politico-historical coherence. In both cases, seriality in time is the main structure. Except that, in the case of the state as portrayed in the *Muqaddima,* other conceptual layers come into the constitution of the famous *'aṣabīya* which will be discussed in detail later, but which do not alter the empirical determination, 'in the real', of that which is denoted by this term.

Daula, we have suggested, is the central concept in the *Muqaddima.* Its centrality is demonstrated both by the position it occupies in the narrative order (see below, pp. 49-50)[32] and, of more relevance in this context, by the way in which other concepts are geared towards it. This conceptual orientation is manifested both in the centrality of the state as a topic in the *Muqaddima* and in the impossibility of other, ancillary, concepts without it, and in its specific contours as those which designated the continuity in time of a uniform structure of power.

This conception of the state conserves the notions of the state held in the only two cultural locations where this notion exists in Arab-Islamic culture: historiography and what may loosely be termed 'political thought'. Had the state not been, in the latter genre, the play of an abstract power actor, then we would not have encountered the persistent statement on the sovereign as the upper limit of a hierarchy built upon obedience. The sovereign is not only the conserver of religion and of the worldly order alike. He is the representative of the ultimate order that is guaranteed by God himself–this is the sense of the conception of sovereignty as *istikhlāf* (see below, p. 55). Order is, and could only have been, imposed within the bounds of the state by the use of real or imagined coercive power, and it is in terms of such power of coercion that sovereignty is defined, for human nature is fundamentally anarchic and order will inevitably break if a final custodian and arbiter did not exist. That is why the king of Tlemcen Abū Ḥammū (d. 791/1388)–who knew Ibn Khaldūn and employed his brother Yaḥyā at his court–states in his *Fürstenspiegel* that the first support of a sovereign is an army. This is naturally the reflection of a man who ruled skilfully for thirty years; but this does not exhaust its significance: a *Fürstenspiegel* is a contribution to a genre and, as such, is compelled to conform to the conceptual profile of this genre which looks at justice, for instance, as but a means for the maintenance of what might today be called a regime.[33] This is based on the axiomatic view that without the regime as expressed in the coincidence of the state with the sovereign, worldly order cannot be maintained–with the corollary that order, and hence the public interest, are coincident with the state.[34]

It is this charter for despotism that informs Ibn Khaldūn's discussion of the custodial authority (*wāzi'*) and not some supposed sociological reasoning. This custodial authority, we are informed, is 'the sense of kingship' (Q, 1: 71).[35] It endows that over which it presides with a coherence it would otherwise lack, for that suffers from a perpetual tendency towards disintegration into atomistic units which would go against the purpose of creation, which is best served by the adherence of men to those organized assemblages that guarantee them the necessities of life which can be obtained only by collective effort. Kingship and, therefore, the state, is thus not, as modern political thought would like to envisage, the representative of 'society'. Quite the contrary. If there is at all any possibility of conceiving a representational link between state and society at the time of Ibn Khaldūn, and such a possibility is dubious, it is society which would 'represent' the state. The direction of force between the two is unilineal and unilateral. Without the state, there is no society. That is why Ibn Khaldūn believes the state to be 'the supreme concatenation of the world' (Q, 2: 92),[36] and this is also how change in the conditions of society, which Ibn Khaldūn takes to be a change of customs and of the conditions of daily life, could only be conceived in terms of the change in the presiding powers, each of which determines the conditions of the populace presided over (Q, I : 45 and *passim*).

That the agent that holds power is abstract and in keeping with the exigencies of historical writing (how else could it have become the prime category of historical writing had it not conformed to the culturally possible conception of the state?) can be shown with reference to the concept of *'aṣabīya*. Conventional wisdom on Ibn Khaldūn has it that this notion portrays his sociological thinking par excellence, but it will be shown that Ibn Khaldūn was no more a sociologist than Plato a Platonic lover. Much of the confusion has raged around a fundamental misconception: the supposition that *'aṣabīya* is an invariant *denotatum* which could thus be rendered as 'esprit de corps', as 'group will', or one of the other variants of these renditions.[37] I will now argue that this notion, in the *Muqaddima* as elsewhere in Ibn Khaldūn, is polymorphous, and that all these forms and locations within which it is embedded are geared towards a conceptual order whose locus is the concept of the state as required by historiography, and that, therefore, it is not *'aṣabīya* that dictates the form of the state, but that it is the abstract conception of the power agent which produces a requirement for the various forms in which *'aṣabīya* appears in the text of Ibn Khaldūn. The corollary to this is that all other determinants which could be considered as qualifying the abstractness of monarchy and smearing it with the density of social and economic affairs become unthinkable or, at best, irrelevant, both to the passage in time of the individual state and to the succession of states. History is the history of the state, and the state is the monarchy: there is nothing in history that is external to the state, nor is anything not internal to the monarchy of relevance.

'Aṣabīya is 'a function of lineage affiliation or something that fulfils the role of such affiliation' (Q, 1: 235).[38] The most pertinent thing to note here is that Ibn Khaldūn does not at this juncture (nor, indeed, anywhere else) offer anything by way of ethnographic description of the forms and results of the lineage affiliation or 'that which fulfils its role' but, instead, makes it absolutely clear that, though the love of one's kin is a sentiment

of divine provenance imprinted in the heart of every man, such a feeling of solidarity which falls under *'aṣabīya* is not the work of an abstract altruism. The solidarity of the group is itself a function of the coherence of this group, and such coherence cannot be maintained without the presence of a dominant element with a mandate to coerce (Q, 1: 252)–very much like the physiological compound in medieval medicine, where the equivalence of elements will not produce a definite temper, for which the dominance of one element is imperative (BB, 131-2). Beyond its cohesive charter, *'aṣabīya* is irrelevant, for lineage affiliation as expressed in genealogy, we are told, is a matter purely of the mind whose only relevance to reality lies in that it generates the cohesion of a group (Q, 1: 252-3)–and therefore its capacity to become an actor in the arena of political struggles, of power, and, hence, of historical relevance. The group which achieves cohesion through *'aṣabīya* being totally, as we have seen, represented in its sovereign, it follows that all considerations about its internal coherence point vertically upwards to the royal hinge that endows this coherence with consequence. The theory of *'aṣabīya* accentuates the historiographic exigency that the historical state take on the rubric of a people.[39]

It is patently obvious that, unlike the majority of commentators on our author as well as of students of beduinism, Ibn Khaldūn's interest in, and emphasis upon, the cohesion of social groups is not informed by a gratuitously romantic image of an idyllic and noble *Gemeinschaft*. Indeed, such an image would have been conducive to the production of ethnographic descriptions, which Ibn Khaldūn, sadly, did not give us. *'Aṣabīya*'s occurrences in the Khaldunic text, moreover, are very rarely in connection with the pristine tie of blood among individuals. Throughout, the discussion is geared towards the higher order of the formation of a state. In what may have been a *Gemeinschaft*, the discussion of *'aṣabīya* devolves upon the headship exercised by a member of the group which can only be maintained by the domination which, in the first instance, is provided by *'aṣabīya*[40] (Q, 1: 239). But then this headship is not limited to the small group; it grows, like a wave, in concentric circles: simple headship, *ri'āsa* based on a form of consent, is pronounced by Ibn Khaldūn as unconsummated and incomplete, for all pristine leadership is not a simple state of affairs, but is a vectorial quantity with a definite orientation towards kingship, *mulk* (Q, 1: 252). By its very nature, it requires extension: the subjugation to its will of an everwidening circle of groups with a progressively more obscure and higher tie of kin to the central group which is exercising leadership, a subjugation as if by suction into a vortex whose centre is progressively elevated from headship to kingship to the state.

Needless to say, this progress is accompanied by a terminological shift in the flow of the *Muqaddima*, as we shall see in the next chapter, in which the only constant is *'aṣabīya*: no matter how far the group widens, it is called *'aṣabīya*, and this is attributed to and named after the central clan or even the leader of whatever central group is exercising dominion over others. This expansion not only has the sanction of history, as can be seen from even a cursory reading of Ibn Khaldūn's account of, say, the rise of the Almoravids (BD,6: 373 ff.) or the Almohads (BD, 6: 470 ff.). It also has the sanction of metaphysics, for kingship is the *telos* of *'aṣabīya* (Q, 1: 252–4). In both cases there is not a trace of sociology or of concern with the internal composition of power groups. In the descriptions of the rise of the Almoravids and the Almohads, Ibn Khaldūn presents the picture of a central power group which, suddenly, starts expanding militarily and bringing under its sway groups to which it is genealogically related and, later, other groups which sometimes reject their own genealogies and adopt those of the conquerors.

In this march towards its teleological destiny, *'aṣabīya*, therefore, does not subsist by itself, but is a notion active only in the context of state formation. It is of no interest to Ibn Khaldūn as a sociological concept, in which capacity its importance and significance is grossly overrated anyhow. In terms of the Khaldunic discourse, the orientation of the notion of *'aṣabīya* is strictly focussed towards its being that aspect of a power group which defines it as a power group. Ibn Khaldūn stated that *'aṣabīya* fulfils in the wild the very role that the ramparts and walls fulfil in a city they surround (Q, 1: 233–4).[41] Consideration of *'aṣabīya* is exclusively consecrated to its appurtenance to the point of vertical pull and integration in a given power situation: it is the organizational framework of politics. From being originally a power group on the ascendant, *'aṣabīya* later comes to designate a power group as the beneficiary of the state.

In its two basic moments just mentioned, *'aṣabīya* refers to social groups that do not have a uniform social composition, for the intervention of time and circumstance, as we shall see in the next chapter, produces changes in that which *'aṣabīya* denotes after it has assumed power and founded a state. In the eyes of the *Muqaddima*, it makes little difference if this *'aṣabīya* is composed almost exclusively of kinsmen, as it is when it is preparing itself for statehood, or of a mixture of kinsmen, mercenaries, freedmen, allies, and others, as is the case in the fully constituted state and, more elaborately, in the oecumenical state that we have already encountered earlier in this chapter (see the succinct statement in T, 314-5).[42] In real terms, this state of affairs results in a dislocation of the position occupied by the hierarchy of kin: the Almohad nobility, which occupied such a central position in the early years of the Almohad state, was radically downgraded in later years although, even under the Ḥafṣids, it preserved the same formal organization as it had in its heyday.[43] Ibn Khaldūn was certainly aware of this, not least in his capacity as politician and his activities at the Ḥafṣid court. Yet he does, for instance, say that the Almohad hierarchy was called upon to confirm Ḥafṣid dynastic changes (BD, 6: 280) without bringing out the political anachronism of such a custom. For the anachronism is of the sociological order, and the Almohad hierarchy was still, after all, one component of the Ḥafṣid *'aṣabīya.* And moreover, the Almohad *'aṣabīya* deposited in the Maṣmūda clan after the demise of the Mu'minid house (which belonged to the Kūmīya, a different tribe altogether) still counted as the Almohad *'aṣabīya,* and the Ḥafṣid appellation of the state designated the distinction of a state, of an agency of dominance, rather than of a people over whom domination is exercised (see BD, 6: 560–1, 576–9 on the Mu'minids and the Ḥafṣids). Similarly, the dependence of the Ḥafṣids on Castillian mercenaries and on tribal alliances with groups totally unrelated to the Almohad 'people' in no way alters the fact, held by Ibn Khaldūn, that there is a strict continuity–hence identity–between the Ḥafṣids and the Mu'minids. The irrelevance of the internal composition of *'aṣabīya* is clear. It is the appellation of the state and the identity of its impropriators that are paramount.

There are two primary results to be had from the foregoing. The first concerns the significance to the discussion of *'aṣabīya* of the composition of its *denotatum,* and that by way of a brief conclusion and recapitulation, and the second concerns the criterion for the integrity of the state, which we will see can only be located in the context of succession.

The human composition of *'aṣabīya* is significant only in so far as it constitutes the human armour of a sovereign group–the term is generally in the form of *"aṣabīyat fulān".* The term indicates groups in a power equation whose internal structures and characteristics are neither elaborated by Ibn Khaldūn nor deemed to be of particular significance. The gap, very wide, between the definition of *'aṣabīya* as a function of lineage affiliation and the external description of its fortunes as one unit among others, is never bridged. And the reason for this is eminently justifiable, and the only one probable, in the context of the discourse on *'aṣabīya*: in terms of the physiognomy of the state, it can only, and need only, be an extension of the requirement that the state be regarded as a *sui generis* entity whose relation to 'civil society' is one of unmitigated and unilateral verticality. It is a notion unthinkable except within the semantic ambit of the state, and its want of content reinforces the abstractness of the master category: the state, which engenders it as a theoretization of the paradigmatic requirement that the historically significant unit be the state of a people or a dynasty.

The structure of power, and thence of the state, is independent of that by means of which, and over which, the state presides. This independence is not compromised by the labour of time. On the contrary. The vicissitudes of the state in the context of its temporal passage in fact, as will be demonstrated, confirm its abstractness as a power agent whose criterion of integrity is purely internal to itself. The passage of time has an impact only on the *'aṣabīya* identified with the state, for that which generates the conditions of the atrophy of the state is the state itself, and it is the state in the form of the sovereign *'aṣabīya* that passes through what has been called 'stages' and then on to annihilation.

According to the historiographic paradigm by which the Khaldunic conception of the state is bounded, the integrity of the state is guaranteed by its dynastic rubric and ceases with the waning and disappearance of this name: a state is Coptic, Merinid, Almohad. The structure of the individual state, therefore, is determined by the integrity of succession along a line which is fully contained in the name. In diachronic terms, the state is almost literally a line of force: it is a *sui generis* unit of power which appears suddenly, describes a trajectory in time, and is extinguished. This sudden appearance in the *Muqaddima*, moreover, is prefaced by no more than a cursory discussion of a few rather disconnected traits of the group that becomes a state before this state has been fully formed, as we have just seen. If we were to take this movement from full realization to extinction, the movement described in the trajectory just suggested, as one bounded by two termini which announce the beginning and the end of the state, we will find that the only adequately fitting characterization that can be attached to it is what has been called, in a different tune of Ibn Khaldūn interpretation, an aetiology of decline[44] whose metaphysics is developed in the *Muqaddima*. In other words, on the assumption, substantiated in the previous pages, that the *History*, not least in its First Book, known as the *Muqaddima*, addresses the state in so far as it is an abstract power agency existing in time and disencumbered from what today may appear as the necessary social and economic legacy without which it cannot exist, the story of the state is that of its atrophy. Any encumbrances that may appear to weigh down the state and attach it to social or other provinces of life in the *Muqaddima* are conceived in terms of this very aetiology of decline that attaches to the state. The prime consideration–as well as the prime criterion of integrity–in the brief space between beginning and end is the tempo of the dynasty conceived in terms of the continuity of this dynasty, and this tempo, which in its turn dictates the tempo of the decline of the civilization engendered by the state, is determined by criteria purely internal to the state as an agency of power in the form of a dynasty based upon an *'aṣabīya* of uncertain constitution: the natural life span of the state as determined by the stars and as they correspond to the terrestrial vicissitudes and habits within the state, as will be shown in more detail in the next chapter.

The trajectory traversed by the historical unit 'state' is, in most cases, 120 years long. The state has a natural life span, just as men have life spans, although the latter vary more than does that of the state. While the optimal life of a man, according to the astrologers, is 120 years, this is in fact an optimal maximum. The life span of a state corresponds to that of three median human life spans which, together, amount to a Great Lunar Year of 120 years or three generations, or the equivalent of one-eighth of time lapse between the Grand Conjunctions of Jupiter and Saturn (Q, 1: 305-6). During these three generations, the state passes through five moments.[45] Once again, there is no invariance about this: the stages of the state are five 'in most cases' (Q, 1: 314), and one would assume that any variations on the number of stages is the result of the forcible annihilation of the state, as there is no theoretical provision in the *Muqaddima* for any other interpretation. Each of these moments is characterized by its difference from the others as this is expressed by a distinct ethos (Q, 1: 314). Initial triumph gives way to tyranny, on to the peaceful organization of power, then to peaceful contentment, and finally to the last moment in the life of the state, characterized by prodigality and its attendant ills (Q, 1: 315-7).

It must be stressed here that in the discussion of the moments of the state, the state is fully identified with, and wholly absorbed within, the state as dynasty and as *'aṣabīya*-group as such. The wealth of descriptive detail that accompanies Ibn Khaldūn's chronicle of the decline of this group–and it is never more powerful than it was at its inception and first moment–pertains wholly to the group. This does not save the so-called 'development of the state' from theoretical banality: in the metaphysical link in which the five moments are generically modes of the same substance (as we shall see in detail in the next chapter), 'state' itself pertains only to the power group; the sense of their consecutive connection, that of the aetiology of decline, moreover, is equally of exclusive pertinence to this group and not to the state as such which does not decline, but merely appears and disappears. The link between the moments is purely serial; outside this seriality is nothing but the rather banal observation that the moments follow one another in the process of the dissolution of the state and not as realized in the moments, but as manifested in them. Metaphysical links pertain to the state as such, whereas decline pertains to its manifestation in time, and this manifestation is assured as a unitary movement only through the unity of the state, and this in turn is only assured through its appurtenance to a lineage. Continuity in time is the sole criterion of integrity and unity precisely because no relation between the moments exists except for consecution. Nowhere does Ibn Khaldūn undertake to demonstrate that the five moments necessarily follow from one another. All that the *Muqaddima* does is register the succession of one by another.

This consecution, then, is one in which change is purely accidental and of no consequence. It is change which confirms the main thesis of this chapter: that the object 'state' addressed by Ibn Khaldūn is the abstract power actor that is required by historiography, and that any elaborations of a quasi-sociological nature remain within the bounds of this historiographic requirement and do not (indeed, cannot) supersede it conceptually. Being an aetiology of decline, change between the moments is, in terms of the state and its fortunes, a decline in the power of the state, not a change of an intrinsic nature. The sense of the change and its direction are in no wise and at no stage subject to a reorientation, and not even to deflection: that is why reformist efforts are to no avail (Q, 2: 107). Change and constancy have the same sense, for the former is oriented towards the latter: we have a change in the *status quo*, the state, which remains constant as an historiographic unit throughout the vicissitudes that befall its constituents. Change, in other words, has no effect on the state as a state, which remains itself throughout its trajectory until the moment of its disappearance and is not a medium subject to change. To the appearance and disappearance of the state–the two historical termini *par excellence*–considerations of 'civil society' are wholly incidental. Indeed, the three-generation cycle is by no means an absolute rule in the realm of historical reality. Some states exceed the Great Lunar Year by a matter of centuries: their initial power inculcates conditions which render *'aṣabīya* superfluous, and for proof of this Ibn Khaldūn refers his reader to the Fatimids, the Aghlabids, and others (Q, 1: 264–8; BD, 7: 122–3 and *passim*). And it is because the *Muqaddima* portrays the moments of the state as moments of power and not as changes in political form and in relation to 'civil society' that the frequent comparisons made between Ibn Khaldūn and Polybius or Vico are totally unjustified.

The moments that the state is made divisible into are, in the light of the foregoing, purely circumstantial. That these moments occur in most states that come into existence does not alter this property: they do not so much constitute a theory of history as much as a repeated observation. And just as without the link with the abstract state these moments are linked paratactically, so are individual states that occur one after the other also related by parataxis. There is no question of one giving way to another in more than a circumstantial sense. Preceding and succeeding states are differentiated by a dynastic rubric, and each is infirmed in a self-sufficient island of time, the succession of which occurs very much within history as a paradigmatic structure. As we have seen, each of these temporal islands is given inner structures, both temporal (life span) and extra-temporal (*'aṣabīya*) which are articulated only in terms of the main historiographic parameters of the state: a chain of succession held into a unity by a vertical link built of genealogy. And this genealogical material is represented in the *Muqaddima* as that which sustains *'aṣabīya* by both its truth and its fiction–indeed, the *History* is replete with numerous instances of clans adopting nobler genealogies for themselves when they attain political dominion over others or when they attach themselves to other, more powerful, clans by bonds of alliance and vassality.

Ultimately, therefore, and in the purest practice of historical writing, the state is a name. It is the name that establishes the historicity of an historical group, as it is the name that establishes a ritual expression of order in the wild.[46] The historical narratives of Maghribi history are replete with information on the basis of which sociological considerations could be brought to bear on the construction of causalities other than the fictional and genealogical in historical narratives: matters such as geographical contiguity, institutions such as vassality, facts of geographical position with respect to trade routes, even remarks in the *Muqaddima* about the complexities of relations between kibesmen and sedentary cultures (Q, 1: 276-7)–all such considerations remain unrelated to each other, randomly distributed in the text, and narrated as mere events that come to pass under the ambit of the state. They remain completely unvalorized, being the sheer minutiae of history rather than its structural elements. What matters is the name and the historical power that resides in the name. For the name is the name of a people, and history is the story of a people as expressed in its sovereigns and their succession.

It is because Ibn Khaldūn was such a consistent practitioner of the historiographic paradigm that he considered Berber history as a unit of study. He was indeed the first to posit Berber history as a self-sufficient and integrated historical unit.[47] The Berbers had earlier figured only as a moral and ethical unit–at least in the discourse of high culture–that gave rise to such tracts as *Kitāb mafākhir al-Barbar*,[48] which is much like Ibn Khaldūn's own praise of the Berbers in the *History*, enumerating their qualities and the illustrious men they produced (BD, 6: 104-6). This is parallel to Ibn Khaldūn's consideration of the Banū Hilāl and Banū Sulaim as self-sufficient units of historical narrative–indeed, although Ibn Khaldūn describes the Hilālī migration as a swarm of locusts (BD, 6: 31) very much in keeping with the historiographic legend of his time,[49] he describes in detail their progress, their well-defined territories, and all the other facts relevant to their orderly historicity as states, i.e., as structures of genealogical continuity.

The self-sufficiency of Berber history is naturally premissed on the genealogical integrity and continuity of the Berbers. This is made possible for Ibn Khaldūn by his systematic refutation of Berber genealogical lore which was intent on proving the Arab origin of Berber states such as the Zayyānids and their broader Zanātan confederates (BD, 6: 181).[50] It is only after the lengthy discussion of the self-sufflcient, *sui generis*, integrity and independence of Berber genealogy that the history of the Berbers was a viable project for Ibn Khaldūn. Indeed, it can also be contended that the reason why Berber dynasties in the Maghrib put their genealogists to work on constructing Arab descent for them is not only because, as Ibn Khaldūn constantly says, they consider the Arabs more noble and far more blessed, but because, the high culture of the age being Arab, they could only acquire legitimacy in terms of high culture if this legitimacy were articulated in terms of elements that exist within this high culture, such as Arab genealogies. It is only once the Berbers are established as a name that they can be considered as the possessors of states, and therefore as historically significant. The wealth of anthropological detail hidden by the names and genealogies of tribal groups is irrelevant to Ibn Khaldūn's purposes. And it is in their succession as names that the Berbers are constituted as an historically relevant unit, as states whose mode of existence is temporality and whose internal constitution is a mere adjunct of their succession in time.[51]

NOTES

1 See A. Miquel, *La géographie humaine du monde musulman*, Paris, 1967 ff., vol. 2, pp. 271 ff.; A. Shboul, *Al-Mas'ūdī and His World*, London, 1979, pp. 151 ff. A particularly enlightened and interesting account of India is Bīrūnī, *Taḥqīq mā lil-Hind min maqbūla, maqbūla fil-'aql au mardhūla*, ed. C. E. Sachau, London, 1887.

2 Indeed, even Ranke himself had to posit a metahistorical unit as the prime historical category, and this was that of the 'nation'. See L. von Ranke. 'A Fragment from the 1830's', in F. Stern (ed.), *Varieties of History*, Cleveland and New York, 1956, pp. 59-60, and F. Meinecke, *Historism*, tr. J. E. Anderson, London, 1972, p. 500. On orientalists as historians, see, among others, C. Cahen, 'L'histoire économique et sociale de l'Orient musulman mediéval', in *SI*, 3(1955) 93-6; A. Abdel-Malek, 'L'Orientalisme en crise, in *Diogène*, 44(1963) 115; A. Hourani, 'History', in *The Study of the Middle East*, ed. L. Binder, New York & London, 1976, pp. 97-135.

3 A. Al-Azmeh, *Ibn Khaldūn in Modern Scholarship*, London, 1981, pp. 141 ff., and *idem.* "L'Annalistique entre histoire et pouvoir etc": *Histoire et diversité des cultures*, Paris, UNESCO, 1984, pp. 95-116. The latter contains a discussion of the relation between this conception and that of annalistic writing, which might be thought as disproving it. Biographical literature is an exception, but then it is not strictly historical.

4 'dhikr al-akhbār al-khāṣṣa bi-'aṣr au jīl'.

5 'li-intiẓāmihim fi 'idād al-mulūk'.

6 The corruption of the Biblical text and the existence of three versions of the Bible is common fare in Arab-Islamic culture and historiography alike, and finds its first expression in the Koran (3: 48 and *passim*). See Abul-Fidā, *Al-Mukhtaṣar fī akhbār al-bashar*, Cairo A. H. 1325, vol. 1, pp. 4-6. Although normally ascribed to intentional alteration, Ibn Khaldūn ascribes the corruption of the Biblical text to careless copying and esoteric exegesis (BD, 2: 11). See also W. J. Fischel, 'Ibn Khaldūn: On the Bible, Judaism, and Jews', in *Ignace Coldziher Memorial Volume*, ed. A. Schreiber and J. Somogyi, pt. 2, Jerusalem, 1956, pp. 147-71; W. Bacher, 'Bibel und Biblische Geschichte in der Muhammedanischen Literatur', in *Jeschurun* (Bamberg), 9(1872) 18-47; 1. di Matteo, 'Il "Taḥrīf" od alterazione delle Bibbia secondo il musulmani', in *Bessarione* (Rome), 38(1922) 64 ff., 223 ff.

7 See, for a prototypical example, Iṣfahānī, *Tārīkh siniy mulūk al-arḍ wal-anbiyā'*, ed. Gottwald and Tabrizi, Leipzig, A. H. 1340, p. 9 and *passim*, and the definition given by Ibn Farīghūn, *Jawāmi' al-'ulūm*, ed. F. Rosenthal in *History of Muslim Historiography*, 2nd. ed., Leiden, 1968, p. 459, and cf. Sakhāwī, *Al-I'lān bit-tawbīkh li-man dhamma ahl at-tārīkh*, ed. Qudsī, Damascus, A.H. 1349, pp. 6-7.

8 The mainstream tradition of Ibn Isḥaq (d. c. 150/767) and Ṭabarī (d. 310/923) is countered by another, in which the Arabs do not figure as a self-subsistent entity among the seven original peoples: see Iṣfahānī, *Tārīkh*, p. 6; Ma'sūdī, *Kitāb al-Tanbīh wal-Ishrāf*, ed. M. J. de Goeje (*Bibliotheca Geographorum Arabicorum*, vol. 8), Leiden, 1894, p. 77; Ibn al-'Ibrī, (Barhebraeus), *Tārīkh mukhtaṣar ad-duwal*, ed. A. Ṣālḥānī, Beirut, 1958, p. 3. The mainstream is conveniently summarized in Ibn Qutaiba, *Al-Ma'ārif*, ed. Th. 'Ukāsha, Cairo, 1969, pp. 26-7 and, in more detail, in BD, 2: 11 ff. For an overview in a Western language, see A. Borst, *Der Turmbau von Babel* (Stuttgart, 1957 ff.), vol. 1, pp. 325 ff.

9 Ibn Khaldūn was by no means the solitary holder of this opinion. See, for instance, Hamadānī, *Al-Iklīl: Al-Kitāb al-awwal*, ed. O. Lofgren, Uppsala, 1954, pp. 3-4.

10 The classic statement is in Ṭabarī, *Tārīkh al-rusul wal-mulūk*, ed. M. J. de Goeje, Leiden, 1879 ff., vol. 1, pp. 6–7. A reasoned definition of this, as of much else, can be found in Ibn Ḥazm, *At-Taqrīb li-ḥadd al-manṭiq bil-alfāẓ al-'āmmīyya wal-amthila al-fiqhīyya*, ed. I. 'Abbās, Beirut, 1959, p. 202. This matter will be treated further below, pp. 107 ff.

11 Persian genealogists differ on this point and insist on a separate origin for the Persians–BD, 2: 309–10. Other Persians, however, claimed not only Semitic descent, but direct descent from Isaac: on them, see Mas'ūdī, *Tanbīh*, pp. 108–10.

12 As the Arabs and Berbers are the main personages in the *History*, the histories of other peoples are narrated on their margins and according to strictly chronological criteria. The outline of the Second and Third Books of the *History*, dealing with the Arabs and the Berbers, is as follows. **Book Two:** on the Arabs, their chronological classes and states 'from Creation until the present': (i) first prolegomenon on the genealogies of nations; second prolegomenon on the representation of genealogies in the *History*; (ii) chronological classes of the Arabs: (1) the first class of 'Ād and Thamūd, on the margin of which is narrated the prophetic sequence Abraham-Ishmael-Isaac-Joseph-Lot; (2) the second class of the Ḥimyarīte Tabābi'a, on the margin of which are narrated the histories of the Babylonians, the Copts, the Israelites, the four classes of Persians, the Greeks-Macedonians, the Romans, the Byzantines, and the Goths; (3) the third class comprising the states, principalities and reigns of Qaḥṭān, Quḍā'a, Ḥīra, Kinda, and 'Adnān (Muḍar through to Quraish), followed by Prophecy through to the death of the Prophet. Next in treatment is the Islamic caliphate, which, under this name, applies only to the Medinan regime. Then an account is given of the Umayyad state, on the margin of which the early Khawārij are treated. Next, the state of the Shī'a is dealt with. This is primarily an account of the Abbasid caliphate, with the smaller states that coexisted and waned alongside it being treated according to their synchrony with Abbasid history. The Qarāmiṭa, the Ḥamdānids, the Banū Mazyad, and the Buwaihids are dealt with just after an account of the reign of Al-Mu'taḍid, which is also followed by a first account of the Seljuks up till the dominance of their Sultan Muḥammad over Baghdad. The narrative again focusses on the Abbasids, then switches to narratives on the 'Alawite states: the Idrīsids, the Isma'īlīs, the Banū Ḥamdūn, the Banū Qutāda and, by extension, the Umayyads of Andalusia, followed by the subsequent history of Islamic Spain until the time of Ibn Khaldūn. The *History* then switches back to the Abbasids, in synchrony with whom the histories of the Ṭulūnids, the Ikhshīdids, the Ṣuffār of Sijistān, the Marwānids of Diyārbakr, the Sāmānids, the Ghūrids, the Daylam, again the Buwaihids, the Banū Ḥisnawaih Kurds, again the Seljuks, and the Tartars are narrated. This is followed by a sketch of the Turkic states in the Levant and an account of the Crusades, followed by the histories of the Mamlūks, the Armenians, and the Mongols; (4) the fourth class, comprising the tribal remains of the Arabs in the Arabian Peninsula and elsewhere, followed by a detailed account of the Banū Hilāl and Banū Sulaim in the Maghrib; (iii) **Book Three:** on the Berbers 'and the second people of the Maghrib': (a) their genealogies, (b) their abodes, (c) their virtues, (d) a perfunctory overview of their history prior to the Islamic conquest and up till the time of the Aghlabids, (e) the Butr Berbers: the Zuwāwa, Zuwāgha, and other minor peoples, on the Hawwāra of the Barānis, followed by Kutāma and their association with the Fatimids. A narrative of the four chronological classes of the Ṣanhāja is then given: the Zīrids, the Banū Khurāsān of Tunis, the Banū Ḥammād, and the Banū Ḥabūs, of

the first class, followed by the Almoravids and the Banū Ghāniya of the second class on whose margin the history of the sub-Saharan black African states is narrated. The third class then follows: the Maṣmūda, Barghuāṭa, and Idrīsids, all culminating in the original Almohads of the Mu'minid house and followed by the Ḥafṣids who, one would presume, constitute the fourth class of Ṣanhāja. Then follows an account of the second great tribal grouping of Zanāta: their first generation which stretches from pre-Islamic times through the Kāhina on to Abū Yazīd in the tenth century A.D., and includes the Zirids of Fez and other minor dynasties, followed by a second class whose most outstanding representatives are the Zayyānids ('Abd al-Wādids) of Tlemcen, and a third which is simultaneous with the second and which contains the Banū Bādīn, the Banū Salāma (in one of whose Saharan settlements Ibn Khaldūn wrote the *Muqaddima*), and, above all, the Merinids of Fez.

13 Ibn Khaldūn's *History* does not improve on the imprecision that characterizes Arab historiographic terminology. *Jīl* and *ṭabaqa* have fluid meanings and are interchangeable, designating at once 'chronological class' as well as 'people' and section of a people. In the latter sense, they would be synonymous with *sha'b*, *umma*, and *jadhm*. In the former, chronological succession need not necessarily be of units of the same people, but these units can appertain to any class of facts. One author speaks of the four *ṭabaqāt* of the caliphate, being Medinese, Damascene, Baghdadian, and Cairene (Qalqashandī, *Ma'āthir al-ināfa fī ma'ālim al-khilāfa*, ed. 'A. A. Farrāj, Kuwait, 1964, *ad. loc.*). The same considerations apply to terms designating smaller human groupings: *'ayṣ, fakhdh, 'ashīra, qabīla, ḥayy, baṭn,* etc.: See the articles on Ibn Khaldūn, Mas'ūdī (d. 345/956), Shahrastānī (d. 548/1153), Fārābī (d. 339/950), and the Koran in N. Nassar, *Mafhūm al-umma bayn ad-dīn wat-tārīkh*, Beirut, 1978. The imprecision in question is a reflection of the highly interesting imprecision of tribal terminology: see Hamadānī, *Iklīl*, pp. 6–7; Maqrīzī, *An-Nizā' wat-takhāṣum fīmā bayna Banī Umayya wa Banī Hāshim*, ed. Najafī, Najaf, A. H. 1368, p. 57; Nuwairī, *Nihāyat al-arab fī funūn al-adab*, Cairo, 1923 ff., vol. 2, pp. 284–5, and J. Chelhod, 'Les structures dualistes de la société bédouine', in *L'Homme*, 9/2(1969) 95–6.

14 See above, n. 12.

15 Although the people of 'Ād were by no means physically exterminated, they were historically liquidated. After their world-historical sway had waned, they dwelt in the Syrian desert at the time of the Babylonians. That they had what the *History* terms as 'kings' can only be taken figuratively, for we are also told that they constitute the remains of the first class of Arabs (BD, 2: 497). Their historicity is therefore vestigial and cannot contradict the present argument.

16 The fourth class of Arabs is the *'Arab musta'jima*, those Arabs tending towards foreignness–so called because their use of the Arabic language is not in conformity with the pristine Muḍarī tongue in which the Koran was inimitably inspired (BD, 6: 8), and who comprise the famous Hilālīs and Sulaimis of the Maghreb.

17 This is discussed in Al-Azmeh, 'L'Annalistique'.

18 In *ibid.*, and *idem.*, *Ibn Khaldūn*, 176. History, *ta'rīkh*, is, essentially, datation: see TK, I : 56, and the convenient summaries and definitions in Sarrāj, *Al-ḥulal as sundusīya fil-akhbār at-tūnisīya*, ed. M. H. Hīla, Tunis, 1970, vol. 1, pp. 135 ff.

19 Al-Azmeh, 'L'Annalistique'.

20 On this process, see E. L. Petersen, *'Alī and Mu'āwiya in Early Arabic Tradition*, Copenhagen, 1964.

21 Qalqashandī, *Khilāfa*, vol. 1, p. 2. Two authors present curious positions in addition to Ibn Khaldūn. Our author's pupil al-Maqrīzī (*Nizā'*, pp. 59–61) compares the vicissitudes of the history of the Israelites with that of the Muslims in a vein that does not laud the Abbasids at the expense of the Umayyads at all. As for Suyūṭī (d. 911/1505), he interprets the *ḥadīth* according to which there will be only 12 caliphs in Islam in a novel way: he declares that this refers only to those caliphs who will do good, and they include Muʿāwiya. Two Abbasids (al-Muhtadī and al-Ẓāhir) are pronounced as mere possibilities, and two of the dozen in question are relegated to the realm of eschatology (*Tārīkh al-khulafā'*, Beirut, n.d., pp. 13–15).

22 This position is not unique to Ibn Khaldūn. See Ibn Ṭabāṭabā (also known as Ibn aṭ-Ṭiqṭaqā), *Al-Fakhrī fīl-ādāb al-sulṭānīya wal-duwal al-islāmīya*, Cairo, 1962, p. 60 and Miskawaih, 'Textes inédits de Miskawayh', ed. M. Arkoun, in *Annales islamologi-ques*, 5(1963) 204–6. See the remarks on this matter by M. ʿA. Jābirī, *Al-ʿAṣabīya wad-daula: Maʿālim naẓariyya khaldūnīya fīt-tārīkh al-islāmī*, Casablanca, 1971, p. 313.

23 Again because of likely respect for Abbasid political piety, ʿAlid descent was normally denied to the Fatimids. Ibn Khaldūn took great exception to this (BD, 3: 757–8), as did Maqrīzī (*Ittiʿāẓ al-hunafāʾ bi-akhbār al-aʾimma al-fāṭimiyyīn min al-khulafā'*, ed. M. Aḥmad, Cairo, 1971 ff., vol. 3, pp. 345–6), at the cost of much misrepresentation and vilification (see Sakhāwī, *Aḍ-ḍau' al-lāmi'*, vol. 4, pp. 147–8). On this whole matter, see P. H. Mamour, *Polemics on the Origin of the Fatimi Caliphs*, London, 1934.

24 This seems to have been in aid of Ibn Khaldūn's assertions concerning the ʿAlid descent of the Fatimids, and of the consistency of this assertion with his taxonomy of early Islamic historical states.

25 The Turks, according to our author, are one of the most plentiful nations on earth (T, 351). By the consensus of Arab genealogists, they are descendants of Japheth (BD, 5: 798). Turkic genealogists took over this view, with the modification that instead of descent from Japheth by way of his son ʿĀmūr, they came from the seed of another son, Türk (R. Dankoff, 'Kašgharī on the Tribal and Kinship Organization of the Turks', in *Archivum Ottomanicum*, 4(1972) 29–30). They occupy a prominent role in historical cosmography: Ibn Khaldūn states that not only have the Arabs and the Turks 'always' alternated in world domination (BD, 5: 4, 799; T, 351), but the whole of the world's habitation seemed to him to be moving northwards (M. Redjala, 'Un texte inédit de la *Muqaddima*', in *Arabica*, 22(1975) 320–23)—towards the dominion of the Turks and the Europeans.

26 'muzāḥimin lahā baʿd ṣadr minhā'.

27 I have argued the essential conceptualization of this point in 'L'Annalistique'.

28 In the same passage, Ibn Khaldūn tells us that the Sūfīs, not unnaturally, assumed this new historical actor to be the Fatimid Messiah (*Al-Mahdī*). Such predictions were not confined to quasi-Maraboutic quacks, but were shared, according to the same passage again, by Ibn Zarzar, a Jewish physician in the Aragonese court (*ṭabīb Ibn Adfūnush*) who had earlier been employed by the Merinid sovereign. See T. Fahd, 'Djafr', in EI², 2: 375–7.

29 There need be no incompatibility between belief in the workings of the stars and those of terrestrial factors except for vestigial remains of the naive Enlightenment polemic. Works by Dame Frances Yates and Alexandre Koyré have shown that no such incompatibility exists with respect to the beginnings of modern scientific attitudes (the Copernican revolution itself was partly born of Hermetic notions). For Ibn Khaldūn as for Giordano Bruno, the material world is full of occult sympathies

descending from the stars on which it is dependent–or at least with which it runs parallel. The terrestrial and the astral are two provinces of being which sometimes converge and sometimes refer to distinct orders. Ibn Khaldūn himself was well known for his knowledge of the *Zā'irja* (a very complex chart from which the future of dynasties could be predicted, described in detail in Q, 3: 146 ff.), a knowledge which one younger contemporary thought was somehow esoteric and something which Ibn Khaldūn preferred to keep to himself (Ibn Ḥajar, *Durar*, vol. 3, pp. 376–7). Astrological calculation and expectation was certainly widely practised among Maghribi intellectuals during Ibn Khaldūn's time (Ibn al-Azraq, *Badā'i' as-silk fī ṭabā'i' al-mulk*, ed. A. S. Nashshār, Baghdad, 1977 ff., vol. 1, p. 154) and widely used at court (H. P. J. Renaud, 'Divination et histoire nord-africain au temps d'Ibn Khaldūn', in *Hespéris*, 30(1943) 213–21), and Ibn Khaldūn's most revered and important mentor, al-Ābilī (d. 757/1356), studied occult sciences under Khallūf al-Maghīli, a Jew considered a great master of the arts, and in his term disseminated knowledge of the occult to his own students (T, 36, 47).

30 Ibn Khaldūn speaks of the necessary correspondence between the prescriptions of the stars and the nature of terrestrial matters: 'al-muṭābaqa bayn ḥukm [al-athar al-nujūmī] wa 'umrān al-arḍ wa ṭabī'atihā amr lā budda minh' (Q, 2: 246). Astrologers not only made pronouncements on the advent of world-historical peoples, but also had their own pronouncements on what Ibn Khaldūn took to be the tendency of organized habitation to move northwards (Redjala, 'Un texte inédit', p. 322, and cf above, n. 25).

31 The conception of sovereignty as absolute exclusivity in matters relating to the exercise of power and authority is well established–indeed, it appears, singular–in Arab-Islamic culture, providing the sole conception of the state. This can be seen, for instance, in the quite casual remarks in a biographical dictionary, where the author discourses rather casually upon the difference between the terms *malik* and *sulṭān* in terms of a hierarchical ladder of exclusivity in the exercise of power (Subkī, *Ṭabaqāt al-Shāfi'īyya al-kubrā*, ed. 'A. Hilū and M. Tanahī, Cairo, 1964 ff., vol. 5, p. 315).

32 See Al-Azmeh, *Ibn Khaldūn*, ch. 1.

33 Abū Ḥammū, *Wasīṭat as-sulūk fī siyāsat al-mulūk*, Tunis, A.H. 1276, p. 118.

34 See the classical statements of, for instance, Ṭurṭūshī, *Sirāj al-mulūk*, Cairo, A. H. 1319, pp. 39–42, 51; of Rāzī, *Muḥaṣṣal afkār al-mutaqaddimīn wal-muta'akhkhirīn*, Cairo, A. H. 1323, p. 176 and the notes in A. S. Tritton, 'Al-Muḥaṣṣal by ... Rāzī (Cairo, 1323)', in *Oriens*, 18–19(1967), *ad. loc.*, 11. I 1–14; and in the sixtieth night of *Alf Laila wa laila*.

35 'ma'nā al-mulk'.

36 'as-sūq al-a'ẓam lil-'ālam'. Ibn Khaldūn's discussion of the *ḥijāb*, the seclusion of the sovereign from his subjects and the various layers of this *ḥijāb*, is a discussion of the vertical exclusivity of power. The same would apply to Abū Ḥammū's exhortation to his son and heir to institute a multiplicity of subtrefuges whereby even his own domestic slaves would not be privy even to the architectural layout of the royal palace (*Wasiṭa*, p. 21). This absolute separation of the ruler is even articulated in terms of the architectural choreography of power: we will notice that the Alhambra, the royal city of New Fez, and the citadel of Cairo married the continuity of a preexisting urban centre with the institution of a remoter type of rule expressed in topographic separation.

37 I have discussed this matter in detail in my *Ibn Khaldūn*, pp. 233 ff.

38 'min al-iltiḥām bin-nasab aw mā fī ma'nāh'. The forms in which *'aṣabīya* appear and variants of its translation are listed in T. Khemiri, 'Der 'aṣabīya-Begriff in der *Muqad-*

dima des Ibn Ḫaldūn', in *Der Islam*, 23(1936) 163 ff. This situation naturally precludes my reference to *'aṣabīya* by any term or in any form other than the original Arabic.

39 Cf. my *Ibn Khaldūn*, p. 143.

40 One commentator has aptly called *'aṣabīya* the 'pendant affectif de la répression'– O. Carré, 'A propos de la sociologie politique d'Ibn Khaldoun', in *Revue Française de Sociologie*, 14/1(1973), p. 122.

41 Cf. Jābirī, *Al-'Aṣabīya*, pp. 248–9, and P. Kraus, rev. art. in *Orientalische Literaturzeitung*, 37(1934), col. 535–6.

42 Throughout the Maghrib at Ibn Khaldūn's time, the human armour of the state was composed of distinct groups, including foreign mercenaries from Catalonia (and sometimes Genoa), and each of which was supported by a distinct type of economic relation to the state. Together, they would qualify as the *'aṣabīya* of the monarch whose importance as a unit of *'aṣabīya* for the state, in the *Muqaddima*, far outweighs the reality of their inner distinctions. Abū Ḥammū, the king of Tlemcen, provides very precious information on the composition of his armies (*Wasīṭa*, pp. 78–80 and cf. the information on the Banū Tūjīn in BD, 7: 338): (1) allied clan leaders, presumably related to the royal house, (2) the monarch's own clan, (3) allies, primarily tribes and clans inside and around the territorial sway of the state, and (4) slaves and hirelings, composed of Christian renegades (*'ulūj* or *a'lāj*), Christian militias imported from the Aragonese court (see C.-E. Dufourcq, *L'Espagne Catalane et le Maghrib aux XIIIe et XIVe siècles*, Paris, 1966, pp. 102–3), slaves proper (*wiṣfān*) and others. The allies, frequently Arab tribesmen, are used to discipline dissenting members of the House. And while the three first categories receive their pay from land and other revenue sources, the fourth category is paid directly by the state treasury (*ibid.*, p. 124). And while there is evidence throughout the *History* that Ibn Khaldūn was well aware of these distinctions within the ruling *'aṣabīya*, this awareness remained at the level of a sheer awareness which did not impinge on the theoretical elaboration of *'aṣabīya* and which dwelt in a theoretically distinct domain.

43 See J. Hopkins, 'The Almohad Hierarchy', in *BSOAS*, 16(1954), p. 93.

44 M. Talbi, in EI^2, 3: 829.

45 I use the term 'moment' for 'ḥāl' and 'ṭaur' in systematic preference to the normal rendition as 'stage'. 'Moment' neutralizes the crypto-evolutionist and developmental connotations of 'stage' as is required by the analysis to follow, while at the same time preserving the integrity, unity, and continuity of the state in question. See the lexical deliberations on 'ṭaur' in LA, s.v. 'ṭ-w-r'. On the technical and semantic wealth of *ḥāl*, which is totally lost in the usual rendition, see TK, 1: 359–60.

46 See the discussion of anthropological considerations in my *Ibn Khaldūn*, pp. 209 ff., and below, ch. 3.

47 See M. P. Edmond, *Ibn Khaldoun: Situation dans la culture arabo-Islamique* (Oran, 1964), pp. 12 ff.

48 Ed. E. Levi-Provençal, Rabat, 1932.

49 M. Brett, *Fitnat al-Qayrawān: A Study in Traditional Arabic Historiography*, unpub. Ph.D. Thesis, University of London, 1970.

50 H. Kurio, *Geschichte und Geschichtsschreiber der 'Abd al- Wādiden* (Freiburg im Breisgau, 1973), pp. 15 f, and cf. Ibn Ḥazm, *Jamharat ansāb al-'Arab*, ed. E. Levi-Provençal (Cairo, 1948) pp. 461 ff.

51 A brief outline of these temporal successions was given in n. 12 above.

CHAPTER TWO

THE PROBLEMATIZATION OF HISTORY

In the previous chapter, the object of Ibn Khaldūn's new science contained in the *Muqaddima* was identified and established as a construct from the conception of state immanent in Arab-Islamic historical writing. It was argued that there is an identity between the objects of all three books of the *History*, that the object upon which both the *Muqaddima* and the historical narratives discourse is one and the same. It was also argued that the terrain in which this identity is located is that of the physiognomy and morphology of the concept of state: what it refers to in the empirical manifold, and how this act of reference is geared towards a specific form of its referent. Historical narrative is one about the history of the world, while the *Muqaddima* is a prolegomenon on the object of historical writing, which is the state. The state occupies a central position in all parts of the *History*.

We have also seen that the first book of the *History*, the *Muqaddima*, stands to historical narrative in a relation of logical priority, much in the same way as the grammatical inchoative is presupposed by any predicate (*mubtada'* and *khabar*). Historical writing, indeed, is 'a narrative of human aggregation (*ijtimā'*) which is the organized habitation (*'umrān*) of the world' (Q, 1: 56). History is the narrative of a specific object which has a logical priority over the act of narration itself although, as we have seen, it is topically derivative of the object of narration. It is this system of dyadic priority–one in which narration is anterior to its object, and the other in which this object is anterior to narration–which allows the *Muqaddima* the freedom to name its object *'umrān*, civilization,[1] and not *daula*, the state, as the analysis in the preceding chapter would have logically warranted. The constitution of the science of civilization takes place according to a system of concepts which is not derivable from historical writing. But this freedom is ultimately bounded by the original historiographic constraint which was the very exigency to which the new science was a response. This chapter will show that the constitution of the science of civilization is dictated by the structure of the consummated form of civilization: the state. In other words, the constituents of civilization as well as its orientation are directly geared towards its end product, the state, and is therefore made of only those components that Ibn Khaldūn considered germane to the formation of the state as required by historical writing. Indeed, as we shall see, this end result is the only way in which we can explain–and justify–the very contents of the *Muqaddima*, if not the manner of its construction.

Before we pursue the techtonics of the *Muqaddima* any further, we should now turn to the very structures of this part of the History. After all, it is the first book of the *History*, the *Muqaddima*, which is Ibn Khaldūn's title to fame, and it is in this section of Ibn Khaldūn's work that the reader can find the precise configuration which is formed by the conjunction of the sciences of his age.

The keys to the *Muqaddima* are embedded in its title. The term *muqaddima* is a highly multivalent one; and its semantic fields stretch out very widely to engulf within their purviews a variety of conceptual systems, as the extensive treatments in encyclopedic works on Arab-Islamic sciences show very amply.[2] A *muqaddima* is a prolegomenon in the very widest and most general sense of the term. It is a prefatory discourse, according to the general belletristic understanding of the term which was in very wide use. It is the beginning of a work in whatever understanding of beginning is employed: as artifice, as in the purely literary-ornamental use. More importantly, and much more in keeping with Ibn Khaldūn's *Muqaddima*, the term takes on a more rigorous colouration in relation to what succeeds it. It takes the sense of a beginning whose priority is not confined to that of textual sequence, that it occurs in the work before other passages, but whose priority attaches primarily to a discursive effect it has on the very structure of subsequent discourse.

A prolegomenon in the sense used by Ibn Khaldūn conforms to the most general definition given of it: 'that upon which something depends in itself', and 'that upon which something depends, be this dependence conceptual, apprehended as being habitual, or conventional' (JT, 342; TK, 2: 1215).[3] In this general sense it can also serve to mean the premise of a syllogism,[4] since this premise contains the result of the syllogistic process. In the same way, Ibn Khaldūn speaks in an early work of 'prolegomena which reveal the truth' of a specific subject matter (L, 18). The *History*, Ibn Khaldūn informs his reader, contains a textual sequence which is graduated. It starts with a discourse on the conditions which make for the events of history and only then presents a narrative of specific historical events and sequences (Q, 1: 7).[5] History being, strictly speaking, a narrative concerning the events of particular epochs or peoples (Q, 1: 50), that which is to act as its prolegomenon is a discourse upon the general conditions obtaining in epochs, among peoples, and in the different climes–a discourse which had previously been provided, in their own times, by Bakrī and Mas'ūdī (Q, 1: 50-51). The prefatorial discourse plays a remedial role in relation to historical narrative, whose inadequacies were what prompted Ibn Khaldūn to problematize history in the first place, as the opening passage of the *History* informs the reader. It acts as a gauge against which narratives inherited from the past are weighed with view to ascertaining their plausibility or implausibility; it acts, so to speak, as a 'control group' from which deviation is arrived at by analogy and which results in a verdict of implausibility.

This sense of prolegomenon, with its properties derived from the sciences of jurisprudence and theology and with its near homology with the notion of *aṣl*, will be taken up in a subsequent section of this chapter.[6] More germane to our present purpose is the logico-natural sense of Ibn Khaldūn's use of prolegomena. An analogy can immediately be drawn here with the Greek *archē*, a term which is not only lexically homologous as 'principle' and 'origin', but equally has the sense of 'cause'. In Islamic sciences, in which such notions as *aṣl* and *'illā* are associated with the sciences of law and theology, and with the sciences of nature, an ambiguity of sense reigns with all the terms associated with acts of beginning which a prolegomenon heralds. An analogous situation obtains in classical and medieval European philosophy, as Schopenhauer argued in his dissertation with respect to the concept of *archē*: a clear and unambiguous distinction between this concept as a logical principle and as a real cause was never made.[7] A logical principle, a premise, is also a cause in terms of the flow of a proof. Logical processes are also causal chains, and a chain of causation in the mind and 'in the real' are both contained within the spectrum of sense contained within the semantic field of acts of beginning and apodicticity contained within the term *muqaddima* and its cognates and associates. It stands for all species of anteriority, logical and real, which are contained in the notion of 'principle', including that of material anteriority in a science–its fundamental principles, *muqaddimāt*, are also its *mabādi' uwal*.[8]

Anatomy of the Muqaddima

The science of civilization, like all other sciences, is built upon basic principles which constitute its prolegomena. This science is the prolegomenon to history, and, like history, it has to have its own prolegomena which go into the process of its constitution as a science. And these prolegomena, as we shall have ample opportunity to see, cover the multitude of senses and ambiguities that have just been observed, and exist at a variety of levels at several points in the flow of the text of the *Muqaddima*. Like all sciences,[9] again, the science of civilization is a *sui generis* science, its object, (*mauḍū'*) civilization, being a natural conceptualized entity (Q, 1: 63). Its object being established, the first step in every science, its founder's task, is to identify and treat the particular topics (*masā'il*) which the science is concerned with addressing–and these are the essential accidents of its object (Q, 1: 61-63). This establishment of the science involves the search for the general conditions which obtain under the aegis of civilization, and the modalities (*kaifīyāt*) in the form of which these conditions obtain (Q, 1: 2). The science of civilization is that which treats of the organized habitation of the world and of the essential accidents that occur within organized habitation (Q, 1: 56). Differently expressed, these modes are equivalent to the modes through which civilization passes: the science of civilization, according to another definition, is that which treats of the modes attaching to civilization, one after the other (Q, 1: 61). The first book of the History treats 'of the nature of civilization and of its essential accidents: of beduinism, of urbanism, of domination, of acquisition, of livelihood, and, finally, of sciences and crafts' (Q, 1: 56). Seen as a textually graduated series, this enumeration corresponds to the actual textual flow of the *Muqaddima* and, roughly, to a temporal series of what occurs before what else. It is equally legitimate to regard them as a graduated series of the essential accidents of civilization, where the relative proximity to the beginning of civilization, in every sense of the word 'beginning', corresponds to the relative proximity to the metaphysical principle according to which the accidents–and their substance, civilization–are construed.

The vocabulary in which Ibn Khaldūn presents the properties of the object of his new science is very decidedly metaphysical. Civilization, like everything else, has a nature (*ṭabī'a*) specific to it and to its modes (Q, 1: 57). The discourse upon nature in Ibn Khaldūn's time presents a complex picture, for at hand is a discourse upon the natures of things, not on nature as such, and the natures of things bear a multiplicity of meanings.[10]

Each specific entity has a specific nature inherent in it, a qualitative nature which has certain properties of a substantive rather than (as in the modern acceptation) a functional nature.[11] It is a *physis* in the classical and pre-classical philosophical senses, one which allows things to happen 'naturally' to a body–such as its falling down because it naturally falls down. A nature in this sense is the substratum for changes undergone by a body, but it is not the passive substratum which simply undergoes change. It is an active disposition, a constitution which realizes itself through change, and an essential property in terms of which a thing is defined and is therefore not simply a technical sense of nature–there was no uniform technical sense–but also a vernacular sense of nature which is still very much in evidence in quotidian parlance today.[12] In the high culture of Arab-Islamic history, this idea of nature was utilized in Avicennan medico-physical discourse as it had been utilized among the Stoics,[13] and denoted also the power which compels an entity to reach its natural consummation which is the full realization of its nature (JT, 145). It is in this sense that, for Ibn Khaldūn, senescence is natural in the state (Q, 2: 106). The qualitativeness of this nature is such that it bears and supports alchemy. This is the sense of Ibn Bishrūn's (fl. c. A.D. 1000) statement quoted by Ibn Khaldūn (Q, 3: 200) that everything in the terrestrial world is potentially subject to alchemical action because the natures of things–their constituents, such as the four elements–are present in everything. And it is also in this sense that Ibn Khaldūn states that knowledge of an entity is knowledge not only of its form and its telos, but also of that which is active within it and the nature which receives such action (Q, 3: 221). So medical and vitalistic is the concept of nature utilized by Ibn Khaldūn that, when speaking of the human mind and its nature, he expresses its dispositions in terms of vapours circulating the heart and the brain.

The nature of civilization which informs the basic structures of the science of civilization, like the natures that inform the objects of other Arab-Islamic sciences, is constituted, as we have seen, by a teleology which expresses the fully attained nature and which is reached by the inexorable and natural movement expressed in the succession of modes through which this nature exists. Each of these successive apparitions of the nature of civilization, and each of the essential accidents of this civilization, equally possesses a nature of its own which yearns for consummation.[14] *'Aṣabīya* is such an essential accident, and it 'naturally requires domination' (Q, 1: 253), as are the less essential habits that, once established, acquire the properties of a nature (Q, 2: 107). Indeed, such is the lot of the conjunction of topics which form the *Muqaddima* and which appear within it as essential accidents of the nature of civilization and thus as the topics of the science of civilization: in order, they are the modes of civilization (beduinity and urbanism), *'aṣabīya* and the types of domination, and the resultant states and kingships and what occurs under their aegis by way of acquisitive and intellectual activities (Q, 1: 56).

The relations between these entities are manifold. They are relations of textual sequence, relations of hierarchy with respect to proximity to the original nature, relations of temporal consecution, and relations according to the categories of matter and form. Excluding the first chapter of the *Muqaddima* which deals with 'human civilization in general', the second chapter, on 'beduin civilization and savage peoples' through to the sixth and last chapter dealing with sciences and education, form a textual sequence where there is a beginning in time (beduinism) generating the *'aṣabīya* that forms the state, either where no state had been or by taking over from a moribund power, examines the constituents, in time and otherwise, of this state in the third chapter ('on states, kingship, the caliphate, and their attendant institutions'), and then keats of urban life in the fourth, fifth, and sixth chapters, as that which comes to be as a result of the testablishment of the state. We have there three temporal units: beduinism, followed by the formation of the state, and then life in the cities. Moreover, the movement in the realm of reality between beduinism and the state and then on to urbanity and its various manifestation is equally one between a natural beginning and the natural end, the *telos* of this beginning and the consummation of its nature: civilization in the form it takes in the cities, *ḥadāra*, is the *telos* (*ghāya*) of civilization as such (BB, 371). Although both modes of civilization, beduinity and urbanism, are equally natural (Q, 1: 220), one is more pristinely natural then the other and much closer to its beginning. Beduinism 'is anterior to urban civilization and precedes it, and the desert is the mainstay of civilization and of the cities' (Q, 1: 223),[15] for there is little doubt that that which is strictly necessary (and hence simple) is anterior to what is supererogatory (*kamālī*) (and therefore complex), and the beduins dwell in the reign of the former, while city life calls for the latter (Q, 1: 224).[16] The natural agency that makes the transition between the two modes of civilization is *'aṣabīya* whose natural goal is kingship (Q, 1: 253). This, in turn, engenders urbanism so as 'to replete that which was lacking in matters of civilization among the beduins' (Q, 2: 204). The second mode of civilization is a completion of civilization, one that is effected by the accretion of properties that make for its inevitable decline, and the diminution of properties it possessed in an earlier phase: the *'aṣabīya* which benefits from the state passes through moments which can be differentiated by their degree of beduinity (Q, 1: 314)–a remark which could be trite and merely commonsensical in the abstract, but which acquires more profound dimensions in view of the teleological structure under scrutiny. Finally, civilization is the matter of the state and, equally, the state provides matter for civilization (Q, 2: 92, 96).

Relations between the textual units that make up the *Muqaddima* are, therefore, very complex and are located at distinct levels. Two very noteworthy points indicate clues as to why the work is constructed in such a complex manner: it has been noted that beduinism not only occurs before urban life, but that it is also anterior to it, and that civilization and the state stand to each other reciprocally both as matter and as form. The anteriority of beduinism to urbanism is not only a serial anteriority involving mere textual and temporal precedence, but is also a conceptual anteriority, a sort of logical presupposition which the term *muqaddima* evokes. The latter cannot happen without the former. Indeed, the transmutation of *'aṣabīya* into a power group is by no means a certain eventuality. Urban life only takes place in cases when kingship is attained by beduinism (Q, 1: 309). The flow between beduinity and urban life, when actually affected, is one which is totally dependent upon its beginning, just as a conclusion is dependent upon its premise. And indeed urban life and its inevitable atrophy is very much the conclusion of beduinism. It concludes it in the sense of ending it in precisely the manner that its nature requires. The natural movement whereby beduinism passes through the medium of the state and engenders urban civilization is one in which a beginning is consummated according to a teleological view of the destiny of civilization. The metaphysic of decline–one commentator has very aptly called the *Muqaddima* an 'aetiology of decline'[17]–which concretizes the movement of civilization to its inevitable doom is one in which the metaphysic of nature takes on a form which is very homologous to that of a logical process, one in which the end is fully contained in the beginning. So much so, indeed, that the conditions obtaining at the beginning of the full unfolding of a civilization are determinant of the detailed outcome that characterizes the fully formed product. The numbers involved in the formation of a certain state, for instance, are determinant of the geographical extent and other properties regarding the sway and 'strength' of that particular state (Q, 1: 327 ff.). The homology of this view with the everyday vernacular conception of nature is readily apparent: a nature inheres in an entity at its beginning, and the outcome cannot but be coincident with the original natural input: a rather banal idea in itself, but one which fulfils a precise conceptual role in the *Muqaddima*.

The homology between logic and nature that has been indicated also informs the reciprocal apparitions of both civilization and the state as matter and form at one and the same time. This reciprocity, indeed, points even further towards the supports that different textual components of the *Muqaddima* provide for each other and the changes of form which these components are subject to and which depend on the precise level at which their relation is placed. And this reciprocity is further testimony that, in the *Muqaddima*, the serial structure of text which seeks to transcribe the serial unfolding of the empirical manifold at the same time personifies the unfolding of nature as a metaphysical concept. Indeed, it can be said that the temporal movement of nature to its consummation is the empirical mode in which a movement of a higher, metaphysical, order is accomplished. It is a movement of categories in the guise of time, one in which metaphysical categories are embodied in the form of textual units (beduinism, *'aṣabīya*, the state, urban life) which, in their turn and by their sequence, simulate and register the movement of reality directly and in keeping with Ibn Khaldūn's nominalist intent.

What may be seen as a contradiction, or at least a dubiousness, when both the state and civilization reciprocate representing matter and form to each other, is thus a necessary discursive tactic: neither of these textual units is matter and form at the same time but metamorphose according to their location in the overall structure and flow of the *Muqaddima*. The metamorphosis is located at the point of transition between the two modes of civilization. The state is the agency which brings about this transition and which experiences this change. The state is the form of civilization: it is so because it is the primary concern of the science of history–and of civilization–and thus the apex of its investigations, and because its formation is the fulfilment of a potential and the completion of the nature of civilization. In this sense, it is the form not only of beduin civilization, but of civilization *tout court*. It closes the most important chapter in the history of the nature which is civilization and which, from the point where the state is formed onwards, begins to decompose and atrophy as a result of its sheer dead weight. But this process of disintegration inevitably leading to the eventual nullification of the state and (sometimes) of civilization is also that in which the state–and, consequently, civilization–attains its fullest expression in the form of city life and its splendours, its wealth, its power, and its arts, crafts, and sciences.

So weighty are these manifestations of the state that they take up three of the six chapters that compose the *Muqaddima*.

In real, empirical, terms, the magnificence of urban life is in direct proportion to the power of the state that gives rise to it, and the state itself is prior even to the cities (Q, 2: 201), in the sense that even long-established cities are insignificant without the presence within them of the state. Urban life revises its identity as form: it transmutes itself into matter, the matter of civilization, under the pressure of the empirical form taken by the metaphysical movement of the *Muqaddima*. This movement here acquires a simple causality, a causality connecting a before with an after. And it is precisely here that the real *denotatum* of civilization appears most clearly, the *denotatum* of the metaphysical and logical march of the *Muqaddima*. For 'in the real', Ibn Khaldūn does not set about fishing conceptually. He merely identifies and registers the sensuous properties of his denotatum and summarily decrees it a metaphysical category. Nowhere does one encounter an actual definition of beduinity, of *ḥaḍāra*, or of the state. What he presents is the successive register of what sensuously appear to be successive moments, which he calls modes, of a temporal chain. *Ḥaḍāra* is merely the aggregate of its sensuous properties: the manifestations of luxury. This is the sole definition of *ḥaḍāra* that we have (Q, 2: 251), and it is just as vernacular and simple as that presented by Ibn Khaldūn's onetime friend Ibn al-Khaṭīb: *ḥaḍāra* is identified with jewellery, perfumes, palaces, orchards, clothes, and festivities.[18] *Ḥaḍāra*, like the other modes of civilization, is the mere assemblage of its visible characteristics, and hence its rendition here as 'city life' and not by a more technical term is fully justified. Being such an assemblage of visible characterizations, the moments of civilization, in their empirical being, are fully divorced from their metaphysical moment with which their connection is forced and completely external. For as *denotata*, these modes are merely identified and characterized, not in any necessary way posited as moments of their metaphysical being.

The modal unfolding of the *Muqaddima* proceeds regardless. The necessity and constancy with which nature actualizes its full essence is, we have remarked, analogous to the arrival from a premise to a conclusion. In both cases, the end product is contained in the beginning. In both cases, the necessity with which the conclusion and end is derived from the beginning is one inherent in the beginning, and is released from its infirmity within this beginning only by seriality: the succession in the form of time of the essential accidents of nature, and a homologous[19] succession of propositions. In both cases, that is, a necessary process unfolds towards a predetermined end under the influence, and in the form, of essential accidents, which are analogous to the necessary succession of propositions, each requiring the validity of the previous one, just as, in the realm of nature, each of the essential accidents presupposes the actualization and the passing of the previous one. The processes of entailment and of teleological actualization are parallel and run with an infallible rectitude–just as logic eschews sophistical syllogisms, so does natural unfolding never admit non-natural interference.

The general structure of the *Muqaddima* is therefore one in which three distinct orders–nature, logic, and time–run parallel to one another. We shall see in the next section of this chapter, and as Diagram One illustrates, the companionship of these three conceptual orders does not run through the entire textual sequence of the *Muqaddima* from beginning to end. Be that as it may, the inner structures of each of these orders are similar: a beginning in which the end is contained–with the exception of the third level, which only derives the necessity of its development from its 'standing in' for nature, for causality and empirical unfolding as such are totally aimless in themselves (Hegel would have called them 'bored concepts'), as a cause does not alone or with any necessity determine the effect it has–and which reaches this teleologically predetermined end by passing through a number of successive moments. In terms of nature, these are essential accidents, in terms of logic, steps in an argument, and in terms of time, points at which the act of seriality is continued.

Now each of the entities involved, in the *Muqaddima*, is a textual group unified by subject-matter and constituting a thematic class of its own. The unity of the *Muqaddima* at each of its three levels is located in the sequence of these groups: the modes of civilization, *'aṣabīya* and the forms of dominion, the state, and the sciences and crafts and other means of assuring livelihood. These textual groups each act as a point which punctuates the flow of the three conceptual orders of the *Muqaddima*.

Moreover, and as we have had occasion to mention in passing, each of these textual groups, such as *'aṣabīya*, itself acts as a nature, as a premise, and as a temporal beginning. Each of these textual groups, in other words, reproduces within itself the structure of the *Muqaddima*: a teleological flow in time. The subsidiary nature *par excellence* here is the state. Its temporal flow is regularly punctuated by the moments of the state, which are its modes, each akin to a different temper (*mizāj*) of a living body (Q, 1: 314)–further demonstration of the very intimate connection between different natural sciences and medicine, sharing the same concept of nature. The successive moments in the life of the state lead inexorably to its atrophy. In a similar way, and as the next section of this chapter will demonstrate in detail, each textual group as a thematic class (the state, for instance) acts as a nature which marches in accordance with its disposition towards its end, and which manifests itself in phenomena which are attendant upon its existence. The state, in this context, does not only pass through its moments, but it also produces institutions such as the chamberlaincy and the vezirate, produces monuments whose greatness is proportional to the greatness, wealth, and extent of this state, and enters into wars which require considerations on military tactics in those textual parts of the *Muqaddima* which treat of the thematic class 'state'. Wars as such, or the caliphate, for instance, find their discussion within the ambit of the textual group 'state' and belong to the thematic class 'state' not because they are a natural outflow of the nature of the state (as its temporal moments are), but because they occur within the topical and thematic contexts of the state: they are inevitable in the case of wars, and specific to certain states in the case of the caliphate, but are not developments undergone by the essence of the state. They are simply its associates, occurrences which take place in conjunction with it, both necessary and inevitable (as in war) and contingent (as in the caliphate).

Ibn Khaldūn appears to have been fully aware that each of those textual units was a self-contained logical and natural unit in the discourses of logic and of nature. That is why every chapter of the *Muqaddima* (with the exception of the fifth) is given one or more prolegomena, and this it is that inaugurates the reproduction within each textual unit of the structure of the work as a whole. Some attention to the terms used in the preliminary discourses of the different chapters is illuminating: [20] the first chapter consists exclusively of prolegomena, the second starts with premises and preliminaries, the third is introduced by principles, the fourth by preliminaries, and the sixth is once again preceded by a prolegomenon.[21] There is an order to be discerned in this succession of terms, and this is one of decreasing apodicticity, provided none of the terms is being actively misused (and Ibn Khaldūn never misuses terms; the occasional uncertainty of his terminology is due to the conflation of different scientific terminologies within the *Muqaddima*). Closeness to origin confers a conceptual priority, and this is very much in keeping with the structure of the *Muqaddima* that we have been outlining. The cycle which each individual textual group within the *Muqaddima* inaugurates is a duplicate of the overall textual cycle: beginning, premise, cause, leading to *telos*, to conclusion, and to effect. And the beginning of a textual unit is coterminous with the conclusion of the one that precedes it: this applies to the textual units as wholes; within each, we have, as we shall see in the next section, units that are natural conclusions of the beginning, and others whose existence is historically or otherwise contingent, and these last are clustered together topically and relate unilaterally to that which constitutes the beginning of the unit.

Further force is added to the juncture where one group ends and the other begins by the Koranic citations interspersed throughout the *Muqaddima.*[22] These statements–and those from the prophetic Tradition–serve to encapsulate the arguments or points that had just been concluded in the form of a wisdom or a precept. But they are much more than sagely sanctions of the truths enunciated. The invocation of divine and prophetic statements acts as the custodian of the truth of Ibn Khaldūn's own statements, much as God in Descartes' *Discourse* defeats the persistent mystifications of devilish falsehood. In this sense, they serve as additional proof of arguments made, for the epistemological status of Koranic statements is on a par with that of any other sort of demonstration. When such situations occur at the conclusion to a textual unit, they represent a kind of logical end, one which is the ultimate proof of the proof. One must also cite in this connection the use that Ibn Khaldūn makes of historical examples. There are 405 historical examples in the *Muqaddima,*[23] and they serve the function of proof by reference to direct experience which the nominalist disposition of Ibn Khaldūn the thinker and Ibn Khaldūn the politician requires. Historical example is just as palpable as more proximate experience and, in logical terms, is epistemologically on a par with other modes of proof.

There is one textual group, however, which does not have a beginning in the strict sense of the term. The first chapter, which was excluded from the sequence of textual groups and thematic classes in the *Muqaddima,* is the beginning of all beginnings. The chapter consists only of prolegomena, *muqaddimāt,* a term which we have seen as containing the most general sense of beginning and of apodicticity (along with technical determinations). Seven prolegomena make up the first chapter of the *Muqaddima,* 'On Human Civilization in General', and the chapter does not include treatments of the main object which the prolegomena are supposed to introduce, as does every other chapter in this or, indeed, any other book. By this token alone, a special status for the first chapter could have been assured. But there is much more to this peculiarity than nonconformity to a more general pattern. The prolegomena sketched within it fall into three unconnected groups: the first asserts that the aggregation of human beings in organized habitation and the formation of civilization is natural and necessary, the second, third, fourth, fifth, and 'seventh'[24] deal with geography and ecology and the effects of various factors of climate, location, and natural fertility on the type of civilization and the specific characteristics of men, and the sixth prolegomenon discusses at length the phenomenon of prophecy and the cognate phenomena of soothsaying, divination, and other forms of knowledge of the occult. There is no visible common denominator to link these three domains; there is no shared internal principle that could conceivably link ecology, cosmological epistemology, and philosophical anthropology. Yet all three domains, however utterly distinct as objects of knowledge, are yet the partners in the first chapter of the *Muqaddima*, where they all figure as prolegomena to the whole book.

It is in relation to the subsequent development of the book that their connection is therefore to be seen. And it will become clear that their unity can only be known retroactively and by hindsight, so to speak. Without civilization, the seven prolegomena will be absurd, for it is through civilization that they exist as the conditions of civilization, its *sine qua non*.[25] They are all geared towards providing those conditions without which the development of civilization and its consummation cannot be explained. They constitute an absolute beginning, but not in the natural sense; rather they are the beginning of civilization in a purely logical sense, figuring as the unquestionable first principles of the science of civilization which constitute the science, hence, metaphorically, 'prove' it. Such apodictic principles need not be proved at all, as Ibn Khaldūn was well aware (Q, 1: 71).[26]

The Muqaddima: *Epitome with Glosses*

The *Muqaddima* opens with a prolegomenon which both establishes the object of the science of civilization and derives from this establishment a corollary that constitutes the essential accident of this civilization to which the entire *Muqaddima* is oriented: kingship. Men must form aggregates in order to be able to eat and defend themselves against wild beasts. The formation of human aggregates makes possible the cultivation of crops and the manufacture of weapons, and as such, human life will be impossible without human aggregation. Without it the purpose for which God created man would not be fulfilled, for God created man so that he could dignify creation with the image of divinity. Such is the meaning of the Koranic conception of *istikhlāf*, that which establishes the significance of the creation of men.[27] The necessity of human aggregation is therefore established by recourse to an argument from theology–the object of the science and its fundamentals, we have seen, are established by means other than those belonging to the science itself (Q, 1: 69–71).[28]

With the establishment of the necessity of human aggregation comes the necessity of domination and, by extension, of kingship. Men are naturally aggressive, aggressiveness being embedded in their animal soul.[29] In order to ward off each other, they appoint one among them who performs the role of a custodial authority which checks such aggressive instincts by its domination, its rule, and its heavy hand.[30] This is a very classical idea in Ibn Khaldūn's culture; so much so that it became a dictionary definition of the term *wāzi'*, custodial authority.[31] This is the sense of kingship (Q, 1: 71–2).

The second prolegomenon discusses and delimits the share that habitable territory has in the overall configuration of the earth. This configuration is structured by the division into seven zones current in Ibn Khaldūn's culture and which our author took over from al-Idrīsī (d. 560/1165) who wrote his great work at the Norman court in Sicily. The zones are delimited by lines of equal latitude and unequal longitudes, with the first zone having the greatest longitude and the seventh the smallest (Q, 1: 75 ff.).[32] The prefatory discussion which precedes the very detailed description of world geography indicates the locations of the major peoples, rivers, seas, and deserts, and is followed by an addendum, which establishes that the northern part of the world is possessed of an ampler habitation than the southern part (Q, I: 83 ff.). The reason is simple and is derived from contemporary medical concepts: the heat in the southern part offsets the action of humidity and thus impedes the process of generation, as there is no generation without the action of humidity. There is little habitation in the first and second zones, therefore. There is a moderate amount in the third, fourth, and fifth zones, and an amplitude of it in the sixth and seventh.[33] Beyond the septentrional limit of the seventh zone, which comprises all the area between 64 and 90 degrees north, habitation is totally absent, for heat and cold occur completely separately and at separate times, thus being incapable of combining and leading to generation.

The second prolegomenon thus can be seen as a discussion whose aim is to eliminate certain parts of the globe from being party to civilization. Indeed, the term *'umrān* is commonly used to denote habitation and habitability in the geographical sense.[34] The task is to delimit those areas which are habitable, and are therefore capable of producing manifestations of historical significance. With this in view, providing an interesting parallel with Hegel,[35] the third prolegomenon narrows down the discussion and focusses it further: it discourses upon moderate and inclement climates, and the influence that climate exercises on the colour and complexion of people. Not unnaturally, Ibn Khaldūn ascribed full humanity to the inhabitants of the moderate zones (the third, fourth, and fifth zones), which are quintessentially moderate in Iraq and the Levant. It is the inhabitants of these parts of the world that are the most moderate (in the classical sense of *sophrosyne*) in everything: in complexion, in tempers, in religions (being the only peoples who produced prophets). In addition, this moderation is also the perfection of civilization: architectural perfection and the possession of the two 'natural currencies'(gold and silver). These people comprise the North Africans, the Levantines, the Iraqis and Persians, the Sindhis, the Indians, and the Chinese. In addition, the people who form the paradigm of human perfection comprise the Andalusians and the peoples adjacent to these most moderate of nations: the Franks, the Catalans, the Greeks, and the Romans. In contrast to these, Ibn Khaldūn finds that the Black Africans, Slavs, and other inhabitants of inclement zones are removed from the median perfection of the moderate peoples. They do not possess a currency based upon gold and silver, they have no sciences, their cuisine is elementary, and some even eat one another. Their complexions are as immoderate as other aspects of their life. Black Africans are black from the sheer effect of heat in the first and second zones, while the fair people of the north are pale because of the lack of heat.[36] There must, however, be an exception to the curse of ecological immoderation, for the inhabitants of the Arabian Peninsula which lies in the second and first zones not only produced a rich record of historicity, as we saw in the last chapter, but also produced Islam which, as a complex of histories, civilizations, sciences, and much else, can only represent the most perfect of historical manifestations. The seas that surround the Arabian Peninsula effect the dryness that is concomitant with heat, and thus assures the action of humidity (Q, 1: 151). This is, of course, a sophistical argument based on abstract association between 'humidity' and 'water'. But it was scientifically viable in terms of Ibn Khaldūn's medical knowledge, which was based on precisely such abstract notions of quality.

The immoderateness of tempers in relation to immoderate climes is the thesis that informs the fourth prolegomenon. As tempers depend upon humours, and as these last are dependent upon the proportions of heat add cold, it follows that those living in hot climes have hotter humours and therefore hotter animal souls.[37] That is why Black Africans are ever dancing, foolish, and light of demeanour and in their bearing. The people of Fez, by contrast, constantly appear as if in mourning and take excessive care to prepare for every possible eventuality. That is why they store inordinate amounts of grain in their houses (Q, 1: 155–7). But foolish and barely human as the Black Africans may be, this is not the result of their feeble-mindedness, as Mas'ūdī followed Galen and Kindi (d. after 252/860) in maintaining.[38] The mind is affected by environmental factors, however, and this is where the paradigmatic humanity of the inhabitants of the moderate zones is dented. The fifth prolegomenon maintains that a people's disposition, both physical and mental, is directly connected with the type of food they eat and thus with the surroundings in which they live. And the reasons for this are, again, medical. Excessive food, and especially excesses of meat, produces inordinate and unnatural amounts of rotten waste and endows the intestines with humidity in excess of that which naturally attaches to them, with the consequence that people who are accustomed to excessive eating are much more susceptible to diseases and to death from famine. Those, like the Andalusians, for instance, whose staples are oil and corn tend to have much better bodies, and much more educable minds.

The 'ecological group' of prolegomena thus establish the limits of habitation. They also narrow down the possibilities for this habitation to bloom into fully-fledged civilization and bring in a number of constraints that typify various characteristics and manifestations even of habitation that takes place in temperate climates, and which is therefore capable of natural flowering. In general, these prolegomena conform well to the model of universal description which Ibn Khaldūn admired so much in Bakrī (d. 487/1094) and Mas'ūdī, and which he considered the *sine qua non* for transforming history into a field where the veracity of received information can be checked against such 'general conditions'. The relevance of this general description of the world to the grand design of the *Muqaddima* is not obscure.

The same cannot be said for the sixth prolegomenon. This shifts the terrain of apodicticity very radically to that of prophecy, divination, visions, miracles, and cognate phenomena. There is no historical constancy about prophecy. It is not, as the philosophers represented by Avicenna (d. 438/1037) argued, a function of the faculties of the soul. Ibn Khaldūn had expressly rejected this view at the conclusion of the first prolegomenon and in a small digression (Q, 1: 72–3). Prophecy is not in the nature of man as such; if it were, then the philosophers' argument that custodial authority rules by means of divine ordinance would hold, for divine ordinance as delivered through prophecy would also come naturally to man through the faculties of the soul.[39] Ibn Khaldūn states quite clearly in the context of his refutation of this argument that custodial authority does not need divine ordinance, and that peoples with prophets are few in comparison to peoples without. The argument that prophecy has a prefatory role in considerations of civilization because of its naturalness is thus foreclosed. Prophets are individuals chosen by God to be given special knowledge of things divine and to discourse upon things that will happen in the future (BB, 91). They are individuals whom God sent to mankind so that men would be told of their own good and shielded from hellfire (Q, 1: 165). But although Ibn Khaldūn thus distances himself from the philosophical view of prophecy, this does not render his own theory any more appealing to conservative circles. For, as we shall see, he presents a gnoseological theory of prophecy whose elements are derived from hermetic and gnostic elements common to the three great monotheistic religions and which in the Islamic context, flourished on the margins of official knowledge among sūfī sages and ecstatics, among sorcerers, and among astrologers.

But there is something uncannily natural about this knowledge that God allows certain individuals to have, and which is also obtainable in a less ample degree by lesser beings such as fortune tellers. Ibn Khaldūn is obviously eager to reject the suggestion that prophecy was natural to man,[40] a position which may make it his by right. Prophetic knowledge is a species of knowledge which is made possible by the position that mankind occupies in what has been termed the Great Chain of Being.[41] This is a graded scale of imperfections starting from the four elements going through metals, plants, animals, mankind, and then, across the elemental threshhold, to various spiritual beings, and ending in the perfection of God.[42] It is a scale along which elements and entities are convertible, or at least capable of elevation, and it is this that makes possible the transformations of alchemy, the sūfī theory of the unity between microcosm and macrocosm and of God and man, as well as the occult knowledge that is made possible by knowledge of astral and numerical sympathies in the elemental world and the knowledge of the future that prophets and certain lesser beings can attain. The elements that make up this scale are linked by a thread that assures their continuity in such a way that the essences of some have the capacity to go over the lower extremity of ones that are superior to them.[43] It is this that makes the souls of some human beings capable of detaching themselves from humanity and actually passing over into angelicalness for an instant, in which they are possessed of knowledge unfettered by time, and beholden to divine discourse (Q, 1: 174–5 and cf. S, 22). It is such moments of possession that are one outward characteristic of prophets–the Prophet Muḥammad had fits of sweating and hallucination that some modern commentators have seen as symptoms of epilepsy. Other outward signs of prophecy are goodness and uprightness of character, proselytism, the possession by the prophet of some sort of protective *'aṣabīya* such as lineage (on this matter the *Muqaddima* adds much detail later), and miraculous works (Q, 1: 165 ff.).

To assure the integrity of prophecy and to distinguish it from soothsaying, Ibn Khaldūn resorts to a sophistical argument.[44] Both types of knowledge, as well as that of visionaries, of holy fools, of that informing the utterances of the dead at the moment of death, are acquired from the Chain of Being. All of these types of knowledge exist at the third of three levels at which knowledge is to be had (knowledge of sensibles, gnoseological knowledge of 'the heart'[45] current among mystics, and knowledge unfettered by bodily connections–Q, 1: 175 ff.). But the prophet is alone among those who are naturally capable of crossing the boundary of humanity. Soothsayers cross the boundary by their effort of the will. Not being naturally inclined towards angelicalness, they cannot perceive things perfectly, hence they express their knowledge oracularly, aided by Satan, and try and spur on their perception by the use of rhymes which distinguish them as soothsayers. Their knowledge is thus sometimes correct, and sometimes not. The same unnaturalness and non-innateness of contact with the beyond applies to other types of occult knowledge, only Satan does not play a role there. Like that of soothsayers, the knowledge of mystics, holy fools, fortune tellers, and others is sometimes correct, but by no means certain. (Q, 1: 181 ff.). The distinction of prophecy, therefore, is a distinction of the moral order dictated by a theological act, for it is God who directly chooses a prophet and endows him with the nature that allows him to cross the boundaries of the elemental world. The distinction of prophecy is thus also truly cosmological, for the prophet possesses very peculiar properties along the Chain of Being.

Prophetic knowledge is thus natural in so far as it belongs to the Chain of Being, not in so far as it is natural to human beings, to human knowledge, or to manifestations of human aggregation, such as civilization. Whence, then, the apodicticity that justifies its treatment as a prolegomenon to the science of human civilization? It is difficult to determine why Ibn Khaldūn thought it necessary to include his discourse on prophetic knowledge among the prolegomena to his new science. After all, an entire section of the sixth chapter deals with human knowledge, and the same chapter contains ample locations for a discourse on prophecy. Yet one can suggest three possible considerations. It is quite possible that one feature of prophetic and cognate knowledges had such a strong political density at Ibn Khaldūn's time that its relevance to the science of civilization seemed selfevident: this is the determination of the beginnings and ends of states.[46] Another could be that the centrality of prophecy to the histories of both Arabs and Berbers justified an investigation of the phenomenon, although this seems offset by the non-centrality, even by the peripheral position, that the caliphate plays in the thematic content of the *Muqaddima.* Lastly, it could be argued that this was the continuation of the polemic against the philosophical view of the prophecy that was commenced towards the end of the first prolegomenon, a continuation or some kind of footnote whose length became uncontrollable. The detail with which prophecy is treated could be seen as warranted by the importance that this aspect of knowledge had among the very influential mystics of Ibn Khaldūn's time, whose view of prophecy runs parallel to their views of mystical knowledge and of spiritual gnosis which our author attacked so vehemently in a special work (S, 55-7, 110-11).[47]

It is now clear that the general orientation of the prolegomena is that towards the full development of civilization. This con sideration imposed the discussion of whatever topics were treated–witness, for instance, the thrust and focus of ecological and geographical considerations that were identified above. Yet these do not lead to civilization; they are only presupposed by it. Their action is not genetic; they constitute conditions and requisites. They therefore do not constitute the nature of civilization, but simply provide some of its indispensable constituents. In other words, the flow of the nature of civilization does not start with the prolegomena, but cannot start without them. They are logical apodeictic states. Nature starts flowing in the second chapter of the *Muqaddima.*

The second chapter of the *Muqaddima,* entitled 'On bedouin civilization, savage peoples, tribes, and that which obtains along with them', begins where the parallellism between the purely logical structure of the *Muqaddima* and its modal and naturalphenomenal structure commences. This point of transition is located in the first section of this chapter. Entitled 'That beduin and urban folk are natural', it states the entire subsequent content of the *Muqaddima* as well as its graduation according to nature from simple necessities to that which is complex and supererogatory. In a statement that has constantly been misinterpreted as implying an economic view of civilization, the chapter opens with the declaration that the differences among peoples under different conditions is an aspect of the difference in the means by which they secure their livelihoods (Q, 1: 220). But this seemingly economic statement is immediately contextualized in terms of the first prolegomenon of the first chapter: the difference between peoples is formulated in this way because that which brings about the aggregation of people–and hence their formation into civilization–is their need to secure their livelihood. Hence the type of livelihood is an important element in the determination of the differences between them. With those peoples who make do with the elementary necessities, they can either engage in some form of animal husbandry with its various divisions (beekeeping, cow rearing, etc) or in agriculture, again with its various divisions. When such a point is reached as to attain a situation of supererogatory and luxurious life style, once again the principle which made aggregation a necessity comes into action: people come together to produce and consume luxuries. At this point the fullest flowering of civilization with its silks, its palaces, its foods, its crafts, and its sciences. The nature of beduinity is no more rigorously conceived than the nature of urbanism that we have encountered above (p. 57). The naturalness and originality of beduinity is demonstrated by recourse to ordinary observable phenomena, and the nature of beduinity is really the aggregate of the visible characteristics of beduinism. They are really the vernacular conception of beduinism about which a semi-settled shepherd in today's Mesopotamia could be as enlightening in his enumeration of the characteristics of the beduin (courage, 'naturalness', etc.) as Ibn Khaldūn was. The difference is that the *Muqaddima* juxtaposes a modal and a logical order along with this vernacular order of things.

This will become clearer as we proceed. More directly germane to the present argument is the fact that, strictly speaking this first section of the second chapter is not a prolegomenon to the second chapter only, but to the whole *Muqaddima.* Indeed, it should be said here that the textual units investigated in the previous section (pp. 53–54 above)–structured by prolegomena and developments thereof–do not always fully correspond to what Ibn Khaldūn designated as chapters. Neither are these prolegomena always placed together at the very beginning of each unit. But these minor aberrations do not justify the redrawing of boundaries between the chapters of the work. The proper prolegomenon to the second chapter of the *Muqaddima* is contained in its second and third sections. The third states that beduinism is both older and logically anterior to urban life, and explains this by the categories, again, of the simple leading to the complex, and the necessary leading to the supererogatory. The second section is really a logical statement: it states that Arabs are 'natural': they, and peoples akin to them (Kurds, Turks, Turkmen, Zanātans in the Maghrib), are the simplest and most bound to necessities. And this is because they tend camels, which require particular conditions of ecology and demand very extensive transhumance (BB, 121). The Arabs seem natural because they seem the most elementary, the 'original' and complete state of beduinity.

The originality of beduinity as such with respect to urban life, however, is of a different nature. The anteriority is not only logical. Beduinity is also original in the strict sense, in that it is beduin folk that supply the humanity of the cities. That is why, Ibn Khaldūn tells us, the inhabitants of any given city originate from the beduins of the surrounding countryside, who gravitate almost naturally towards life in the city (Q, 1: 224)– and it must be stressed that beduinism in the Khaldunic acceptation does not imply nomadism. Beduins live not only in the desert, but in the mountains as well (Q, 1: 67; BB, 121), as can well be seen in the beduin origins of states such as the Almohads. Urban life exists in the city and its immediate surroundings. The originality, in the logical and the natural senses, of beduinism over urban life is also represented by the discussion of *'aṣabīya.*

The originality of beduinity is also assured by two more vernacular concomitants. Beduins are closer to goodness than urban dwellers. For the human soul in its pristine condition is an ethical and moral *tabula rasa* ready to receive whatever is imprinted upon it. It is important to note that Ibn Khaldūn does not identify beduinity and goodness: beduins are merely better than urbanites. And this is so not because of the intrinsic goodness of beduins, but because of the evil that attaches to man when, in an urban setting, he pollutes himself with his unchecked desires. Urban civilization itself is 'the end of civilization, its passing over into decomposition, and the quintessence of evil and remoteness from the good' (Q, 1: 226). Another beduin characteristic that diminishes with the advent of urbanism is courage. That is why a tribe fresh from its remote fastness is more than a match for the army of an effete state (Q, 1: 251).

'The habitation of areas and territories where a beduin livelihood is exercised is confined to those tribes in possession of *'aṣabīya*': [48] this is the title of the seventh section of the chapter under consideration, and the thesis stated is proved by recourse to principles enunciated in the prolegomena. Ibn Khaldūn assumes that each group will naturally be aggressive toward other groups, just as individuals will behave aggressively towards each other. While cities are protected by walls against external aggression and by the high hand of the sovereign against internal strife, internal peace in a beduin setting is guaranteed by the elders. External defence is assured by *'aṣabīya*–used here to designate a group and as a homologue to an association of common kin (Q, 1: 233-4), and as a synonym of *'uṣba.* Common kinship of course can never be ascertained and is always at the mercy of a great number of distortions (a relative exception is the more isolated Arabs and like peoples) which Ibn Khaldūn explores with some detail and with reference to various peoples of the Maghrib (Q, 1: 236 ff.). The important thing is belief in this common descent, the belief which, as God willed things, induces men to care for their kinsfolk (Q, 1: 235-6).

The thrust of the discussion of *'aṣabīya* is clearly geared towards the 'aṣabīya group, being a context in which the military activities of beduin tribes are exercised and has nothing to do with sociology. It is the tribe as a power actor, the *'aṣabīya* as a *'uṣba,* and it is constituted within the tribe itself by sheer power. And the conception of power informing this understanding of *'aṣabīya* is none other than that amply investigated in the first chapter above. *'Aṣabīya* after all, 'belongs' to somebody. This Ibn Khaldūn makes very clear in his discussion of the constancy of *'aṣabīya* in one genealogical line (BB, 131): that which belongs to the strongest line in a tribe is the prime and dominant *'aṣabīya* in the whole tribe, overpowering and dominating the other *'aṣabīyāt* which appertain to other groups, and serving as the most prominent *'aṣabīya* among the subsidiary and stronger ones which exist at what today would be called a lower level of segmentation. The prime *'aṣabīya* of this type can be transferred among the lower ones, as long as this remains within the same general group. Had things been otherwise, the group would not cohere: the temper of a mixture cannot exist without the dominance within this mixture of one of its elements, and without a definite temper there is no generation, and no reality (BB, 131-2). The dominant house normally persists through four generations, for it starts to rot and distance itself from the excellence and vitality of the process and person of foundation almost as soon as the house is established–the only exception where the reality of noble lineage is absolutely continuous and reaching up to Adam is that of the Prophet Muhammad–for, like all of creation from the elements through plants and animals to man, nobility of the house will eventually rot and go (Q, 1: 247-9).

The natural process continues through the second chapter: the *telos* of *'aṣabīya* is kingship (Q, 1: 252). *'Aṣabīya* naturally seeks royal domination: starting out as custodial authority, it takes on the aspects of forcible domination by one section of a group, which thus elevates its status from chieftaincy (*ri'āsa*) to enforceable royal authority, a situation which affects the coalescence of disparate but related groups and houses into a larger unit, the grand *'aṣabīya*. It should be noted that, although 'in the real' this is a process of centralization which was as visible to Ibn Khaldūn as it would be to an observer today, the concomitant stratification is not rendered relevant enough for specific mention by Ibn Khaldūn. The thrust of the Khaldunic discourse is slanted towards the nature of *'aṣabīya*, and this is derivable from the nature of man which seeks domination over others, not from the nature of social strata, as well as from the nature of the telos of *'aṣabīya* which is royal domination. Centralism for Ibn Khaldūn happens naturally, and not because of sociological imperatives. Once dominant within its own tribal boundaries, this *'aṣabīya* aspires to dominate the proprietors of another *'aṣabīya* by virtue of its very nature. Once this other has been brought under the dominion of the triumphant *'aṣabīya* it tends to coalesce with it and fortify it further. This process cascades further until the grand-*'aṣabīya* has acquired power equivalent to that of an established state, in which case it takes over the state, either by outright conquest, or otherwise by taking it over in all but name–as happened to the Seljuq and other Turks in relation to the Abbasids (Q, 1: 252–4). It is noteworthy that Ibn Khaldūn, just as he ignores the sociological considerations of stratification, similarly does not register the social, legislative, and other concomitants of the transition between chieftaincy and royal domination.[49] These changes are registered in the *Muqaddima* as things that somehow and very suddenly obtain when the dynasty has established itself in the city. And this is another demonstration of the thesis that the orientation of the unfolding of the *Muqaddima* is rigorously confined to those manifestations of civilization which are of direct relevance to the theme of power: the attributes and characteristics of royal domination are only relevant in so far as they are concomitants of the topic 'royal domination', not in so far as they have a history which precedes kingship.

The seventeenth section of the second chapter, which has just been outlined, is the prolegomenon to all that is left of this chapter, and is one that is closely related in logical terms to principles enunciated and established elsewhere: in the third and eighth sections that we have already reviewed (on priority of beduinity, and on *'aṣabīya* and lineage). And what is left for this chapter to do is describe some properties of kingship and sketch some thematic digressions which are made pertinent by historical experience. One impediment to the attainment of kingship is the too hasty acquisition by the growing *'aṣabīya* of the accoutrements of urban life and before they have established their sway in their own right. This is a situation that corrodes the roughness and naturalness which make for the strength of *'aṣabīya* until it is altogether on the wane. The same effect is brought about by failure to dominate the established state, which leads to the sense of powerlessness and the humiliation that are concomitant with this situation and which remove the hard edge of *'aṣabīya*. The overall conclusion is that cooptation into the system of the state that falls short of dominion over the state is a sure recipe for the non-consummation of the natural urge to attain absolute power (Q, I: 255 ff.). Domination has other malign effects on peoples. People lose their own customs in imitation of their masters or of those stronger than they, and here the case of the Granadans imitating Castillian and Aragonese dress and other aspects of life, such as the erection of statues, is brought to light (Q, 1: 267). Most seriously of all, once a people has fallen under the dominion of another, this invariably heralds its historical extinction that will come with the extinction of *'aṣabīya* in favour of the stronger one. It is in the nature of man to dominate, for his habitation of the world is in accordance with the *istikhlāf* that we have already encountered (above, p. 55). Once he is incapable of exercising or sharing in dominance, his spirit will weaken, and his hopes will wane, and his incentive to increase and to build will proportionally decline (Q, 1: 268).

A necessary concomitant of kingship is its high moral standing. In the twentieth section of the chapter under consideration, Ibn Khaldūn undertakes to prove that a sign of kingship (actual or imminent) is the moral stature of the *'aṣabīya* to which kingship appertains. The proofs adduced are of various kinds and different orders. The rational soul, as distinct from the animal soul of mankind, is closer to good than it is to evil. Kingship and the art of politics being eminently human traits (as distinct from animal traits) belonging to the rational soul of man, morality appears to attach to them of necessity. Furthermore, since the glory attaching to the greatness and dominance of a house is built upon a base (*'aṣabīya*) and the complements of this base, which consummate it and which are ethical observances, the *telos* of *'aṣabīya* is also the *telos* of these complements. The consummation of kingship is also the consummation of morality. A firmer proof, Ibn Khaldūn adds, is a theological one which is ambiguous as to its wider signification: as kingship and the art of politics are really a custodianship that God gave to man to ensure that His will is maintained, anyone whose *'aṣabīya* qualifies them for kingship and who, additionally, have the moral stamina to enforce the divine will, are qualified for the *khilāfa* of God (Q, 1: 259-61). Now whether this *khilāfa* is simply the custodianship in the name of God, or the caliphate as the custodianship of Islamic law and devotions is not clear. If the latter is meant, this passage could be taken as a demonstration that the caliphate is the supreme form of kingship, and not one form of it. Such an interpretation is highly unlikely in the context of the *Muqaddima* as we shall see, but may well be the result of a personal predilection on the part of its author, one which remains without discursive effect on part or all of the book.

As further demonstration of the indissoluble link between worldly glory and lofty morality, Ibn Khaldūn cites the ethical practices of the powerful: clemency, hospitality, patronage, regard for the learned and the pious, and others. It appears that our author, like other observers of his time and ours, noted what would today be called the accumulation and redistribution of wealth and of status.[50] But this he singularly deflected and transformed into an expression of morality and its connection with the cosmic and worldly orders. In terms of the second chapter of the *Muqaddima* however, this discussion plays a peripheral role. It is consciously deduced from earlier discussions, but does not alter or otherwise effect the course of the subsequent flow of the work. It is in the manner of a digression, like other digressions which have no intrinsic and compelling reason to be the topics treated in the work. Their logic is entirely *hors du texte.* Such are the sections that conclude this chapter and which deal with the Arabs, one would assume, not because they are the norm, but because they figure prominently in Ibn Khaldūn's universe. The Arabs can only conquer plains; if the Arabs conquer a territory it is soon laid bare; the Arabs are the furthest among nations from kingly politics; and kingship only accrues to them in a religious form (Q, 1: 269 ff.). These observations are all seen as results of the Arabs' savage temperament which comes from their isolation in the deserts, which makes them predators from the point of view of city residents. Their cleanliness of heart and of disposition, however, makes them very receptive to goodness. And since they rarely discipline themselves under a leader, religion makes the *wāzi',* the custodial authority that is leader, a matter of inner belief rather than an imposed order. And that is why kingship only comes to them in religious form.

The beginning of the third chapter, on states, kingship, the caliphate, and state institutions, does not provide us with the neat introduction of new themes. The discussion, like that in the second chapter, takes up the theme of *'aṣabīya* in various aspects and contexts and extensively sketches the elements which make up for the atrophy of the *'aṣabīya* that has founded a state. But we do have new themes, such as the vicissitudes of this *'aṣabīya* once it has become the state, and the institutions that are concomitant with this state of affairs. In both cases, however, even with themes encountered previously, we have a new node that pulls them together, a new thematic class: the state, which is the agency which effects the transition between beduinity and urban life and, indeed, the subject of this transition. Aspects of beduinity–which, as we say above, diminish gradually and with the flow of time–remain with us until the fifteenth section of the chapter is reached, that dealing with the transition between the two modes of civilization. From that point hence, totally new territory is covered, that of the state as existing in urban civilization, and a totally new thematic class (urban civilization) is commenced, which will continue throughout the subsequent flow of the *Muqaddima*. These aspects of thematic content (textual sequence) are contextualized in terms of logic (up to the end of the first section of the chapter and in the form of third order prolegomena), of nature, of time, and of thematic contiguity which justifies digression. Through all this, we can discern the overriding power of the general orientation of the *Muqaddima* and of the nature of its object: the aetiology of decline. It should be noted, in line with comments made about beduinity and other essential accidents of civilization that, like these accidents, the theme of decline is vernacular. It is a theme present among all peoples and in all historical epochs that the city is a corrupting and effete order in comparison with the vigour, purity, and simplicity of the country. The theme is neither specific nor original to Ibn Khaldūn or his culture, but is a universal commonplace which, in the *Muqaddima*, is given the metaphysical cover of natural teleology.[51]

Nature flows through this third chapter in two streams. The one links it with the previous chapter by way of section one ('that kingship and oecumenical states can only be accomplished through the tribe and *'aṣabīya*'), through the fifteenth section (on the transition of the state from beduinism to urban life), on to the subsequent, fourth chapter, which deals with life in the cities. This terminal point, therefore, is the point at which the flow of nature stops and ends. For the nature of civilization is consummated with its consummation in the city, and the decline that is observed is not the decline of the city as such so much as the corrosion of the state which has its impact on the city–which could always be revived by the takeover of a new and vigorous state. The first section acts as principle of the chapter in another line: it extends into the tenth section (on the progressive tyrannization of the state), through to the crucial thirteenth section (that the nature of kingship, once consummated, heralds the senescence of the state). It is this line which puts the definitive end to the flow of nature in conceptual terms, while the actual process of dissolution in empirical time is continued in subsequent textual development. In addition to these principles, the chapter, like others, contains developments of these main units, either developments logically warranted by them, or seen pertinent because they are thematically related to them. Discourse within these sections is unified by deliberations based upon simple causality.

Variations on the theme of *'aṣabīya* follow the initial principle of this chapter, and these deal with auxiliaries to *'aṣabīya* in the formation and maintenance of states. Some states can dispense with *'aṣabīya* after they have been formed. This comes about when a state has been established for a very long time, with the *'aṣabīya* being transferred and passing over from one branch of the house to another, branches that make up so many states united by a great house. Such was the lot of the Abbasids and the Aghlabids, for instance, under whom the leadership of these two houses became natural and appeared to their supporters as sure as religious beliefs. A complement to this thesis is that such states, if they should wish to conquer other states, can count on an already established reputation and on a ready constituency, so to speak, for power: such was, for instance, the state of the Idrīsids in the Maghreb, and the Fatimids in their conquest of Egypt (Q, 1: 279 ff.).

Religion also plays the role of enforcing *'aṣabīya*: states of oecumenical sway and great power originate in religion, be this religion a prophetic religion (Jews, the Arabs, the Almohads) or just an exhortation to goodness–the last, we saw, is intrinsic in men and in kingship. And that is because religions enhance the internal unity required for combat in a power situation, and an internal element of faith in the fighter. One could say that if two *'aṣabīya* groups were equivalent in all but the existence of a religious message within one of them, this one will win by virtues of this difference. Ibn Khaldūn adduces the example of the Qādisīya battle between the Arab armies and the Persians, when the 30,000 Arabs are supposed to have routed the 120,000 troops of the latter. But while *'aṣabīya* can act alone without religion, the opposite is not true under any circumstances. History and contemporary events supply Ibn Khaldūn here with ample illustrative material to support this thesis, although this material is not that which demonstrates the thesis. It is demonstrated by recourse to principles already proved, namely, that there can be no kingship or political power without *'aṣabīya*, a proof which is also supplemented by another, a quotation from prophetic tradition: that God never sent a Messenger except steeled by his people (Q, 1: 284 ff.). Also important with respect to the extent and the life expectancy of a state are the numbers involved in the conquest of the original *'aṣabīya*, to which both extent and life are directly proportional: the first because the state is governed by its geographic division among sections of the *'aṣabīya*, and one cannot dilute that original *'aṣabīya* and overstretch it too much, and the latter because numbers imply genealogical lines and houses among whom the state can be rotated, going to one after the state of another of the same lineage has waned. And in any case, the strength of any creature is proportional to that of its temper. The temper of an *'aṣabīya* being dependent on the greatness of numbers, it follows that the larger the numbers, the stronger the constitution, and therefore the wider and longer the sway of the state. The empirical, materially causal explanation (*sabab*) of this is that, since the state starts to fail when its extremities start either declaring themselves independent or being eaten away by others, the distance of the extremities from the centre and this weakness of the peripheries are directly proportional (Q, 1: 292 ff.). The spatial and temporal magnitudes of the state are therefore functions of a fundamental concept of the state: the state as its centre, its empirical existence being the spatial and temporal extensions of this centre, the ruling power group.

The second principle in the chapter under exposition is the thirteenth section, and this section recovers, and acts as a node and conclusion to, the three sections that preceded it: it states that it is in the nature of kingship to become tyrannical, that it is in the nature of kingship to acquire luxury, and that it is in the nature of kingship to acquire a quietistic and docile disposition. All three natures are signs of the senescense of the state and herald its atrophy. The tyrannization of kingship follows very clearly from foregoing arguments which looked at the progressive centralization of leadership in a group. With the conquest of the state, this goes further and results in the tyranny of one individual who, spurred by his animal soul, adopts a haughty attitude towards those who used to be his peers and the pillars of his *'aṣabīya*. The animal soul, of course, serves here as an explanation of this trend with reference to principle, for simply to state this as a fact would be inadequate to contextualize it, as the 'sociological' order which we perceive today was clearly absent from Ibn Khaldūn's world of categories. Moreover, if the matter were simply stated as an observed development, it would likewise not satisfy the logical exigencies which the *Muqaddima* set itself. Concurrently with this, the group which takes over the state from its previous proprietors inherits the luxuries available in the city, and enjoys them to a degree directly proportional to the power of the new state and to the degree of accomplishment in luxury left behind by the outgoing state. The third and last component in this catalogue of symptoms of decline is given the proof that is most pertinent in terms of the *Muqaddima.* Kingship immediately induces docility and quietism in its proprietors because, since it is attained solely by struggle, and since this struggle has domination as a *telos,* that which leads to the *telos* becomes superfluous the instant the *telos* is fully attained. The aggressive spirit that fires the pursuit of the state wanes as the luxuriant fruits of its attainments are enjoyed (Q, I : 299 ff.).

Thus consummated, the nature of kingship constitutes the beginning of the process whereby the state enters its period of senescence. There are three ways in which this senescence manifests itself, and these manifestations take place in relation to *'aṣabīya,* which constitutes the substance as well as the armour of the state. They are, moreover, commonplace empirical manifestations, whose explanation is purely serial and causal, for their rationality (in the eyes of the *Muqaddima*) resides in their relation to the three natural manifestations of consummated kingship and auguries of decline that have just been sketched. A psychological component of *'aṣabīya,* courage and daring, is corrupted when the members of auxiliary *'aṣabīya* groups take their share of the benefits of the state as mere reward for services rendered, thus severing their sense of shared proprietorship of the state. The luxury and extravagance engendered by the nature of kingship, moreover, create an imbalance in the books: expenditure comes to exceed income, the king demands control over outlays, and anyway favours those personally attached to his service to his erstwhile associates. And finally, with the *'aṣabīya* on the wane and distance from beduinity and courage on the increase, the king naturally resorts to troops other than those who 'naturally' belong to him, such as mercenaries, thus dealing a blow to the natural armoury of the state (Q, 1: 303 ff.).

The exacerbation of this state of affairs and its attainment to its ripest form usually takes three generations. For states, like individuals, have definite life spans, likewise corresponding to the heavenly conjunctions. Three generations or one hundred and twenty years is the usual life-span of a state. A generation is the time taken for nature to form fully the constitution of a person–and it is this sense of 'forty' that holds the real truth of the Israelites' forty years in the wilderness, for it signifies that they roamed the desert for just enough time for the generation accustomed to indignity to go, and for a new and vigorous one to mature. A state normally (abnormalities do exist, one would presume, due to the stars) lasts for three generations because one generation is spent in the full possession of beduin virtues, including the collective glory imparted by the state. The second generation matures under the privatization of giory and under luxury, while the third matures under conditions where men are akin to women and children in their need of protection and where *'aṣabīya* and its concomitants have waned altogether. It is thus that nobility lasts for only four generations, the fourth being presumably being lived under the shadow of past memories and glories (Q, 1: 305 ff.).

The accomplishments of civilization are not created *ex nihilo*. The state takes over an urban civilization left behind by the vanquished state, as the Arabs took from the Persians habits of luxury which they elevated to even greater heights under the Abbasids, or as the Almoravids took from the Andalusians, or the Turks from the Abbasids. This is the thrust of the fourteenth section of the chapter under review, on the transition of the state from beduinity to urban life (Q, 1: 309 ff.): it is not the creation of an urban civilization, but the acquisition of an urban civilization. It is this acquisition of something external that determines the transition, and it is this that plunges the vigorous state onto the path towards its end. It is this acquisition that allows the state to consummate its nature and which leads to the last moment in the life of that nature: the moment taken by the vicissitudes of the state when it is installed in the city. These vicissitudes, moreover, are all part of one moment and belong to one mode of the development of the nature of civilization. Their connection among one another, therefore, cannot be expressed in terms of a nature or of logic, for the march of both has been consummated. It can only be expressed serially, as one of succession and as one of typology. The remaining thirty-seven sections of the third chapter of the *Muqaddima* thus add nothing conceptually new, but comprise a discussion of the changes brought about by time, and one of the types of kingship along with their institutions.

When the state first instails itself in an urban context, the luxury that accrues to it has a beneficial effect on the *'aṣabīya*. For since the state is still vigorous, the increase in fertility, brought about by luxury and the sense of accomplishment resulting from power, has the effect of adding to the numbers at the disposal of *'aṣabīya*. The same effect is caused by the greater acquisition of clients and servants brought about by luxury. And at this pristine moment, when the *'aṣabīya* is still a unit of combat, the increase in numbers is an increase in the power of the state (Q, 1: 313). And it is naturally the numbers involved in the beginning of the state that determine its power and, by consequence, the greatness of the edifices it builds and the vastness of its wealth. It is this that accounts for great edifices, and not, as Mas'ūdī and a great number of others maintain, the gigantic bodily proportions of their builders (Q, 1: 327 ff.).

The numbers involved in the beginning do not, however, seem to have an impact on the moments through which the state passes between consummation in the city and atrophy, also in the city. These moments are, in most cases, five in number, and each is defined according the character (*khulq*) it confers upon the state. Each is a different temper of the existent which is the state, and this temper Ibn Khaldūn sees as residing in the attitude of the state towards its charge: power. This is at best a metaphorical employment of both the notions of temper and of nature, the latter notion being implicitly present in that a temper is a mode in which this nature exists. But it could nevertheless be said that some rigour is achieved by Ibn Khaldūn's statement that the conditions and character of the beneficiaries of the state in its successive moments differ in their beduinity (Q, 1: 314). The first moment is that of victory and vigour. But the rot starts eating away this vigour almost immediately, for the second moment is that during which the vigour of the state is directed against its own kind in its bid to privatize power. This accomplished, the state enters the third moment, that in which its power is established, and its magnificence manifest in wealth, in architecture, in the arts, and in sciences. The magnificence imparted by wealth persists through the fourth moment, but it is during this phase that the strength of the state is diminished by its quietism and sense of well-being and self-satisfaction. But the weakness of the state in the fourth moment is aggravated in the fifth, characterized by prodigality and waste at the court which consume all revenues at the expense of armies, and which alienate whatever remains of the *'aṣabīya* (Q, 1: 314 ff.).

The conditions obtaining during these moments occupy much of the remainder of this chapter. These include observations on a variety of matters which a courtier would be aware of. Such, for instance, is the observation (to which a short section is devoted) that clients, be they clients through slavery or through alliance, are not all alike in their relation to the head of the state. Clientage, Ibn Khaldūn says, is just like *'aṣabīya* and fulfils its role, the difference being that the latter does have a natural component of filiation whose real naturalness is less relevant than its conception, for its importance resides in its being conceived as the tribe or the power group. Clients have a graduated seniority, the older the association implying a closer connection (Q, 1: 332). It can happen that a client could dominate the sovereign from a position of power–say the vezirate or the chamberlaincy. But under no circumstances does such a formal client assume the royal title. For the royal title is one among a complex of what we would today call symbols of authority, order, and legitimacy, whose destruction may well mean the destruction of the state. There is no kingship without *'aṣabīya*, and the *'aṣabīya* of the client, even though it may extend beyond his own person, nevertheless falls under that of the sovereign and is articulated in its terms. Indeed, should this client attempt to seize the royal title, he cannot remain long in power (Q, 1: 336 ff.). This intrusion on the prerogatives of royal authority prompts a definition of full kingship as opposed to kingship *manqué:* a true king is only he who dominates his subjects, who collects revenue, who sends embassies, who protects border positions, and who is answerable to none other than himself. A true king is only he who has full and unadulterated power over ail the territory he claims as his (Q, 1: 341–2).

Another group of topics is now introduced by Ibn Khaldūn, one that deals with the caliphate. In order unambiguously to affirm the naturalness of this institution, the *Muqaddima* precedes it with a short recapitulation of the principles of kingship: kingship is effected by an aspect of the animal soul which desires dominance. It follows that, left to itself, kingship will by definition be unjust. And since pure injustice prevents kingship from accomplishing itself, rules of the political art must be employed. Most commentators have misapprehended the passage in question and taken it for a disquisition on the types of states after the manner of the Greeks and of Fārābī, but his analysis is confined to the real states governed by laws which are either religious or purely rational. In both cases, there is no mention of a classification–let alone one based on moral merit as with Fārābī, for Ibn Khaldūn distinguishes himself from Fārābī clearly (Q, 2: 126–7)–as much as a discussion of two ways in which the art of politics is practised. The distinction is in governance and its art (*siyāsa*), not in forms of the state, which are all the same as we saw. If an historical antecedent were at issue, one would surely seek it in the *Fürstenspiegel* tradition running ail the way back to the earliest Islamic times.[52] Having distinguished the caliphate from other manifestations of kingship by maintaining that the former is in accordance with the divine will and is directed towards the good both here and in the hereafter, Ibn Khaldūn presents a detailed account of the theory and institutions of the caliphate.

There is no reason to linger over a discussion of why the caliphate was made into a topic of the *Muqaddima*, as the answer is straightforward. The caliphate had become a scholastic motif in all writings concerning the state at the time of Ibn Khaldūn which at times could be valorized politicaily.[53] The caliphate was also an historical monument of paramount importance in Ibn Khaldūn's culture. The caliphate was, finally, an historical manifestation of kingship which is under discussion in the *Muqaddima.* Caliphs are those who perform the tasks of prophets after the waning of prophecy, and this task is to ensure that men obey divine ordinances (Q, 1: 344). Its necessity is a matter of belief and cannot be demonstrated rationally (Q, 1: 345-6). This was the view established by Ghazal' (d. 505/1111) to which conformity was the predominant norm.[54] Indeed, Ibn Khaidun does not deviate from the Sunni legal doctrine of the caliphate, and explicitly says he will not dwell too much on its doctrine as this was adequately covered by the standard treatise of Māwardī (d. 450/1058).[55] Nevertheless, he does give a fairly detailed statement of the doctrine of the caliphate and of the various disagreements that it engulfed and entailed, including a succinct and very urbane statement of the Shiite doctrines of the Imamate (Q, 1: 345 ff.).

In spite of his adherence to the standard doctrine, including the view that descent from the prophetic tribe of Quraish is a prerequisite for holding the office, Ibn Khaldūn introduces a novel component which makes the topic of the caliphate very much his own. In commenting on the opinions of Maghribis and Andalusians, as well as those of Juwainī (d. 478/1085) and Isfirā'īnī (d. 418/1027) in the East, that it is permissible to have more than one caliph at the same time provided they coexisted at considerable distance from each other, as well as Bāqillāni's (d. 403/1013) rejection of the necessity for a caliph to be descended from Quraish, he undertakes an explanation of these views. They reflect, he contends, a bowing of scholars before reality: the reality of the coexistence of caliphs, and the reality that the *'aṣabīya* of Quraish is no more, which Juwainī and Bāqillāni' merely register. But this does not produce enlightened views of the matter, for the caliphate is intertwined with *'aṣabīya* positively as well as negatively. Quraishite descent was considered an exigency not because of the necessity of receiving divine grace (*baraka*) through connection with the prophet. The unity of Mudar in early Islam was expressed through the *'aṣabīya* of Quraish, and Quraishite descent was therefore imperative for assuming the caliphal position. Our author then proceeds to use this argument to attenuate his own position on Quraishite descent and the caliphate: the lawgiver wanted to ensure that leadership devolved only upon those with a strong *'aṣabīya* and who are, consequently, capable of ruling (Q, 1: 348 ff.). This is the sense and the principle (*'illa*) which is included in the Quraishite requirement. The law elucidated by the Prophet, however, is not bound to the time it was enunciated but is universally valid. Ibn Khaldūn stops here and does not go further into admitting that Bāqillāni's position is valid. His discussion is not conclusive, and could not be. For it admits extra-doctrinal argumentation into doctrinal positions, a thing that, as we shall see, Ibn Khaldūn disapproved of very unambiguously. This may be admissible as part of the science of civilization, but it cannot reach conclusions that contradict doctrinal positions. The only possible position that mediates the two is the eschatological position that Quraish will produce a man at the end of time. In dealing with this position towards the end of the third chapter, Ibn Khaldūn points out the indeterminacy from which it suffers. For Quraishite *'aṣabīya* had waned, and what remains of Quraish in the Arabian Peninsula must be the origin of this messiah–if indeed the doctrine concerning his appearance is valid (Q, 2: 172–3, and see below, p. 80).

Regardless of caliphal doctrines, the caliphate always turns into kingship. This happened both with the Umayyads and the Abbasids. And this happened according to the nature of *'aṣabīya.* But there was no alteration in the basic commitment towards religion on the part of the state when the caliphate changed hands and went from the Medinese regime to the *'aṣabīya* of the Umayyads and then to that of the Abbasids. Ibn Khaldūn's long defence of Mu'āwiya in the *Muqaddima* (Q, 1: 370 ff.) is parallel to the consideration in the narrative part of the *History,* where he even calls him one of the Rāshidūn (BD, 2: 1140–1). Mu'āwiya may not have been as right as Ali in his claim to the caliphate, but that does not by any means disqualify him–and here Ibn Khaldūn is obviously continuing his polemic against the mystifications of historians.[56] There is no way of avoiding the transformation of the caliphate into kingship; in the case of the Umayyads and the Abbasids, there was a change in custodial authority: while in the pristine Muslim state it was religious fervour, it changed into the sword of *'aṣabīya.*[57]

The caliphate, therefore, existed without kingship, then in combination with it, until the *'aṣabīya* of kingship was separated from that of the caliphate. But it is clear that Ibn Khaldūn feels that many of the functions of the caliphate–as that state which directs its subjects towards conformity with divine will–are taken over by kingship, regardless of whether the caliphate is regarded as contained in kingship. It is functionally represented by kingship. Had the caliphate and its institutions been confined to the ideal caliphate–possibly the model of the Medinese regime–Ibn Khaldūn would have found no justification for the treatment he gives of its institutions. These are the religious institutions which are ancillary to it (prayer, the administration of law, the organization and institution of legal and political legislation (the *fatwa*), holy war, and the *ḥisba*, the institution which controls and ensures everyday compliance with the precepts and prescriptions of doctrine), of which a rather cursory account is given (Q, 1: 394 ff.). The account of the caliphate is then concluded, and to it is appended a discussion of the positions of Cohen, Patriarch, and Pope, which gives an historical account of these titles and remarks that their holders live very much on the margin of the state,[58] because Judaism and Christianity, unlike Islam, do not prescribe the fusing of religious and state institutions which is necessitated by the obligation to wage holy war(Q, 1: 415 ff.).

The secular institutions of the caliphate are discussed in the context of royal institutions–for, among the Muslims, the institutional prescriptions and requirements of the caliphate were displaced and transferred to kingship, which made them its own (Q, 2: 3).[59] This state of affairs had existed since the days of Māwardī, and the legal aspects of such institutions in relation to caliphate and to royal rule are adequately stated in his *Aḥkām*, and kingship in the context of the caliphate, Ibn Khaldūn tells us, as Māwardī said long before, is the appropriation of power that belongs to the caliph. The institutions of this position, such as the vezirate, the chamberlaincy, the financial, fiscal, intelligence and various other administrative institutions, as well as the organization of armies, navies, and the police, are discussed. The reader is presented here not with a comprehensive, but with a selective, historical discussion of these institutions, complemented with a very rich portrayal of their conditions at the time of Ibn Khaldūn, especially in North Africa and Spain. This is then followed by a somewhat detailed and very invaluable description of what one would today call the symbols of power employed by Maghribi sovereigns of Ibn Khaldūn's time: banners, bands, thrones, seals, clothes, tents, and praise from the pulpit of the mosque (Q, 2: 3 ff.).

Before going on to the next textual group, the *Muqaddima* presents a fairly detailed description of war and its arts. Wars are of four kinds. Wars of envy and competition and wars of aggression take place between contiguous tribes and are waged by tribes on hapless neighbours, and these wars are perfidious. Wars in the cause of God or in the cause of a state, on the other hand, are wars of justice. Along with this classification, Ibn Khaldūn presents another, that according to tactics, of which there are two basic types: that of the closed formations of the phalanx used by Europeans and Persians (indeed, Castillians were recruited by Maghribi monarchs for the purpose of waging such war), and that of lightning raids involving rapid attack and withdrawal (*karr wa farr*) used by the Arabs and Berbers. The former have more solidity and are physically more resilient, but triumph in war is not dependent upon visible factors such as these. Victory is dependent on intangible fortune (*bakht*), which is not a supernatural factor but simply the confluence of factors of the psychological order (*'aṣabīya*, for instance) and of ruse (Q, 2: 65 ff.).

After these thematic digressions into the caliphate and kingship, the *Muqaddima* once again rejoins the march of the nature of the state towards its extinction. It rejoins this march towards its end with the symptomatics of extinction and its mechanisms. Primary among these is the effect of the state's fiscal policies on the city and, consequently, on the wealth of the sovereign himself and of the state in general. At the outset of its tenure of power, a state normally imposes very little by way of taxes, and these are either the small, philanthropic contributions required by Islamic law or those in accordance with beduin custom. The cumulative revenue from such taxes, however, is great: Ibn Khaldūn argues this point in much the same simplistic, vernacular way as it is argued today by neoclassical theorists of free enterprise, claiming that low taxation gives producers an incentive to work. With the acquisition of luxurious and extravagant habits and with the increase in the number of the state's dependents (administrators, mercenaries, etc.), the need for more revenue leads to the imposition of exactions. The state also resorts to interference in commercial life when in need of revenue: it establishes monopolies in the name of the sovereign and tampers otherwise with the profits that people could make (such as enforced purchases and the fixing of prices), with dire consequences to the prosperity of the city. For the state is 'the great concatenation of the world which provides the matter of civilization' (Q, 2: 92), and when the state drains the wealth of the populace and does not redistribute this wealth in the form of grants to clients who then redirect this wealth to the market, economic life recedes. That is why the Prophet condemned injustice: it causes civilization to decline (Q, 2: 93). All these matters are injustices that herald the destruction of civilization (Q, 2: 79 ff.).

The isolation of the monarch from his surroundings (*ḥijāb*) is also an inevitable occurrence in the life of the state that intensifies with its senescence. It is a natural consequence of the privatization and tyrannization of power that the sovereign should establish a number of concentric screens around himself which shield him away from people with progressive severity and puts a chamberlain in charge of these screens. Such screens are also established by clients who take over the effective running of the state around the titular sovereigns (Q, 2: 101 ff.). Also a sign of senescence is the division of the oecumenical state into two, which happens as a consequence of tyrannization which leads erstwhile associates to form their own states at the extremities of the original one. Such was the establishment by 'Abd al-Rahmān al-Dākhil of the Umayyad dynasty in Spain on the margin of the Abbasid caliphate, followed by other states on the same margins: the Idrīsids, the Fatimids, and others in the East (Q, 2: 103 ff.).

Such are the manifestations of the decline of the state, and they are irreversible. Reformist activity is thus by definition doomed to failure, for these things occur naturally and, being natural, are unalterable. They can all be classified as disorders in one of the two pillars of the state: the soldiery, which weakens with the weakening of *'aṣabīya* and the lack of revenue, and money, which is necessary for the maintenance of the soldiery and the establishment of all the marks of royalty and statehood (Q, 2: 106 ff.). The weakening in the power of the state spurs on pretenders who belong to the original state as provincial governors, or peoples who are outsiders and take over the state as conquerors. In both cases, the state is taken over not by a decisive battle, but by a progressive attrition during which the aspiring power bides its time until the established state is clearly enfeebled even in the eyes of its own subjects (Q, 2: 118 ff.). And it is during such a period of mortification that death daims the victims of famine and pestilence. For the end point in the life of the state is also that during which population is at its greatest and its density at its highest. The exactions imposed upon agricultural produce lead to a diminution in production, a consequent spiralling of food prices, and the attendant famine; while the density of population in the city leads to the spread of decay in the air and leads to a miasmic effect on the constitutions of people, afflicting them with the plague and other diseases (Q, 2: 125–7).[60]

The fifty-first section which immediately follows the discussion of famine and pestilence appears very much out of place. It consists of a recapitulation of a previous statement on the difference between purely rational and religious political arts, repeating that the two are intertwined in Islam, and quoting the full text of a long epistle on the arts of politics and justice written in the years 205–206/821[61] by a general of Al-Ma'mūn to his son upon the appointment of the latter to a provincial governorship (Q, 2: 127 ff.). The section clearly belongs earlier on in this chapter along with the twenty-third section. The chapter ends with two sections discussing at considerable length and with immensely valuable detail the eschatological lore regarding the advent of the Fatimid Messiah (the *Mahdī*) and the occult lore concerning the advent of states and religions and their demise.

Accounts about the appearance of the Mahdī, a member of the Prophet's family, at the end of time, and that of the Antichrist (*dajjāl*) and of a multitude of events to happen then are legion among Muslims of all ages, Ibn Khaldūn tells his reader. And these accounts fall into two categories: those based upon prophetic tradition, and those occurring in mystical works.[62] On the basis of this classification, Ibn Khaldūn proceeds to discuss this matter. Matters of tradition are parts of the science of tradition, and Ibn Khaldūn, consequently uses the techniques of this science to deal with them. With a merciless application of the principle of the primacy of the reliability of transmission over the content of the narrative report transmitted, Ibn Khaldūn sets about to show that all chains of transmission of such reports are faulty, and that, consequently, the reports themselves are untrustworthy (Q, 2: 142 ff.). The inflexibility with which the fundamental principle of tradition criticism is employed by Ibn Khaldūn has been the subject of a very severe criticism, but this criticism does not touch on any substantial issues.[63] Ibn Khaldūn is not alone in his scepticism, for two truest of the six canonical recensions of tradition, those of Bukhārī (d. 255/870) and Muslim (d. 261/875), do not contain sections on the Mahdī. Neither was he the sole person to criticize the introduction of Christian and Jewish elements in Koranic exegesis. But he had the audacity to question the judgements of such tradition authorities as Tirmidhī (d. c. 275/888-9), Abū Dāwūd (d. 275/889), and Ibn Maja (d. 273/887) and, more important perhaps, infringed upon the unwritten rule of tradition criticism which prescribes the obligation to be charitable to narrators of tradition.[64] One is at a loss to interpret this zeal, but it may not be too hazardous to submit that our author was engaged in invalidating the claims of the mystics and depriving them of any support from the respectability of tradition.

The mystical position is ascribed to the influence of extreme Shiite doctrines of the Imamate which involve the divinity of the Imam and the incarnation of divinity in the person of the sūfī saint. The awaited Fatimid is of this cast. A plausible historical picture of conduits that Shiism had into mystical doctrines is then complemented by a sketch of the position of great mystics such as Ibn 'Arabi (d. 638/1240), Ibn Sab'in (d. 668 or 669/1269-71), and Ibn Qasi (d. 546/1151)–all three of whom are Andalusians–whose doctrine is often encoded in esoteric symbolism. Briefly, they believe in the doctrine of eternal return: they take seriously the history of the future whose components are propounded in the *ḥadīth* corpus attributed to the Prophet and assume that things have to go back to the way they were.[65] Prophecy is followed by the caliphate, this is followed by kingship which degenerates into tyranny and falsehood, after which prophecy will be resuscitated by sainthood. This is followed by the Anti-christ, until the world of God is restored by the Mahdī. This, they say, will be a descendant of Fatima, and in this contention they use some elements from and techniques of the science of tradition. The time at which this saviour (although some do not specify the identity of this person) is expected is computed by gematric techniques (those later associated with the kabbala and involving the assignation of numerical magnitudes to letters of the alphabet). Needless to say, these calculations never proved correct, and they often had to be reinterpreted to accommodate the non-fulfilment of such millenial expectations and supplemented by further astrological computations. None of this daunted the faithful, however. Throughout the Maghrib of Ibn Khaldūn's time, the belief in the coming of the Mahdī led to the rise of many a Mahdist movement, and to the maintenance of shrines where it is believed the Mahdī will appear (Q, 2: 164 ff.).

Equally prevalent at Ibn Khaldūn's time and throughout Arab-Islamic history was political divination (*malāḥim, jafr*). Such, Ibn Khaldūn tells us, is only natural, for the human soul always yearns to know the future, especially the date on which the world will end and the durations of states, religions, and peoples. Calculations of the duration of the world as such are unreliable, as they rely on gematric techniques, and these involve mere conventions, for the correspondence of numbers and letters is neither rationally demonstrated nor is it a natural correspondence. The effect of the stars on historical events, however, is a different matter altogether. Ibn Khaldūn's sketch of the outline of the significations of heavenly conjunctions is neither critical nor proscriptive. It is followed by a unique outline of (and by quotations from) some of the divinatory poems (*malāḥim*) available from the Maghrib as well as from the East.

The fourth chapter of the *Muqaddima* contains nothing that is conceptually new. Dealing with conditions that obtain in urban life, the chapter discusses a situation whose nature has already been accomplished and the principle of whose dynamism belongs to a moment in the flow of nature that had already been discussed. All that remains is some indications of how this state of affairs atrophies. Otherwise, the chapter can only contain a serially arranged discussion, without any necessary inner coherence: it consists of descriptions of aspects of urban life which have no necessary connection with each other and whose unity is one imposed from outside. They cohere thematically around the textual group 'urban civilization', but are not the only topics which so cohere. For the fifth and sixth chapters of the *Muqaddima* also have this type of thematic coherence. The specificity and unity of the fourth chapter is purely textual. It is no surprise that it starts with mere preliminaries (*sawābiq*), and these recapitulate arguments presented earlier on in the textual sequence of the work. The very physical structure of a city which comprises private and public buildings is a requirement of the accomplished state and is by no means a necessity. Public buildings, in particular, have to be constructed by a communal effort which does not come naturally but has to result from 'the truncheon of kingship' or else from the promise of heavenly reward.[66] Once established, the life of the city, its permanence or extinction, is dependent on the state which founds it or which takes it over: Fez and Cairo, for instance, are continuous centres of states and their populations are ever replenished by beduins in search of comfort. The Qal'at Banī Ḥammād on the northern edges of the Sahara is an example of a city that disintegrated with the disappearance of the state that founded it (Q, 2: 201 ff.).

Ibn Khaldūn then sketches with more detail than in the previous chapter his ideas on the proportion between the power of the state and the size and magnificence of the edifices and cities it causes to be built, remarking on the great works which were constructed and consolidated by successive states (Q, 2: 207 ff.). The discussion which follows on the strategic and climatic factors that should be taken into account in choosing the location of cities (Q, 2: 210 ff.) is succeeded by an account of fact and fiction in the histories of three great locations: the Ka'ba in Mecca, the sanctuary in Jerusalem, and the city of Medina (Q, 2: 215 ff.). The next three sections deal with a different group of topics, being an historical commentary on the density of urban establishment and architectural wonders in the Middle East and North Africa: both the Arabs and the Berbers had no proper urban tradition before Islam, and that is why the architectural accomplishments under Islamic rule are meagre in relation to the power of Islam and in comparison with those of older established peoples, such as the Persians or the Copts. And in any case the purely Arab urban establishments soon go derelict, for the Arabs do not choose 'natural' locations for the building of cities, but, as the examples of Qairawān and Kūfa demonstrate, are more interested in proximity to grazing ground for their camels. What great cities and edifices the Arabs had, they took from the Persians or had built by Persians (Q, 2: 229 ff.).

The next topical group that Ibn Khaldūn tackles is the wealth of cities. This he conceives as an arithmetic sum which is directly proportional to the quantity of civilization, i.e., population and size: the 'differential in the meagreness and greatness'[67] of civilization is directly proportional to the wealth of cities. Thus a Qāḍī in Fez is wealthier than one from Oran. A beggar in Fez was once observed by Ibn Khaldūn asking for the price of a sheep during the Aḍḥā feast, a request which in Tlemcen, for instance, would have brought him severe rebuke (Q, 2: 234 ff.). The 'quantity of civilization' also has a decisive effect on prices in the cities. Barring crop failures and monopolies, the prices of necessary staples such as grains and onions are low because very many of these goods are produced. The prices of luxuries such as fruits and meats, however, are high because production is limited while demand is high because of the great wealth of the city. The great demand for artisanal services likewise raises the price of such services, as do the overpayments given to some artisans by wealthy patrons, which induce these artisans to keep their charges higher than they should be. Similar considerations of the quantity of civilization apply to countries and to various geographical units. The great wealth and magnificence of the cities of the East in comparison with the Maghrib is due to population and the consequent quantity of economic activity. And while the greater wealth of the East does correspond to prescriptions of the stars, these prescriptions are in correspondence with terrestrial factors, the primary one of which is the quantity of civilization (Q, 2: 239 ff.).

The discussion of prices shows the awareness that men of the world have always had about the relation of prices to supply and demand, and this has always been singled out by commentators as testimony to Ibn Khaldūn's precocious modernity. But his remains a sheer observation. The argument on prices is unmistakably ethical. A consistent argument in terms of supply and demand would require that the prices of luxuries as well could be brought down, for great demand leads not only to higher prices, but to increased production. The assumption on the part of Ibn Khaldūn that the quantity of luxuries is somehow constant betrays an underlying metaphysical assumption: that the quantitative constancy of luxuries is a function of their supererogatoriness; a luxury must be limited in supply because it is a luxury. That a luxury is not fixed but varies with wealth, and that things luxurious can become necessary under certain circumstances, is something that cannot be accommodated within the context of the metaphysics of the necessary as opposed to the supererogatory. Likewise, an argument in terms of supply and demand would require the artisans who raise their charges to become uncompetitive, not to be joined by other artisans, unless some other, organizational and political, factor is taken into account, which Ibn Khaldūn's argument does not.

The prices in the great cities are aggravated by the impositions of the sovereigns, for artisans and agricultural producers pass on these expenses to the consumer (Q, 2: 241). Poverty and economic deterioration inevitably follow, for the consumers find less goods to buy, while the high prices prevent the producers from disposing of their products. From this a veritable cascade of evil follows, and it is a cascade that corrupts humankind in general. Need brings about chicanery, deception, and trickery. People acquire the habits of cheating, mendacity, thievery, and become false witnesses and usurers. Not only do they acquire these habits to cheat others, but do so to defend themselves against the exactions of the powerful. Once this sets in, it corrupts the whole of civilization and corrodes its constitution. This is why the city bides the end of civilization (Q, 2: 255 ff.). The corruption of the state, as we have seen, is responsible for this state of affairs in the city. Ibn Khaldūn here recapitulates a previous argument and epitomizes it in the metaphysical terms that belong to the structure of the *Muqaddima*: the state stands to civilization as form does to matter. The inextricable connection between them dictates that the atrophy of the one is the atrophy of the other (Q, 2: 264 f.).

The chapter ends with the observation that, when the power of a state wanes and recedes from outlying cities, these cities are taken over by local power groups bound together by various ties such as kinship. These behave like *'aṣabīya* groups out in the wild, and only one emerges victorious and repeats on a small scale the cycle of kingship: tyrannization, symbols of power, and hereditary succession. Examples of this in Ibn Khaldūn's time are the short-lived city-states of Tripoli, Tozur, Gafsa, Biskra, and others (Q, 2: 267–8). Finally, Ibn Khaldūn's discussion of dialects speaks of the corruption of classical Arabic by pre-Islamic languages in the Levant, in Persia, and in the Maghrib. Under the Turks, Arabic survived only because it is the language of the Koran. Indeed, when the Mongols took over India, Transoxiania, Khurāsān, and Persia, Arabic only persisted as a literary language which has to be taught rather than be naturally acquired as a living tongue (Q, 2: 269–71).

The fifth chapter of the *Muqaddima* deals with livelihood and its provenances, such as gain from crafts and other mechanisms of acquisition. It has no prolegomena in the logical or even in the natural sense of the term. It consists solely of thematic discussions (masā'il), as its title informs the reader. The prefatory discussion and elucidation of the main topics involved is internal to the thematic group in question and does not in any way link it to previous sections and discussions of the *Muqaddima*, which gives some indication that matters arising in the thematic context of livelihood–with the exclusion of natural livelihood as obtains in beduinity–are situated within the context of accomplished life in the city, and are as such manifestations of a nature that has run its course and in no further need of a deductively serial elucidation.

Yet, like all that is produced by this nature, its dynamic is embedded in the first principles that inform the nature. It is thus that Ibn Khaldūn establishes the fact of exchange as the principle that explains all types of gainful activity: since people share the provisions of the world in a situation of mutual dependence, that which accrues to one can only be obtained by another through the provision of a return (*'awaḍ*). Like the idea of cooperation and kingship, this idea of cooperation in exchange seems to have been fairly common.[68] Sustenance (*ma'āsh*) is the fundamental category in what we may call, for lack of a better term, the economic field: it is a field where the major consideration is individual consumption. Hence sustenance consumption, as the most elementary and the one in accordance with need, is fundamental.[69] That which exceeds this need is called wealth (*riyāsh, mutamawwal*).[70] It is surely an ethical conception of wealth that informs the typology of gains that Ibn Khaldūn presents here: besides sustenance and wealth, the categories of acquisition and gain are introduced. All wealth that is not utilized for the direct benefit of its owner is acquisition (*kasb*),[71] as is the wealth of a deceased person with respect to that person. Once the inheritors put it to useful purpose, it becomes gain (*rizq*). This, Ibn Khaldūn tells us, is the sense of the term as used by religious scholars as a concensual usage, remarking that the Mu'tazila exclude from the category of gain all that is wrongfully obtained (Q, 2: 272–4).

All gain is the product of gainful activity. Even animal products involve gainful activity on the part of men, an activity which remains invisible in comparison with artisanal activity, for instance. Livelihood is a product of the solicitation of gain, and it is this that gives the activity the status of an equitable return: it is one among other elements which have returns and whose reciprocal exchange is required by human cooperation. Labour enters into the prices of things as one element among others which are ultimately reducible and convertible to the two natural returns (not equivalents) of wealth: gold and silver, the stuff of wealth. It is not, as in the labour theory of value which commentators are wont to see in Ibn Khaldūn, that labour is the source, fount, and very substance of value. There is no quantitative conception of value here, but a qualitative return,[72] and moreover, labour is only one among a family of possible returns (Q, 2: 275).

Livelihood, according to the precept informing the categorization of gainful activity, is thus utility. The solicitation of this utility takes various forms: it could be a forced acquisition which is called taxation and imposition, it could be had by hunting, by animal husbandry, by agriculture, by crafts, or by trade. These forms are standard in works of belles lettres and political wisdom, Ibn Khaldūn informs us. Moreover, all of these forms are natural except the first, lordly form of gaining sustenance and livelihood which is therefore excluded from the discussion and had already been sketched earlier in the *Muqaddima*. Of the natural ways of obtaining livelihood, agriculture is of course the most natural, being anterior to all other forms, as well as being simple and native to the intelligence of men, it not requiring any form of knowledge or schooling. Crafts, by contrast, require knowledge and thought, and are both more complex and posterior to agriculture. That is why crafts are rarely found among beduins. Also natural is trade: it is natural in so far as it is a manner of obtaining livelihood, albeit not being so in the methods it uses to obtain this livelihood, such as monopolies, hoarding, and transfer of commodities from one place to another in search of a favourable return (Q, 2: 275-8)–rather than of a just return, which is what would make it natural. The conception of a just return is the hidden notion that silently orients Ibn Khaldūn's discussion.

It thus appears that the unnatural character of commercial methods is a product of the non-immediacy with which equivalences are sought and obtained. Strictly speaking, this non-immediacy of a rewarding return should apply to commerce *tout court* and condemn it to unnaturalness. This, however, was patently impossible for Ibn Khaldūn for reasons not altogether clear and ultimately impossible to determine. Islamic law, for one, condones profit, although it is akin to gambling, because it is not a seizure of money without a reward. Too exacting an application of natural criteria would, moreover, have made it imperative that commerce be placed on a par, in ethical and other terms, with lordly acquisition or usury. No such problems of nature obtain in the discussion of two unnatural means of sustenance, service and treasure-hunting. The former is the complement of the political acquisition of the lord and sovereign, and is additionally contrary to nature because the manliness natural to pristine humankind is offended by dependence and effeminacy. Equally unnatural is treasure-hunting, if for other reasons. Like service, it is the solicitation of livelihood by those incapable of natural pursuits. While sketching some of the treasure hunting lore current during his time,[73] Ibn Khaldūn insists that treasures are only found by pure coincidence and remarks that, even if it were granted that hoarders ensure the secrecy of their hoard by magical means, it is unlikely that they would leave talismanic or any other clues for liberating the treasure from its secret (Q, 2: 278 ff.).

A new thematic group is introduced at this point, one that deals with some conditions that make for wealth. Ibn Khaldūn points to an important fact concerning pre-modern societies: that wealth, power, and status are virtually coterminous. He says that men of patrimonial status (*jāh*) are wealthy and get wealthier because they have access to the services of others without necessarily having to reciprocate the service with a reward. It is in this sense that lordship is a manner of acquiring livelihood, and lesser instances of which are the more prominent men of God. Traders, however, who possess no qualities of status, of grandeur or of power, are only wealthy in proportion to their own individual efforts, and this seems to place them at the bottom of the power hierarchy. For every context includes a hierarchy of patrimonial status which makes possible the dictation of prohibition and of permission, parallel to which is the hierarchy of wealth (Q, 287 ff.). Persons active in the religious professions–the administration of law, teaching, preaching, and the like–are not likely to get wealthy, because the demand for their services is meagre. Their wealth is ultimately dependent upon the will of the sovereign, who does not normally impart to them the same wealth he imparts to his political backers and allies. These persons are, moreover, engaged in the purveyance of particularly honourable goods and would not, as such, humiliate themselves in the service of men and things of the world (Q, 2: 295–6).[74] Traders, for their part, have to be in possession of at least some courage in order to ward off the extortions of those in power and the avarice of their peers, while they also have to humble themselves in the interests of business. This makes their moral and ethical stature altogether very inferior to the standards required by the nobility and gallantry (*muru'a*) of the powerful (Q, 2: 302 ff.).

The third and last thematic group in the chapter under consideration concerns crafts and includes the sixteenth through to the final thirty-third section. A craft is defined as a skill (*malaka*), in the Aristotelian sense of *technē*, which is acquired by the repetition of an exemplary and model act until the practice of this act becomes ingrained in the practitioner. And like all other things, crafts are graduated on a scale of complexity which starts with the simple and elementary, such as exists among the beduins, and progresses towards the higher complexities of crafts that only exist in accomplished urban settings. Crafts are also divided according to a different criterion, that of relation to livelihood, which distinguishes crafts of sustenance (butchery, carpentry, weaving, and so on) from those of thought, such as book-binding, poetry, education, and politics. In all instances, the more accomplished the civilization, the more ample, qualitatively and quantitatively, are the crafts. And the accomplishment in the field of crafts is in direct relation to the duration and rootedness of civilization in a given city. This is clearly to be seen in Tunis and Andalusia, Ibn Khaldūn says, where the duration of civilization has led to the perfection of crafts due to the constancy of its repetition over centuries (Q, 2: 306 ff.). Moreover, the quality and quantity of crafts is dependent on demand, with the consequence that civilizations on the wane are characterized by the diminution of their crafts (Q, 2: 311 ff.). The ineptitude of Arabs as craftsmen is a reflection of their beduinity, although some countries, such as the Yemen and Oman, which had Arab rule over thousands of years, are still important centres of accomplished craftsmanship (Q, 2: 313 f.).

In the discussion of the various crafts, Ibn Khaldūn chose to ignore all those crafts which are neither necessary, such as agriculture and tailoring, nor honourable, such as midwifery, medicine, scribing, stationery, and singing. The last three are honourable because of their association with kingship and the court (Q, 2: 316). The most original of all crafts, of course, is agriculture, which is the exclusive specialty of beduins. The first of urban crafts, equally naturally, is construction. Its accomplishment is graduated between the most elementary shelters and the most exquisite of palaces, and one sees how Ibn Khaldūn has forced his arguments about nature somewhat by claiming, totally unjustly, that all beduins dwell in caves or otherwise natural dwellings, and then proceeds to give a valuable and, I believe, unique sketch of what appears to have been the standard outline of house building during his time. Carpentry is equally essential, not only for urban civilization but for beduinity as well. In the latter, it is used to make staves for tents, saddles for animals, and lances for warfare. In the city, carpentry is the complement of construction and extends its utility to shipbuilding. The naturalness and necessity of weaving and tailoring is the result of the need for warmth and the later need for the items of luxury. The discussion of the necessity of midwifery is the occasion for an aside on Avicenna, Fārābī, and Ibn Ṭufail (d. 581/1185-6): while agreeing with Avicenna in his critique of the latter two in the contention that the species of creation can actually be wiped out from the face of the earth (hence the necessity of midwifery among humankind), he disagrees with an opinion which he imputes to Avicenna but which is closer to that of Ibn Tufail, that there is a possibility for regeneration from a brew consonant in its temper with that of mankind and with the aid of an animal that will raise the first of the new humanity under the influence of divine inspiration. Medicine is needed less in the conditions of beduinity than in the city. In the former, the simplicity of alimentation, purity of atmosphere, and frequency of exercise facilitate digestion and thus lead to a better and purer constitution. The honourable character of writing and copying derives from its being specific to man to the exclusion of other animals. Ibn Khaldūn's brief discussion of Arabic paleography in its historical contexts and of royal cryptography, leads to an account of the fundamentals of stationery: copying, binding, correcting, and cognate activities. The discussion of these matters is largely one of how it is that the activity of the stationer is coterminous (or should be so) with preserving the integrity and exactitude of cultural transmission (whence its nobility), and the low state of this art in the Maghrib of Ibn Khaldūn's time. The account of music and singing provides a sketch of the theory of notation and harmony current at the time of Ibn Khaldūn, an account of some instruments, discussions of music among the Arabs and the recitation of the Koran, anecdotes about early famous musicians and singers, and an account on the effect of music on the soul. The fifth chapter of the *Muqaddima* ends with a section describing how the practice of a craft endows its practitioner with improved mental capabilities, especially writing and arithmetic (Q, 2: 317–363).

The sixth chapter of the *Muqaddima* deals with sciences and education–the most accomplished forms of knowledge, and hence those found only in the most consummate instances of civilization. Like the fifth chapter, therefore, the sixth does not possess a prolegomenon that provides something conceptually new in the context of the general logical and modal design of the *Muqaddima*. The chapter professedly has a full-scale prolegomenon, a muqaddima, but this is unlikely to have any significance as to its status. Moreover, this is likely to be the seventh section rather than the first, that asserting that science and education are natural to civilization, which thus links this chapter with the previous one. The first six sections of chapter six are of the nature of prefatory discussions with no necessary connection with the rest of the chapter and are, in any case, a late addition in the compositional and textual history of the *Muqaddima*.[75] They recapitulate and slightly amplify previous discussions on knowledge. They sketch an Avicennan theory of abstractions with the stages of abstraction as corresponding to types or faculties of the intellect, the discerning and the pragmatic,[76] leaving the theoretical intellect to a sketch later on in the chapter. In addition, a dissertation on sense, on the mind, and on the supersensible as three worlds to which correspond three types of knowledge, is presented, in which it is fairly easy to notice that Ibn Khaldūn was constantly, if not systematically, avoiding the use of the Avicennan terminology, which might have made it unavoidable for him to sketch an Avicennan theory of prophecy. The thrust of this dissertation is a sketch of prophetic-angelical knowledge in which our author stresses that there is no question of actual discursive knowledge of the beyond because the spiritual entities who inhabit it have essences which are inaccessible to the human understanding and accessible only to the 'heart'. And knowledge of the heart is act and, being act, is not liable to discursive knowledge (Q, 3: 27–8). The Avicennan claim to discursive knowledge of transcendental intellects is thus unfounded, for prophetic knowledge, like the knowledge of mystics, is a gnostic act. The only discursive knowledge that mortals are capable of having about the beyond is through the medium of dogmatic discourse (Q, 2: 364 ff.).

Training in the sciences is a craft among others. It is this principle, enunciated at the outset of the seventh section of the sixth and last chapter, which provides for the relevance of the chapter as such in the eyes of the *Muqaddima*. Training in the sciences, or education, is a craft because it provides the skill by means of which the science is practised: the skill consists here of the thorough knowledge of the principles, procedures, and topics of the science, and the ability to deduce its particulars from its generalities. This skill does not constitute comprehension properly so called; like all skills, it is a bodily attribute; in this case, it is embedded in the brain (Q, 2: 376). Being a skill and in need of continuous instruction, it is little wonder that the tradition through which knowledge is transmitted and preserved in its integrity is so highly prized.[77] This, we have seen, was one task of the craft of stationery, and it is also preserved in the educational certificate (*ijāza*) granted by professors to their pupils and which gives the pupils licence to transmit a particular text or a number of texts. This was the fundamental form of paradigmatic consistency at the time of Ibn Khaldūn and in his culture.[78] Turning his attention to his contemporary Maghrib, Ibn Khaldūn bemoans the situation regarding the traditions of learning which, he says, have all but disappeared. Tunis and Bougie remain the best endowed, while Fez is almost completely cut off from any connection with the past, and an invaluable account is provided of the paradigmatic and traditional connections between Maghribi sciences and Eastern traditions, and the contrast with the East contemporary with Ibn Khaldūn is pointed out, the reasons for the discrepancy being attributed to the differential amplitude of civilization and its diminution in the Maghrib (Q, 2: 376 ff.).

Regardless of its amplitude, every civilization possesses two types of sciences, and it should be stressed that Ibn Khaldūn is making a distinction, not establishing an opposition. There are those sciences, generically called philosophical or wisdom sciences,[79] which accrue to mankind *qua* thinking being, and which are accessible to the intelligence native to the nature of human thought. Distinct from this group is that which assembles the sciences based upon the absolute truth of certain narrative texts (*akhbār* and *uṣūl*): these are the traditional positive sciences which, unlike the universally uniform wisdom sciences, are specific to eaeh religious community. The positivity of these sciences resides in their fundamental proeedure which is the employment of a sacred text as the repository of truth and the measurement of the validity of situations subsequent to it on the basis of this text. Ibn Khaldūn succinctly states the fundamental procedure of analogical reasoning by saying that the saered text 'cannot contain' subsequent particularities, which, therefore, have to be reduced to it (for the purpose of a positive or negative judgement) by an analogical process. It is from the sacred text that validity is transferred. The corpus of sacred texts is made up of the Koran and tradition, and the first sciences within the positive group are those geared towards the study of these texts: the philological sciences lead to the proeedures of exegesis and the science of Koranic textual variants (*qirā'āt*), the seience of tradition completes the certain establishment of the sacred text and makes possible the science of the principles of jurisprudence whose task is the procedures of the deduction of legislation from the sacred text. A corpus of beliefs and obligations is thus assured, and the science which elucidates them is the principles of religion or theology (Q, 2: 385–6).

The logical progression and connection of the positive seiences is testimony to Ibn Khaldūn's systematic sense; it is an unusual form of stating and expressing the enumeration of these sciences but not an original one. But there is nothing particularly noteworthy about their identification, nor about the identification of the wisdom sciences and their distinction from the positive. The identification of particular sciences corresponds to the paradigmatic existence of these particular sciences with very well-defined boundaries,[80] and their hierarchical organization in the *Muqaddima* seems to correspond to the rationality of contemporary library classifications.[81] The classification of sciences does not merit the almost metaphysical status given it by many commentators;[82] it is not *the* classification of sciences, as is almost invariably contended, but is one of many current in Ibn Khaldūn's culture, even barring what some see as the great divide between this and similar classifications, based on the distinction between the wisdom sciences and the positive sciences and that which admits no such distinction.[83] Ghazālī, for instance, classified sciences in no less than five ways and according to five criteria: methodological, formal, material, juristic, and morally utilitarian.[84] The sciences are each distinct within its paradigmatic boundary, and the manner in which they are grouped together into types is dependent upon the purpose of the classificatory act and its context.

The didactic classification of sciences presented in the *Muqaddima* starts with the positive sciences. Positive and religious sciences of peoples other than the Islamic are ignored, not only because the author was concerned with giving an account of those sciences prevalent in his age. They are ignored because the religion of Islam–and, by implication, all the sciences that give it support and articulation–stands to other religions of the book as the Koran stands to other holy books and as the prophecy of Muḥammad stands to the prophecies of his predecessors. This is one described by the term *naskh*, which denotes abrogation without invalidation, and hence has the sense of supercession, the best equivalent in a European language being the German *Aufhebung* in its Hegelian acceptation. Ibn Khaldūn cites the Koranic injunction to neither believe nor disbelieve what is stated by the People of the Book. The positive sciences have thrived and reached a very consummate level of development. The first to be discussed are the sciences of the Koran (Q, 2: 387-8).

The account of the Koranic sciences first demarcates its object: the seven accepted variants of the holy book, and the procedures of exegesis, be they based upon ascertaining traditions about meaning, or the auxiliary methods of philology. This is followed by a sketch of the main strands in the literature on these topics, the traditions through which they reached the Maghrib, and the contemporary state of the art (Q, 2: 388 ff.). A similar treatment is given to the science of tradition and its procedures (Q, 2: 395 ff.) which, like the account of the Koranic sciences, does not contain much that is remarkable, except in so far as it is a particularly succinct statement of the topic. The discussion of jurisprudence, *fiqh*, similarly starts with an account of the rise of different tendencies within the science and an outline of the basic literature of each. The genesis of the four main schools (and the failure of the fifth, while the sixth and short-lived school of Awzāʿī (d. 157/774) is not mentioned) is followed by a discussion of their geographical distribution across the lands of Islam–where he ascribes the predominance of Mālikism in the Maghrib to the beduinity which it shares with Mālik's Ḥijāz, and then gives an account of the various Mālikite tendencies and traditions in North Africa and the Andalus until his own time (Q, 3: 1 ff.). The science of inheritance division, a subsidiary of jurisprudence, is then brieny sketched, and is sketched again from a different perspective as one of the sciences of wisdom and as a branch of arithmetic (Q, 3: 14 ff., 99 ff.).

A higher plane of complexity attaches to the group of sciences that follow jurisprudence. The first to occur is the principles of jurisprudence, *uṣūl al-fiqh* which, Ibn Khaldūn says, is one of the most exalted, most honourable, and most useful of positive sciences. Ibn Khaldūn's account of this science is crucial for the purposes of modern scholarship, as it brings out the scientific amplitude of the principles of jurisprudence and provides a unique sketch of its history, as expressed in its traditions, transmissions, and literature, which can be used as a basis to restore it to the crucial historical role and cultural location it occupied and which, in modern scholarship, is almost completely ignored. This science is particularly wealthy: it contains and organizes topics derived in a variety of other scientific and paradigmatic locations. Its purpose is the study of the four principles from which jurisprudence is derivable and to which judgement has to be reducible: the Koran, tradition, concensual tradition (the Islamic nation is infallible), and the analogical procedures. For the study of the first of these principles, exegetical procedures are a prerequisite. For the second, it is essential to have a mastery of tradition procedures and concepts, such as criticism of transmission, the sciences of narrative (*khabar*) which entail the study of *naskh*-relations between narratives. The science also requires knowledge of the philological sciences which are used in all matters concerning narrative. As for the central topic of analogy, this requires knowledge of the logical theory of predication, of definition, and deduction. The brief historical discussion distinguishes the tradition of the theologians in this science from that of the Ḥanafī scholars which was subject to a fertilization from the former, and shows how the latter tendency excelled also in the auxiliary sciences of controversy and dialectics. Controversy is the science containing the procedures for pursuing the arcane controversies between the four schools of jurisprudence, while dialectics concerns the procedures of controversy in general, and consists to a large extent of syllogisms intact as to their formal aspect but deficient in their substance, like sophistical syllogisms (Q, 3: 17 ff.).

The discussion of theology is similar to that of the foregoing sciences except for a polemical aside more reminiscent of discussion yet to come in this chapter. Theology is concerned with the defence of the fundamental dogmas of Islam which should be believed by the heart and admitted by the tongue of every Muslim: the belief in God, angels, the holy Books, prophets, predestination, and the day of judgement. The defence that theology carries out is against deviationists, and the reference here is clearly against a deviationism within Islam and not in the face of other religions. The core of Islamic dogma is the unicity of God, and knowledge of this divine property can only be had through belief and not by way of demonstration: not only is the divine realm not accessible to the human understanding, as we have already seen, but the determinants of human action are also inaccessible. For they are internal and specific to the actor, and they are, in addition, of divine, and thus indeterminate (for the human intelligence) origin. In this, Ibn Khaldūn restates the standard occasionalistic position of Ash'arīte theology current at Ibn Khaldūn's time throughout the Islamic world, and especially among Mālikīs.[85] Not only are the determinants of action unknowable, but, even if they were, or if some were, total knowledge would be required to acquire the knowledge of the action, for the series of determinants is infinite. We will encounter the argument about the infinity of determinants in the refutation of astrology later, and will elaborate on it there.

This preamble to the discussion of theological science was clearly aimed at the theologians contemporary with Ibn Khaldūn who, as he correctly remarks, imported many of the topics proper to the paradigm of philosophical science into theology. Such are the questions of divine attributes for instance, or of prophecy. Such matters in theology should be confined to the realm of belief and are not amenable to discursive elaboration after the fashion of the philosophers. It is this philosophization of theology at the hands of the later systematic theologians, such as the consummately scholastic 'Aḍud al-Dīn al-Ījī, Ibn Khaldūn's older contemporary, and what he considered to be its excessive formalization that Ibn Khaldūn sought to combat before he commenced his sketch of the science. The distinction, to Ibn Khaldūn as to the mainstream represented by Ghazālī, was clear: a body to the theologian is a sign of its creator, and to the philosopher it is an object that moves.[86] The oversystematization that Ibn Khaldūn detected he patently thought was unnecessary, as was theology itself: there was no longer need to combat deviation, as there was none any more (Q, 3: 27 ff.). The self-perpetuating systematization of theology transgresses the bounds within which the discourse of the human intellect is valid and possible.

The unseen angelical realm which cannot be reached by the human understanding is accessible to the direct apprehension of the soul. The noumenous is apprehended by the heart, and this apprehension is of the same character as the apprehension of happiness, of pain, or of sadness, and thus cannot be translated into discursive articulation. For discursive articulation requires the convention of a semantics, and the personal gnostics of mysticism are not communicable and exist at a special and distinct sphere of reality altogether, one that is akin to prophetic apprehension. This explains the miracles that occur among mystics in the section on mysticism that follows the discussion of theology. Mysticism, Ibn Khaldūn says, was originally a practice of the pious, and it was not until Ghazālī that it became a science. It later developed, with Suhrawardī (d. 578/1191) and Firghānī (fl. c. 700/1300), for instance, a fully fledged theosophical cosmology of the emanationist type which spans the whole of creation down to the elements–in effect, a very complex and areane chain of being. There is very little judgement on this matter contained in the discussion of mysticism; the strictures of many scholars against sūfī pronouncements upon angels and the divine Throne, for instance, are deemed by Ibn Khaldūn to be irrelevant because all sūfī experiences are intuitive and thus not subject to either demonstration or refutation. When the mystics try to articulate their experiences discursively, such articulations are veiled with an impregnable opacity which, Ibn Khaldūn obviously thought, refutes the very viability of their discursive project.

Ibn Khaldūn is decidedly unsympathetic and ungenerous to the newer manifestation of mysticism in the writings of Ibn 'Arabī and Ibn Sab'īn: the doctrines of the unity of God and man through theophany, and of the Primate of the Time (*quṭb*).[86a] The former, in which God takes possession of the gnostic in the act of gnosis and speaks through him, Ibn Khaldūn sees as identical at once with the Christian doctrine of incarnation and with the Shī'ī doctrine of the Imamate. The Primate of the Time, for his part, represents the bequest of divine truth to a particular time through the person of the Primate, who achieves the most profound and complete union with the divinity, and Ibn Khaldūn identifies this doctrine again with that of the Shī'a, and especially the Ismailis, and points to Avicenna as the first to theorize it in his *Ishārāt.* Ibn Khaldūn admits freely the glimpse of angelical noumena in the course of the gnostic metapsychism which marks mystical experience. But the ideas of incarnation and dissolution within the divine essence drew from him a *fatwa* pronouncing them heretical and outside the limits and boundaries of Islam (the text is in S, 110). And while he disagrees with the critics of mysticism who attack it on account of certain discrete heretical-sounding pronouncements, he is prepared to condone these pronouncements on the assumption that they are uttered in states of entrancement and that, therefore, their pronouncements are invalid, as they are not in possession of their minds: it is in this context, Ibn Khaldūn says, that the execution of al-Hallāj in Baghdad in 309/922 took place: he uttered heretical statements while in full possession of his faculties (Q, 3: 59 ff.).

There is one condition under which the noumenal glimpse can be discursively articulated, and it is this that is the task of the science of dream interpretation. Dreams, like visions, are occasioned by such a glimpse, and are of three kinds. That which is inspired by the devil is based solely upon the regurgitation of images already stored in the dreamer's memory, and is naturally misleading. The two other sorts are benign and genuine dreams, acquired during sleep by a gnostic process of the mental soul and promptly translated into the form of an image. Those inspired directly by God are clear and explicit and in no need of interpretation, whereas those dreams occasioned by angelical will are encoded and require the decipherment of a dream interpreter. This scientist works from the basis of what Ibn Khaldūn unconvincingly calls general principles: a utensil does not only represent a woman, nor does the sea only represent a king: the latter can also encode anger, worry, or a calamity. It is the task of the interpreter to decide which interpretation fits the context of both sleep and wakefulness (Q, 3: 80 ff.).

The seven rational sciences, in contrast to the positive, are natural to man. They do not, like the positive sciences, originate in a sacred discourse which is merely elaborated by the science. That is why logic is the most original of all rational sciences. It is the principle upon which other sciences are based as to their form, just as the Koran and other sacred texts are the principles of all positive sciences. Logic is the absolute and apodeictic given in the field of rational sciences, and that is because it runs parallel to the nature of the mind. Immediately following logic is what the medieval Europeans knew as the quadrivium, consisting of arithmetic, geometry, astronomy, and music. Reason can then progress to the knowledge of natural science, and then on to crown its activities with the complexities of metaphysics.

With the subject matter and structure of the rational sciences thus outlined, Ibn Khaldūn goes on to outline the fundamentals of their history and literature, both discussions being in conformity with the practice adopted in all the sections of the *Muqaddima* dealing with sciences. The rational sciences are universal and the advent of Islam does not have the effect it had on positive sciences, which it transcended in its higher expression of the truth. The Islamic nation–meaning the civilization of Islam–inherited and continued the tradition of rational sciences from the Persians and the Greeks.[87] The Persian legacy has disappeared because–and Ibn Khaldūn purveys here a version of a rich legend–the Arabs are supposed to have destroyed the libraries of Persia at the time of the conquest. It was the Persians, according to one opinion, who had given these sciences to the Greeks, who themselves, according to Ibn Khaldūn, claim that their tradition goes back to Luqman the (legendary) Sage, and from him to Plato, Aristotle, Alexander of Aphrodisias, Themistius, and so until the Romans, to whom the state had been transferred, embraced Christianity and abandoned the rational sciences in keeping with their religious beliefs. The tradition was taken over by the Arabs and Muslims and flowered with Fārābī, Avicenna, Averroes (d. 595/1198), and others who specialized in mathematics and its astrological, magical, and talismanic cognates, such as Majrīṭī and (the legendary?) Jābir Ibn Ḥayyan. Much as with the positive sciences, the state of the art in the Maghrib at the time of Ibn Khaldūn, he says, is very poor because of the diminution of civilization; what remains is invigilated by religious scholars. By contrast, these sciences thrive in eastern Iraq, in Persia, and in West Europe (Q, 3: 86 ff.).

First in the expository order of the rational sciences are the sciences of number: arithmetic, algebra, accountancy, and inheritance division.[88] The quantitative sciences also include geometry, which deals with discrete and continuous quantity as such, and its subdivisions (conic sections, spherical figures, mechanics, surveying, and optics). Geometrical procedures form the fundamental concepts used by astronomy, which is then discussed along with the science of astronomical tables. Throughout these discussions of numerical sciences, Ibn Khaldūn provides a quick sketch of the basic subject matter involved and a cursory sketch of the standard works on each. The science of music is not discussed beyond the very brief definition given to it in the section where the rational sciences as a group are discussed (Q, 3: 93 ff.).

Logic comes next in the expository order of the rational sciences.[89] It is composed of rules that distinguish the true from the false among the two elements that compose every science without exception: definitions and arguments.[90] Ibn Khaldūn then provides an account of the components of the Aristotelian *Organon*, its combination with Porphyry's *Isagoge* (which he does not identify as such, but merely designates as an amendment to the original work), and the further transformations in the organization and delimitation of logical knowledge among the Muslim thinkers. This he sees as a formalization which received a particularly strong impetus from theological criticisms of the science, which particularly attacked the concepts of universals and categories from a nominalist perspective, and which saw in the opinions of some very prominent early theologians (Bāqillāni, Ash'arī, and Isfirā'īnī) that the refutation of a proof necessarily implies the refutation of the proposition that is so proved, a grave danger to the very elements of dogma. Later theologians, especially Ghazālī and Rāzī (d. 606/1210), refuted this last doctrine.

The natural sciences are treated after logic. Natural science is the science which deals with all things which are in movement and subject to change. It deals with the elements, their combinations, and the metals, plants, animals, and mankind that spring from these generative compositions. It deals also with natural phenomena such as lightning, earthquakes, clouds, and thunder. Aristotle is singled out as the main author in the field, the translations of whose works are readily available for all. Among the Muslims, Avicenna wrote extensively on natural science and disagreed with Aristotle on a large number of issues, in contrast to Averroes, who merely wrote epitomes and commentaries on the First Master.[91] Medicine, a branch of natural science, was a field which originated with another Greek, Galen, and on which Avicenna also wrote prominent works. The second and last branch of natural science which Ibn Khaldūn sketches is the science of agriculture, the main principles of which are derived from Nabatean books translated into Arabic. (Q, 3: 116 ff.).

Metaphysics (and not philosophy *tout court*) is the last of the rational sciences, being the most complex and the one with the widest sweep: it is concerned with being and the concepts associated with it, such as corporeality and spirituality, essence, unity, necessity, possibility, and others. The science, as Ibn Khaldūn says, and in a correct depiction of the peripatetic Neoplatonism which distinguishes Arab-Islamic philosophy, posits spiritual entities as fundamental and conceives of existence as a hierarchy posited by emanation. Identifying the science with the paradigm within which it properly belongs–that of philosophy–Ibn Khaldūn adds that a task of this science is the study of the return after death of the soul to its origin, and the happiness that is caused by knowledge. The basic literature on the topic is contained in the works of Aristotle, Avicenna, and Averroes. After the Ghazālīan polemic against philosophy, Ibn Khaldūn again reminds us, metaphysical and theological topics were confounded. Rāzī's *Al-Mabāḥith al-Mashriqīya* and all theological writing posterior to it included a very substantial amount of metaphysical topics, although the order of their occurrence inside treatises was changed.[92] The integrity of the methods and aims of theology is foremost in Ibn

Khaldūn's mind and assists him in incisively demarcating the paradigmatic boundaries involved: some of the objects dealt with in the two sciences may overlap, but topical overlapping does not imply an identity of purpose which, to Ibn Khaldūn, was clearly a component of every paradigm. The argument goes further: there is, in fact, no identity of object, but merely an overlapping of topics in the course of argumentation,[93] meaning divinity, unicity, and associated concepts. The objects are as distinct as the aims and purposes are distinct or, as one could put it today, as the methods are distinct. Ibn Khaldūn here recapitulates the distinction between rational sciences and positive sciences *tout court*, and presents it as the context within which the distinction between metaphysics and theology is located. The concern of philosophy is to demonstrate that which had not been previously demonstrable.[94] The certainty of the propositions that theology demonstrates is pregiven and already unmistakeably demonstrable. The same violation of scientific boundaries occurs in mystical theory, which utilizes metaphysical concepts, and especially in discussions of prophecy, unicity, and incarnation. Metaphysics and mysticism both also violate the boundaries of the human intellect, which has no access to the realms occupied by religion (Q, 3: 1210).

Also striving beyond the bounds of what is permissible and possible for mankind is the group of very highly developed fringe sciences, a sort of high sub-culture whose fundamental concepts were known to and shared by all, but whose specific configurations of these concepts and the social and sectarian associations of their practice as crafts were never officialized by the high culture of the state. These are the sciences of magic and the talisman, of Letters (*al-ḥurūf*), and of alchemy.[95] All these sciences that are based upon the properties of the four elements, agreed by and known to all, and the influences of astral and spiritual factors upon these properties, also a proposition known to and agreed by all. Being non-Islamic, they do not qualify as positive sciences, for these had superseded all the positive sciences of other legitimate religions. These are fringe sciences which, while very highly developed and while each has a well-defined paradigmatic space, were officially frowned upon and associated with unsavoury doctrinal, confessional, and social spaces.

The origin of magical literature is non-Islamic. It comes from the Copts, the Babylonians, the Chaldeans, and the Indians, and the Muslims Jābir Ibn Ḥayyān and, later, Majrīṭī, recensed these books and epitomized them. Magic is an indubitable fact, and Ibn Khaldūn mentions a good number of magical acts of all sorts that he personally witnessed, or that he had heard of from first-hand reports about happenings in India, black

Africa, and among the Turkic peoples. Even at the most popular of levels, magic seems to have been well organized, and Ibn Khaldūn provides invaluable information on specific types of magicians in the Maghrib of his time who had their own esoteric treatises. Regardless of the variety of magical specialties, they are reducible to three, and in this Ibn Khaldūn follows the typology of the philosophers. The typology is derived from the nature of the science of magic: it is knowledge of the potential that some souls have to effect the world of the elements, i.e., the corporeal world. This potential can be activated independently, and this is sorcery which has the same psychic properties as soothsaying: contact with the beyond, a contact that is parallel to that of prophets and saints, only a contact with the wrong side of the beyond, that of satanic forces. The potential could also, in some, be activated, but only with the help of an agency such as the stars, the tempers of the elements, or the properties of numbers, all of which have sympathies in the corporeal world, and this is talismanic magic. The third type, prestidigitation (*sha'wadha, sha'badha*), is not really magic but the effect of legerdemain and optical illusions.[96] In distinction from philosophy, Islamic scholarship does not distinguish sorcery from talismanic magic, but considers them as one impermissible category of acts. Jurisprudence, therefore, decrees the execution of the sorcerer, while he who lays the evil eye is left unscathed because the effect he has it not intentional (Q, 3: 124 ff.).

The difference between the soul of a sorcerer and that of a saint is parallel to that between a prophet and a soothsayer: the soul of a sorcerer can only attain its gnosis–and action–by way of training. This training, moreover, is effected by the performance of devotions to the astral spheres and to the devils, and sorcery is *ipso facto* heretical. Not so, of course, the effect of saintly miracles, for they are effects of divine and prophetic guidance. Mystical training leading to direct apprehension of the beyond itself makes possible the science of Letters. Ibn Khaldūn nowhere says that this is reprehensible, and indeed differentiates it from talismanic magic by likening it to the effect of a miracle in substance, although he does not explicitly make such a comparison, and although he had expressed his disapproval of the mystical procedures (see above, 95-96.) involved in gaining the knowledge upon which the secrets of Letters are based (Q, 3: 134-5, 137-8, 141).

Be that as it may, the science of Letters is made possible by divine emanation and the sympathetic relation that this establishes between all the rungs of the chain of being, from divinity through the astral spheres down to the sublunar world with its words, letters, and the elements. Letters of the alphabet are considered by some to be classifiable in correspondence to the elements and to heavenly objects: letters can belong to fire, to air, to water, or to earth, and combinations of letters are used to produce specific effects in specific situations. Fiery letters, for instance, strengthen the effect of Mars in a situation of war, or can serve to repel cold diseases. Others see the action of letters as residing elsewhere. They believe that every letter of the alphabet has a numerical magnitude, and that the proportions between these values govern the effects of the letters on things of the world. The precise nature of the effect, and the way in which the effect is realized, is impossible to determine. Mystics who practise and write about this art, such as Ibn 'Arabī and Būnī (d. 622/1225), claim it is spiritual, esoteric and not accessible to logical discourse (Q, 3: 137 ff.). A particularly intricate and developed form of the science of Letters is the famous *zā'irja*, a procedure of deducing auguries in response to questions by means of the numerical magnitudes inherent in the letters composing the question and of the labyrinthine connections between these and the zodiac, the astral spheres, and the elements (Q, 3: 146 ff.).[97] Other methods and procedures of the science of Letters are also sketched, but Ibn Khaldūn does not credit them with the scientificity of those discussed earlier, referring to them as games (Q, 3: 179 ff.).

The third and last of these marginal sciences to be dealt with is alchemy. Like the other marginal sciences, it seeks to intervene in the workings of nature–in this instance, by making possible the transformation into gold and, less frequently, into silver of a mineral substance which, along the chain of being, has the potentiality of being the recipient of the form of gold or silver, i.e., of becoming gold or silver. This metamorphosis is caused by the effect of a substance called the Elixir, and its effect is based upon the humours, tempers, and natures of various substances, and the reduction of these substances by chemical operations like evaporation and condensation to their fundamental natures, then the combination of these natures into those of gold or silver. The fundamental natures of gold and silver are therefore first isolated, then speeded up to their natural consummation as real gold and silver. These are the fundamentals of the craft, perfected by Jābir Ibn Ḥayyān and continued by Majrīṭī, Ṭughrā'ī (d. *c.* 515/1 121), and Ibn Bishrūn, the most prominent student of Majrīṭī, whose treatise is quoted almost in full in Ibn Khaldūn's section on alchemy. But all these authors have couched their alchemical writings in cryptic forms, for alchemy is a species of magic and has nothing to do with nature, and is as such proscribed by the authorities of all religions (Q, 3: 191 ff.).

With the account of the marginal sciences completed, Ibn Khaldūn takes them up again in turn, including philosophy, and subjects them to a very thorough refutation. It must be emphasized at the very outset that this refutation never touches upon the practical results of these sciences (except for philosophy). It is an eradication of their principles as sciences, but not as crafts practiced at all times. The refutations of philosophy, of astrology, of alchemy, and the illumination of the truth about them is essential because they are very common and extremely harmful to religion and to civilization (Q, 3: 209–10). The refutations are all based upon a basic idea, that these crafts run against the natures of things: against the nature of the human intellect, against the nature of properties of matter, and against the truth, and therefore nature, of dogma. All three natures are epistemologically equivalent: a dogmatic nature is no less, nor differently, true than a logical or an elemental nature. Each of these orders of refutation will be discussed as one unit and the following account will not be bound by the division in the *Muqaddima* of the arguments into three sections on philosophy, astrology, and alchemy.

All three orders of refutation had been introduced at earlier stages of the *Muqaddima* and in different contexts. But it is only in the thirtieth, thirty-first, and thirty-second sections of the sixth chapter that they are presented as a unified body of argumentation articulated in three paradigmatic spheres: that of philosophy, that of astrology, and that of alchemy. The argument is particularly useful to the modern scholar in that it identifies those elements which together form the sciences in question into paradigmatic formations, which renders them liable to refutation as sciences rather than as a formless constellation of categories and statements. Modern orientalist studies of the non-positive Arab-Islamic sciences, and especially of philosophy, have generally adopted a spurious and Manichean division between 'reason' and 'belief' in terms of which arguments are woven like yarns, and this has led them to look for the 'infiltration' of 'philosophy' into other sciences (or vice versa) and thus to eclipse the true criteria according to which an idea is philosophical or not. Many are at once philosophical and extra-philosophical, belonging simultaneously to more than one science.[98] The distinguishing element that marks pure philosophy is Neo-Platonism which partly results in the three counts Ibn Ḥazm (d. 456/1036) pronounced as heretical and which Ghazālī canonized as such,[99] and the constant configuration of thematic groups which define it as a paradigm: logic, psychology, natural science, metaphysics, theology, and morality.[100] A philosopher is a scholar who thinks all these topics together as a system, and not anyone who uses concepts from one or more of these topics. Concepts of logic or of metaphysics alone do not qualify as philosophical. Ibn Khaldūn uses much of the conceptual armour used by philosophers, and Ibn Khaldūn is not a philosopher and is paradigmatically alien to philosophy.

Philosophy violates the nature of the mind because it claims to transcend it. It is thus that philosophy is theoretically wanting, for it posits an impossible project–knowledge of the beyond–and seeks to achieve it by impossible means–abstraction and discursive reason. Ibn Khaldūn's adoption of Aristotelian abstractions throughout the *Muqaddima* notwithstanding, his critique of philosophy does utilize this polemical motif which was so comni.onplace in Arab-Islamic culture.[101] In this way, the Khaldunian critique of philosophy, in this specific aspect, is quite deliberately an orthodox one, and there need be no contradiction between the critique of abstraction here and its adoption elsewhere, for the two stances are operative within distinct paradigmatic and polemical contexts. The contradiction is purely formal and irrelevant to either of the two stances.

Be that as it may, an essential fault with philosophy is that its attempts to grasp the whole of existence, both corporeal and incorporeal, and contends that it can be apprehended by the mind as to its essence, to its modes, and to its causes. This epistemology is wedded to a psychology: the philosophers claim that the mind exercises its powers of abstraction to arrive at primary and secondary intelligibles which are combined and ultimately are capable of producing the state of moral perfection: this is the happiness attained by rational intellection. Throughout, the philosophers presuppose a Neo-Platonist ontology in which the whole of being is ultimately deducible from the First Intellect (Q, 3: 210–11, 213). This whole paradigm is knocked by recourse to a severe sensualist nominalism. Ibn Khaldūn postulates a strong doubt about the very possibility of any correspondence between the sensuously perceived empirical manifold as corporeal particularity, and the concepts to which these should correspond if one were to talk meaningfully of a process of knowledge. When correspondence does occur, it does so tautologically, because this correspondence is sensuously perceived, because it is intuited, and not because it is in any way demonstrable.[102] This severe nominalism has important results with respect to the theses of philosophy under attack. The emptiness of genera renders impossible knowledge of incorporeal entities by the mind. Access to such entities is only possible by means of gnostic apprehension, not discursive argumentation, and is as such incommunicably individual to each and every man. Access by the mind to incorporeality is blocked by the 'veil of sense'–whose eradication was a main concern of mysticism–and Ibn Khaldūn supports his argument by recourse to Plato.[103] The impermeability of incorporeal being to discursive reason not only faults the psychology of the philosophers, it also has repercussions on their moral theory. The same impermeability to the incorporeal by the corporeal refutes the philosophical theory that happiness is the result of the demonstrative and discursive knowledge of intelligible essences, for these are not accessible to reason (Q, 3: 214–7).

The two remaining sciences to be refuted do not share with philosophy what Ibn Khaldūn saw as its epistemological and psychological preposterousness. But they do share this with it, that they violate the natural order and thus create implausibilities with regard to themselves as sciences–though not as crafts, whose efficacity, as we have seen, was not scientific, being inspired by forces from the beyond which directly intervene in the world of experience, but the manner of whose intervention is not amenable to reason. Alchemy violates nature in postulating the possibility of aiding the transformation of base materials into the higher nature of gold. Such an artificial intervention is totally non-homeopathetic, for if it were true that the work of nature can be speeded up, nature herself would not have left this direct route to others but would have made it her own and as part of herself. Ibn Khaldūn strengthens this rather sophistical argument by dismissing out of hand as inappropriate the theory of the Elixir as the analogue in alchemical transformations to the action of yeast in the making of bread: yeast transforms dough into material ready for digestion, and thus is an agent of corruption and not of generation, as the Elixir is claimed to be (Q, 3: 238–9).

But there are more serious and more profound ways in which philosophy, alchemy, and astrology do violence to nature, and the seriousness of this violence is reflected in the seriousness of the refutation that Ibn Khaldūn directs at them, in line with a very well-established line of argumentation in Arab–Islamic culture which, however, seems to have been confined to anti-astrological polemic.[104] Astrologers claim that they have knowledge of astral effects and correpondences in the elemental realm from long experience. Likewise, alchemists claim that their art is based upon the full knowledge of the elements, humours, and other aspects of alchemical action. Both base the scientific certainty of their procedures and results upon omnipotent, integral knowledge, which does not obtain in either case–for the factors involved in alchemical operations are countless, and the regularities of astral conjunctions and other heavenly phenomena are so rare as not to lend themselves to knowledge as regularities

(Q, 3: 221–3, 237–8). This is the same type of violence that philosophy does to nature when it confines existence to a ramification of the First Intellect, to the exclusion of all else (Q, 3: 213), and is of the same class of impossible ambition to total knowledge of causes which leads to infinite regress and which marks much of the philosophical project (Q, 3: 27–8).

The thrust of this line of refutation is not epistemological. It must not be thought that Ibn Khaldūn and the many other scholars of his culture who had recourse to this polemical motif were contemplating a Humean problematic on incomplete induction. Hume, for one thing, settled for a conventionalism akin to that of the Ash'arites, albeit without their occasionalist ontology. Ibn Khaldūn or Ibn Ḥazm would not settle for the indeterminacy of truth and causation postulated by conventionalism, and the question of the finitude of instances known as opposed to the infinity of integral knowledge is located not on the terrain of the problematic of empiricist epistemology, but rather in the context of a notion of possibility implicit in the anti-astrological polemic and its expansion into other topical domains by Ibn Khaldūn. What is being denied is not the possibility that the results of astrological predictions or philosophical speculations or alchemical operations might correspond to the aim with which they were made, that is, that they might turn out to be right. They often are. What Ibn Khaldūn is denying is the certainty that they will turn out to be right. Behind this distinction lies a classical idea that goes back to Aristotle: that the possible is not only the opposite of the impossible, but is at the same stroke the opposite of the necessary. The necessity for astral sympathy with the elements may indeed reside somewhere, but it is not accessible to the human mind. By this token alone, the human mind renders it impossible because of its contingency.

The scientificity of the three sciences under consideration is, finally, belied by their contradiction to the prescriptions of religion. We have seen that religious statements and those of science are epistemologically equivalent. They are both true, and therefore cannot contradict one another. In this way, that which contradicts divine statements or prescriptions and statements based upon them cannot be true, and cannot therefore have scientific status. It is thus that the astrological assumption that the heavenly bodies effect worldly events is refuted, for it is contradicted by the theological dogma that God is the only actor and the occasionalism attendant upon this dogma (Q, 3: 224). Of the same class of arguments is the Avicennan refutation of alchemy which Ibn Khaldūn brings to bear in his own polemic: God intended gold and silver to be rare, otherwise they would not perform their functions as repositories of wealth (Q, 3: 238). Alchemists are therefore charlatans who not only rob the faithful of their money, but they also corrupt currency in circulation (Q, 3: 231-2)–a possible reference to contemporary counterfeiting activity.

The next block of sections, the thirty-third through to the forty-fourth, deal with education and science. Ibn Khaldūn commences his sketch with an account of the Aristotelian conception of scholarship which he adopts from obscure sources: scholarship is exegetical, or commentary, or compilatory, or any of the four other types mentioned (Q, 3: 245 ff.).[105] What follows is a discussion of certain educational topics backed by invaluable information concerning conditions prevailing in the Maghrib of Ibn Khaldūn. He starts with a discussion of the harmful educational effect of epitomes and of the profusion of books intended for curricula. The attendant confusions of terminology, of casuistry in matters of detail, and of undue compression are inimical to the learning process (Q, 3: 248 ff.). The best way of achieving a successful education is to follow the natural processes of the mind and of the acquisition of skills: repetition, graduation, and the acquisition of the prerequisites of education as expressed in logic and grammar (Q, 3: 254 ff.). The auxiliary, instrumental sciences of logic, arithmetic, and grammar should not, however, be studies for their own sake nor in very great detail. They merely serve to aid the educational process (Q, 3: 258-9). The confusion of paradigmatic topics in Tunisian education is contrasted to the situation in Morocco (Q, 3: 260 ff.), and then a curriculum suggested by Abū Bakr Ibn al-ʿArabī (d. 543/1148) is favourably quoted with the sad note that it contravenes established habits: it suggests a graduation from Arabic to arithmetic to the Koran, then on to theology, to the principles of jurisprudence, to dialectics, and only finally to tradition and its sciences (Q, 3: 263-4). The discussion of education is rounded off by a criticism of excessive severity on the part of the teachers, with a disquisition on why scholars make inept politicians, on the educational benefits of travel, and a repetition of the discussion on the role of non-Arabs in Islamic scholarship.

Finally, the sixth chapter of the *Muqaddima* takes up language and its sciences. The sciences and realities of Arabic–the language with which Ibn Khaldūn is concerned–follow from a basic definition of language: that it is the method of conveying sense and meaning. Words and languages, in this acceptation, are therefore mediators between individual minds (Q, 3: 274-5). Language is thus a process of translation of sense, and linguistic sciences elucidate the rules of translation. As with other sciences, the general conceptual outline of linguistic sciences is sketched along with the historical debates waged within each of them. Linguistic sciences are the sciences of grammar, which studies the composition of words; lexicography, the science of language, which delves into the realms of sense in a manner that goes far beyond the simple assignation and referentiality of words to wider semantic considerations; what we may today call linguistic rhetoric (*bayān*), which goes beyond lexicography in unveiling the distortions, substitutions, associations, and displacements which can effect words in relation to meanings (Q, 3: 278 ff.). The fourth linguistic science is literature, but it is not strictly a science, for it is not concerned with establishing and consolidating the object of a science and dealing with its essential accidents. The essential thing about literature is performance, and the excellence of performance is directly proportional to the amount of skill in verse and prose composition according to canons of taste established by the Arabs (Q, 3: 294–5). A disquisition on the vast differences between the original Arabic of Mudar and contemporary Arabic is then given, as is one on colloquialisms. This is followed by a discussion of the learning of Arabic, and how non-native speakers never acquire proper taste on the basis of which literary excellence can be judged. And finally, the chapter ends with discussions of poetry, its canon, the acquisition of its skill, and with expositions of contemporary classical and dialect poetry from the Maghrib.

The Analogical Regime

The conclusion of the *Muqaddima* completes the constitution of the new science of civilization. The completion of the sixth chapter of the book is followed by a short concluding announcement: Ibn Khaldūn states that he is the progenitor of the new science, the constitution of which was completed in the first book of the History. As the progenitor of the science, Ibn Khaldūn tells his readers, he was only called upon to provide those elements that, as was sketched in the earlier part of this chapter, constitute its fundamentals: establishing its object and identifying its topics. The detailed elaboration of the topics relevant to the new science of civilization is the task of successors, and the completion and exhaustive elaboration of the science is a gradual process requiring time and the accumulation of individual efforts (Q, 3: 433–4).

The conclusion of the fundamentals of the science of civilization fulfils the main task that this science is called upon to do: the problematization of history. The science of civilization allows the temporary detachment of historical narrative from its status as mere narrative whose truth is occasioned by its transmission. In order to fulfil its true task, the craft of history itself must needs have recourse to a detour through extra-historical territory. It must pass through the science of civilization which, Ibn Khaldūn tells us, is the sole means by which the veracity of historical reports, especially those transmitted over long stretches of time, are weighed. In other words, historical narrative is problematized in extra-historical terms with the aim of valorizing this narrative in conformity with the exigencies of truth required from historical narrative. The extra-historical detour of historical narrative therefore describes an epistemological passage, and this epistemological passage is dictated by two concurrent parameters embodied within the concept of correspondence (*muṭābaqa*): the correspondence of narrative to reality and the correspondence of this reality to the grid of plausibility dictated by the science of civilization. And while the former correspondence obeys rules provided by the psychology of the historian, the latter is thinkable only in terms of the system of deductive ratiocination which goes by the name of analogy (*qiyās*). The former is connected with the relation between chronicler and his events, the latter with that between text and its ostensible referent. The latter corresponds to the relation between book one of the History and books two and three of the same work, between the *mubtada'* and the *khabar*.

Of the multitude of refractions and distortions which an eyewitness can effect on the events he is describing, Ibn Khaldūn and his culture could think only of cupidity, i.e., the displacement of the 'true' account of an event and its replacement by an altogether different narrative. The correspondence of narrative and event is therefore conceived, much as it is in the largely moribund European historiography of the nineteenth century, which still thrives among orientalists, as a full and direct transcription of the event within the narrative. Truth is identical with verisimilitude: that is why untruth is the direct antonym of truth, not one that is shaded by considerations such as equivocation, criteria of relevance, interpretive focus, and so on. Untruth is the replacement of a veridic narrative by another, its replacement either by a complete fabrication, or else by direct and visible modes of distortion such as exaggeration–the last being almost natural, for the soul is fascinated by that which is strange, and the human tongue is easily given to transgressing the truth (Q, 1: 12). That is why Ibn Khaldūn ascribes the naturalness of untruth to historical narrative (*khabar*) to factors in the psychology of the historian, rather than to the historian's discursive practices and relations to the events; he singles out *pris de partie*, sycophancy, and various species of gullibility (Q, 1: 56–7). Even the root cause of all these psychoepistemological adversities, which is oblivion of the natures inherent in civilization, is reduced again to the psychology of the historian, acting as its generic type: this oblivion is not a product of the nature of narrative or of any other factor inherent in writing or the relation of writing to reality, but is the product of sheer ignorance (Q, 1: 57).

Underlying all this is, naturally enough, a nominalism which we have already seen in action in the polemic against philosophy. It is a nominalism which, as we have seen earlier in this chapter, sees an identity between mental and real causality in which the latter is determinant, and which is echoed in Ibn Khaldūn's early epitome on Rāzī's theological treatise when he affirms that existence and the existent are coterminous (L, 25).[106] To such a nominalism, the Aristotelian theory of abstraction, of which Ibn Khaldūn makes a conventional sketch, is convenient but inconsistent (Q, 2: 364 ff, 3: 108–9). Indeed, the nominalism that accompanies the epistemology of historical narrative is totally at variance with the theory of knowledge upon which the foundation of the science of civilization is based: for the postulation of an identity between reason and the facts of sensory perception[107] is totally inconsistent with the identification and elaboration of genus, of cause, of form, of matter, of accident, of definition, of specific difference, and of the other concepts necessary for the foundation of the new science and the identification of its object (Q, 3: 221, 241–2)–concepts which we have encountered earlier on. But this nominalism is necessary because of the paradigmatic space within which the entire question of *khabar* is located and without which no problematization of history can take place. For history is a species of a larger body of sciences whose fundamental object and operational ingredient is narrative.

The transmission of the Koran itself is, in real terms, a *khabar* of the original text–hence the importance of the science of Koranic variants. The Koran and Tradition, as well as consensus, are composed in origin and in effect of performative statements (*inshā'īya*) which are posited by the legislator (Q, 1: 61), be that a text or consensus.[108] History, however, is distinct from this in that it necessarily attaches to events. Its narrative is a factual narrative which carries no compelling necessity:[109] it is thus that there can be no necessity to be attached to the fact that the South is inhabited by the progeny of Ḥām, for instance. For this assertion, though true, is merely a factual narrative and has no connection with a deductive necessity (*ṭard*) as is supposed by the genealogists who claim that all southerners are the descendants of Ḥām because they share certain ethnographic characteristics (Q, 1: 154). Factual narrative cannot be the product of a deduction, as the narrative leading to obligation derivable from sacred and veridic texts can. Factual narrative has no necessity: that is why, for instance, Ibn Khaldūn declares that genealogies are not, and cannot be, liable to *naskh*, which would include a necessary and compelling sense which would focus textual variation, with the result that the only way of ascertaining their veracity is factual investigation (BD, 2: 10)–contrary to the positive sciences which require the correspondence to their prescriptions of the referents of these prescriptions, the rational sciences, of which history is one, require their content to correspond to the outside referent (Q, 3: 268).[110]

The substance of statements whose veracity is inviolable–such as those which occur in the positive sciences–is not in any way liable to alternation or rectification. Their sole guardian is the integrity of their recording and of their transmission. But while the integrity of transmission is equally germane to factual narrative, the substance of its statements is in no way unalterable. Indeed, it can be altered all the way to the ultimate alteration of rejection. The only guardian of the veracity of factual narrative is correspondence to fact (Q, 1: 60-61), and this correspondence is paradigmatically understood with reference to the nominalism that has just been discussed (TK, 1: 918-19). Correspondence is a notion that received its original demarcation and sense in the context of Arab-Islamic linguistic sciences, from whence it was introduced into other sciences of narrative criticism, of which *uṣūl al-fiqh* is a most important one. One juristic theorist defines correspondence as the reference of a word to the entirety of its referent,[111] in much the same way as Ibn Khaldūn, in keeping with the common acceptation of his culture, regarded eloquence as the consummate–that is, complete–correspondence of word and meaning (Q, 3: 291). And this correspondence can only be the result of the correct and full transcription of the event into the narrative that purports to relate it. But there is clearly no way in which verisimilitude can be guaranteed. Indeed, there is no guarantee that an event, in fact, took place and that the eyewitness did not actually invent it. Veracity is therefore only approximative and never compelling except by virtue of its consensual acceptance. Veracity, in other words, is reduced to plausibility. One very perceptive author, long before Ibn Khaldūn, admitted into the province of historical plausibility all that is not impossible, and saw the only sure remedy in the reliability of sources and their proximity to the events they purport to narrate.[112] And the ever illuminating Ibn Ḥazm stated very explicitly the logic behind this argument: that, contrary to many of today s historians who presume they can actually seize reality itself in their writing, a historian admits the veracity of a narrative because of the constancy with which it is reported.[113] This statement recovers- almost the entirety of the semantic field in which the notion of historical narrative, *khabar*, finds its real, paradigmatic determinations: the complex of concepts and procedures for textual criticism of a linguistic, rhetorical, and logical nature which inform the sciences of tradition, of exegesis, of theology, and of jurisprudence, and which intersect with the greatest density in the Principles of Jurisprudence (*uṣūl al-fiqh*). Like the science of tradition, history is a science of transmitted narrative; and such is the similarity between the two that one apologist for history could insist that it was the handmaiden of the science of tradition,[114] reiterating a not uncommon, and therefore convincing, argument. And like all sciences of narrative, its concern is with this narrative, not with the identification of narrative with fact or the elaboration of narrative. What it does is narrate, not investigate, as one of the most 'rationalist' of Arab-Islamic writers put it.[115]

This is why Ibn Khaldūn had to have recourse to the analogical regime on which the positive sciences are based. There was no means at his disposal to valorize his insistence on the necessity of testing narratives by means of correspondence except by recourse to the procedures and concepts of the positive sciences, and that is because, ultimately, historical science shares the main structure of the positive sciences: its being a science of narrative. The only difference is that, unlike the positive sciences, history is at liberty to reject narratives–but this rejection is only made possible by the analogical methods of the positive sciences. The nominalist correspondence required to assure verisimilitude is established by means of the procedures of analogy. The departures from the paradigmatic requirements of the positive sciences–the sciences of *khabar*, of which history is part–are ultimately functions of Ibn Khaldūn's intent which did not have conceptual means of articulation, as will be presently demonstrated.

Ibn Khaldūn's theoretical rejection of the standard historiographic procedure of criticism of authorities is accompanied by a programme for the rectification of historical narratives with regard to the substance of their statements. *Prima facie*, this programme conforms to the schema of 'scientific history', enthusiastically claimed for Ibn Khaldūn by his modern commentators. The task of the science of civilization is to act as a gauge for the veracity of individual historical narratives–the metaphor of 'gauge', borrowed from characterizations of logic contemporary with Ibn

Khaldūn, is probably deliberate (Q, 1: 61-2). The movement between the *Muqaddima* and the rest of the *History*, we are told, is one: between conditions (*asbāb*) in general and the individuality of particular narratives (Q, 1: 7). This is how Ibn Khaldūn strives to establish the relation between history and civilization: history, as we have seen more than once, is 'a narrative of human aggregation' (Q, 1: 53).[116] It is a narrative which carries the memory of events whose context is human aggregation in general, and organized habitation or civilization in particular. Plausibility is therefore ascertainable in terms of this civilization; whatever is implausible in terms of the characteristics of this civilization and goes counter to its nature should, according to Khaldunic criteria, be ejected from historical narrative. Such, for instance, are the reports with which Arabic historical works are replete about the conquest of China by the Ḥimyarites of South Arabia, or the narratives on the numbers involved in Israelite armies which, when examined, would reveal that they would have overflown the territory where they are supposed to have been and fought (Q, 1: 9-16). While there can be little doubt that Ibn Khaldūn did entertain the possibility that his new science would supply its user with indubitable results based upon demonstrative principles (Q, 1: 61), the new science was not applied to facts of sensory perception, but to narrative reports. The relation between what is natural to civilization and historical narrative is derivable from the rules of narrative, although this narrative is ontologically dependent on the nature of civilization. The process by which truthfulness is gauged is, again, analogical. But this is so not only because of the compelling historical and paradigmatic structures of *khabar* that we have encountered, but also for equally compelling reasons of the logical order.

In its most general sense, *khabar* is any statement that is not performative (imperative, interrogative, and others). It is comprised of two terms, the relation between which is external to the statement itself (TK, 1: 410-11). In this sense, it is analoguous to the logical proposition, in that from it follows a positive or negative judgement–in the case of historical narrative, a judgement on its veracity.[117] In short, *khabar* is a statement which bears no necessary relation to its referent, in that a necessary connection between it and its referent is beyond the pale of conceivability. Its veracity is a function of the status that it has on both the ladder of credibility drawn up by exegetes and traditionists–in which case certain species of narrative are just as necessarily credible as the sensibles, as intuitive knowledge, and as that which is widely acknowledged[118]–and the credibility of the individual chain through which a narrative is transmitted in time. Credibility and veracity are an open question, whose determination is a matter for criteria extrinsic to both the individual narrative and that which it narrates. Hence the universal definition of narrative, in all sciences without exception, as that which can be either true or false.[119]

All species of transmitted narrative are considered true either because they are certain, by means of specific and complicated criteria of certainty discussed in the principles of jurisprudence, or because they are considered as true, again due to specific criteria of veracity which are connected with the transmission of the narrative.[120] In both cases, and regardless of the avenue through which veracity is established, the outcome is the same. Indeed, such is the status of transmitted statements in the context of establishing veracity that these considerations are not confined to factual statements: the great Fakhr al-Dīn al-Rāzī, in a refutation of astrology, cites arguments of Avicenna and Fārābī without comment, adding that 'this is what is transmitted', and supplements them with a rational refutation of his own[121]–thus, not having commented upon their refutations, having endowed those refutations with the status of a *textum sanctum* which does not suffer for being such, but is, rather, a proof of relevance of the same epistemological status as his own argument. It is not that the cited arguments of Avicenna or Fārābī have a demonstrable certainty in themselves; whether they do or not is irrelevant. The most relevant feature of these arguments, since they are designated by Rāzī as traditional truths, is their authors. So much is this cast of mind a natural one that Rāzī subscribes to it fully, as we have seen, although, in another context when he was polemicizing against Avicenna, he questioned the formal definition of *khabar* that we have encountered, and considered it undesirably tautological[122]–but that was in a different paradigmatic context, that of logic, and the conceptual requirements of logic are distinct from those of history, just as the requirements of history are distinct from those of, say, grammar.

It is clear from this that historical narrative relates to its 'umrānic *archē* in the same way as an event in the present relates to an eternal statement inscribed in an infallible text, and as a proof relates to its progenitor. The *archē* of history, *'umrān,* constitutes the principles of history, its *aṣl,* in such a way that the science of civilization can be said to have been conceived as the analogue of *uṣūl al-fiqh* and as *uṣūl al-tārīkh.* It consists of that body of statements–regardless of their referent, although it so happens that the referent is factual reality–which act as the normative gauge for other statements. Civilization and its modes and the conditions it engenders, as described in the science of civilization, act as the guarantee of individual narratives. They do not constitute the proof of an individual event–for such is impossible–but rather they act as a normative hermeneutic, just as the principles of jurisprudence is a practical hermeneutic.[123] It is one which, in the absence of any means of definite proof short of unattainable personal witness, provides the means for a hermeneutic of value which establishes the possibility of distinguishing a false statement from a true one. But it is a hermeneutic, not a logic, and therefore, its capacity for establishing such a distinction is not binding or final. It cannot prove truth or falsehood, but only indicate it, as a hermeneutic does. The connections between the historical statement subject to the normative examination and its referent is assured by the exemplary (*'ibra*) which civilization and its conditions are.

The question of *khabar* is thus situated in a semantic context which automatically interpellates its own criteria of veracity, which fall outside the context of the referent to which the particular narrative relates: one author classifies veracious reports as those delivered by prophets, as those about which there is general agreement, and those on which there is agreement in a restricted circle of people;[124] another declares a narrative to be false if it is not the subject of general agreement when it should be, or as that which contradicts what is known by necessity or by indubitable demonstration.[125] This second statement could well imply that reports can be disproved in themselves and without reference to the avenue that normally guarantees their truth or falsehood–a view that comes very close to one component of Ibn Khaldūn's position, that which calls for the rectification of historical narratives by recourse to the generalities of the new science.

It has just been intimated that such a conception has a very well-defined inbuilt limit: it can never be completed. For the demonstrative operation involved, as is that in the positive sciences, and as theorized in the principles of jurisprudence, is one of analogy–and this does not, to Ibn Khaldūn or his culture, render it any less attractive or less compelling than the Aristotelian syllogism. The analogical procedure is one for the falsification of narratives, and Ibn Khaldūn stated this explicitly.[126] Proof is out of the question, for proof requires actual witness which is not forthcoming in historical narrative. The hermeneutic is a hermeneutic of exclusion and can never be one for inclusion. It is the comparison of a particular with another particular, one of the two having been declared to have the force of truth. The generality is only present in the *aṣl* and none of the particularities related to this *archē* has any compelling force of its own.

This is amply demonstrated by Ibn Khaldūn's theory and practice of historiography. The *Muqaddima*, he says, will act for his age as the geographical and ethnographic descriptions of Mas'ūdī and Bakrī acted during their own times (Q, 1: 51): the fundamental wherewithal of the historian. Nowhere does Ibn Khaldūn call the materials provided by Mas'ūdī a theory, although it is obvious that he thought it could be theoretically ordered, as his was in the *Muqaddima*. He is quite deliberately aware that the material is a collection–ordered or not–of states of affairs. And it is against these states of affairs that narrative should be weighed to see if they should be beyond the pale of plausibility. The analogy that he draws between himself and Mas'ūdī is telling and significant. His own science is equally conceived as a collection of states of affairs–scientifically and theoretically ordered–against which contemporary and more timeless affairs should be weighed.

In practical terms, Ibn Khaldūn's historical criticism takes the conventional form of valorizing authorities in addition to the rather naïve rationalism which, ultimately, results in the more apparently rigorous application of the rules of the world as transcribed in the *Muqaddima*. When it comes to matters that do not bear comparison with anterior principles, such as rational possibility of plausibility according to the description of general conditions as performed in the *Muqaddima*, and when the task is the choice between two or more versions of an event, all of which are, in themselves, equally plausible, then the only means to which Ibn Khaldūn could have recourse are implicitly and explicitly consonant with the properties of *khabar*. He has recourse to the valorization of hierarchies of authority and refastens the circle outwardly breached by the extension of historical narrative, in the guise of civilization, to territories untrodden by the paradigmatic understanding of history. At one point in the discussion of Berber genealogy, he accepts Ibn Ḥazm's view that Burnus and Mādghīs, the fathers of the Berbers, are of a common origin, over the view of Berber genealogists, with the remark that 'Ibn Ḥazm is more correct because he is more reliable' (BD, 6: 176–7). He valorizes fully the hierarchy of authorities in the determination of truth throughout the History: he prefers a biblical version of an event to that of Orosius because it is biblical (BD, 2: 79 and *passim*), and prefers a datation given by Orosius to that provided by Ben Gorion because, he claimed, the source from which the former culled his information was Islamic (BD, 2: 401–2). Narratives on the beginning and the end of the world to be found in Wahb Ibn Munabbih (d. 110 or 114/728–9 or 732–3), Ṭabari, and Al-Kisā'ī (d. 189/805), and others are rejected because their sources were unreliable (BD, 2: 33; Q, 2: 293).[127] The most spectacular display of this genre is provided, of course, by the lengthy criticism of traditions concerning the advent of the Messiah (Q, 2: 142 ff.), and the demonskation of the 'Alid genealogy of the Fatimids (BD, 3: 757 ff.).

There is, though, another species of historiographic practice in Ibn Khaldūn, and it is this that has attracted the attention of most interpreters, who are usually bent on demonstrating the supposedly anomalous position he occupies in his culture. He criticizes and rejects, on the basis of simple common sense, the reports in Mas'ūdī and others on the fabulous City of Brass (Q, 1: 58 ff.). He rejects the established genealogical connection between Goliath and Qais b. 'Ilān because it goes counter to simple arithmetic: it is impossible to claim correctly that Qais is a grandfather of Goliath when he in fact lived after him (BD, 7: 6). Narratives can occupy a grey area where they might be unuue, but not implausible: the contention that Noah was the first carpenter fits very neatly in this category (Q, 2: 326). Moreover, there are narratives and beliefs that are erroneous because they are implausible: invoking koranic proscription, Ibn Khaldūn explains the Christian belief in the Trinity as due to a superficial reading of the New Testament (BD, 2: 299). Much of what is mistaken in genealogies, moreover, is due to faulty transcription (BD, 5: 798, 6: 309, and *passim*). That is why our author saw fit to include a small section on the transliteration of Berber names and terms at the beginning of the History (Q, I: 53 ff.). Berber genealogists who ascribe Arab descent to the Zayyānids, for instance, are faulted because their contention contradicts an exigency required by the science of civilization: that a lineage can only rule over proximate lineages if these other lineages were its kin from which it forms a grand *'aṣabīya.* Conversely, that which is indubitably accepted but which does not tally with the prescriptions of civilization is relegated to the realm of the miraculous: such is the case with the pre-Umayyad Arab conquests, which violate the statement that a great state, like the Persian, is not taken by storm (Q, 2: 122–4).

The examples cited are instances of the application of the only procedure possible in any science of transmitted narrative or, indeed, any science whose task is to test particularities without elevating them to a higher generic generality, whether this generality is derived from common sense, or the rules enunciated in the *Muqaddima.* This procedure is the establishment of an analogy, and it consists of reducing the particular in question to a principle, *aṣl,* of which it figures as an instance. The connection between the particular and its principle can only be one of acquisition of the former by the latter, adding to its patrimony of instances whose very normative legitimacy (truth, in this case) is entirely dependent upon this act of cooptation. And this cooptation is only possible by extending the legitimacy of the principle to the particular, an extension effected by means analogy, *qiyās* (Q, 2: 385). The analogy itself is established by finding a connective held in between the principle and the particular, a connective which has been aptly termed an 'indicative sign',[128] which provides a criterion of communality between the two. It is a binomial logic that connects the principle and the particular, a logic that connects two terms,[129] two statements, which in fact are particularities, and one of which has the normative status of validity and legitimacy due to criteria extrinsic to its relation to what is taken as the particularity in search of validation. Indeed, one scholar has very convincingly demonstrated how Islamic jurisprudential procedures–and jurisprudence is the paradigmatic locale for the concept of principle *aṣl, archē*, par excellence–constantly displace the centre of gravity of the procedure of legal deduction from the rule to the particularity, to the application of the rule,[130] as is, indeed, required by the logical contingency that necessarily attaches to establishing deductive appurtenance without utilizing the classical Aristotelian concepts of genus and specific difference.[131]

The vocabulary of Ibn Khaldūn's strictures against the historiographic practice common during his time are geared towards these very procedures, with the science of civilization and common sense providing the *aṣl* against which particularities are weighed. This vocabulary is rather eclectic in its outward appearance, deriving from the idioms of metaphysics, of logic, as well as of the analogical procedures of textual criticism and those of argumentation whose scientific terrains are, respectively, the principles of jurisprudence and theology (the principles of religion–*uṣūl al-dīn*, dogmatics). The slavish adherence to received narratives displayed by historians is due to ignorance: historians accept implausible narratives as true because they are ignorant of 'the natures of things that obtain in civilization (Q, 1: 57)[132] Historians treat events without regard to their significance or to the causes of their prominence (Q, 1: 5), and these events remain mere events without reason or cause (*uṣūl*), and are really species devoid of a genus or of a difference (Q, 1: 4). For history is, in fact, knowledge of the conditions that bring about the events, and of their principles and constituents (Q, 1: 2), and the sure method of distinguishing that which is plausible from that which is implausible is to look into a number of things that characterize events and see how credible they are: the historian should look into the materiality of the event, into its causes, conditions, genus, difference, and extent, and measure these according to the prescriptions of reality as presented in science of reality, the science of civilization (Q, 1: 329).

But this metaphysical and logical idiom of matter, genus, constitution, and the like, is a mere adjunct to the eminently non-Peripatetic procedures of analogy. The determination of the logical and metaphysical attributes of an event are a prelude to an analogical operation. The *Muqaddima* and the rest of the *History*, Ibn Khaldūn informs us, are related as a generality to a particularity, moving from conditions that form the context for the unfolding of historical events to the events themselves (Q, 1: 7). That is how, like Mas'ūdī, Ibn Khaldūn sought his *Muqaddima* to be an *aṣl* for the history of his age (Q, 1: 52). The metaphysical attributes of historical events, which form the substance of the science of civilization, and hence the substance of events narrated in history, form the *aṣl* of historiographic credibility, constituting the hinge in the process of verification and the verity to which the particular narrative of an event should be related. The event is reduced to the generality that constitutes its *aṣl*, and if an indicative sign establishing the legitimacy of the particular by linking it to the general is lacking, the narrative is deemed false.

It is this analogical reduction that Ibn Khaldūn prescribes as the manner of relating historical narrative to the verities provided by the science of civilization. And here the idiom of analogical procedure take full sway. The issue is one of soliciting the judgement of 'the constituent principles of what is habitual', of 'reduction to principles' (Q, 1: 9).[133] The event related in the narrative and the principle of its plausibility are like a presence and an absence, like a palpable and proximate entity and one which is invisible, distant and which exists only in the mind: the analogy (*qiyās*) between two particulars which is sometimes called *tamthīl*[134] is adopted by Ibn Khaldūn in one of its procedures, that of the analogy between the palpable and the distant and its obverse, that between the distant and the palpable (Q, 1: 8–9) which was of very wide use in the principles of jurisprudence and in dogmatics.[135] And while Ibn Khaldūn mentions the metaphysical attributes of the natures of civilization in the same breath as he elicits 'principles' and cognate concepts, the conceptual configuration within which the discussion is contextualized is that of analogy in which 'natures' and their metaphysical cognates figure as components of the palpable (as the science of civilization against which the narrative of distant events are weighed) and the distant (as the principle against which the significance of events is gauged–what Ibn Khaldūn termed as the genus, extent, and similar aspects of events). The science of civilization, through the process of analogy, thus verifies its narrative material and orders it in a manner which we have encountered in the first chapter of this book. In both cases, the principles which are the substance of the science of civilization are considered as statements about a subject-matter which is the same as that of history, and which, as statements about that subject-matter, take on the guise of models to which historical narrative is to conform if it is to fulfil the conditions of veracity which vouch for its legitimacy as historical narrative.

Such is the means for the problematization of history, and such are the limits of the operation. Analogy in its various forms is an indicator of a judgement and not the proof of a judgement[136]–for it is not predicative–and is particularly apposite for material such as that treated in the sciences of *khabar* where the matter devolves not upon absolute certainty, but upon the reasoned belief in a narrative.[137] We have already seen that there is no question ever of absolute proof in the context of the science of history, where truth is equated with verisimilitude and this is only assured by reliability. Not even jurisprudence achieves certainty–only definitive belief.[138] Ibn Khaldūn transferred this reliability from reliability of transmission–which required the procedures of the science of tradition–to reliability in terms of an underlying principle, an *aṣl*–and this required the utilization of the procedures whose scientific sanction lay in the analogical regime that reigned in the principles of jurisprudence and, in a form adulterated with Peripateticism, in dogmatics. The science of civilization, as an almost graphic collection of statements about those territories of reality which form the substance of historical narrative, acts as the substitute for the eye of the historian in assuring the possibility of verisimilitude and excluding the admissibility of anything that might contradict the requirement of verisimilitude. The *Muqaddima*, its subject-matter dictated by history, in turn is the principle and custodian of historical truth, ever watchful in its analogical regard over narratives of the past.

NOTES

1 The rendition of *'umrān* here by the problematical word 'civilization' (on which see E. Benveniste, 'Civilization: Contribution à l'histoire du mot', in *Eventail de l'histoire vivante: Hommage à Lucien Febvre* (Paris, 1953), vol. I, pp. 47 ff.) is intended to recover one meaning that 'civilization' has: as the totality of manifestations attendant upon a system of organized habitation. The Arabic word has a rich etymology and rich associations in lexicography as well as in geography, all of which can be reducible to the generality of the opposition between emptiness and its antonym, *'umrān:* see Jābirī, *'Aṣābīya*, p. 460, and M. Mahdi, *Ibn Khaldūn's Philosophy of History* (London, 1958), pp. 184–6. The usual rendition of *'umrān* as 'culture' can only be acceptable, on the basis of etymology and semantics, if one considered culture in the bacteriological sense of abstract, self-nurturing habitation.

2 See the discussions in Qannūjī, *Abjad al-'ulūm*, ed. 'A. Zakkār (Damascus, 1978), pp. 196 ff and TK, 2: 1215 ff.

3 'Mā yatawaqqaf 'alaih al-shay', sawā'a kāna al-tawaqquf 'aqlīyan au 'ādīyan au ja'līyan'.

4 Ibn Sīnā, *Al-Najāt*, ed. M. Makkāwī and M. Kurdī (Cairo, A.H. 1331), p. 33.

5 'Dākhilan min bāb al-asbāb 'alā al-'umūm ilā al-akhbar 'ala al-khuṣūṣ'.

6 See JL, s.v.

7 The *Fourfold Root of the Principle of Sufficient Reason*, tr. E. Payne (La Salle, Illinois, 1974), pp. 9-13.

8 Ibn Sīnā, *Najāt*, p. 158.

9 See TK, 1: 688; JT, 256; GL, 780.2.

10 See the multiplicity of senses isolated by A. O. Lovejoy and G. Boas, 'Some Meanings of "Nature" ', in *idem.* (eds), *Primitivism and Related Ideas in Antiquity* (Baltimore, 1935), pp. 447 ff., and the discussion on the confusions attendant on the notion of nature in A. O. Lovejoy, *Essays in The History of Ideas* (Baltimore, 1948), pp. 69 ff.

11 See the statement of A. Lalande, *Vocabulaire technique et critique de la philosophie* (8th. ed., Paris, 1960), p. 671: 'Il n'est pas possible de ranger les sens du mot *nature*, au point de vue sémantique, en une série linéaire. Ils paraîssent s'être formés par rayonnement en plusieurs directions autour d'une idée primitive, qui serait sans doute celle du développement spontané des êtres vivants suivant un type déterminé'.

12 See the definitions in TK, 1: 908 ff; JL, s.v.; GL, 394; and compare these technical definitions with the fairly similar lexical senses recensed in LA, q.v. 'ṭ-b-''. See the discussions of Ibn Khaldūn's conception of nature in Jabirī, *'Aṣabīya*, pp. 157 ff., and in J. Berque, *Maghreb: Histoire et sociétés* (Algiers and Gembloux, 1974), p. 57, and cf. the more general discussion in P. Kraus, *Jābir Ibn Ḥayyān* (Cairo, 1942-3), vol. 2 p. 165 n. 7. Kraus states that this notion occurs in the works of Majrīṭi–it may not be totally fortuitous to note that an ancestor of Ibn Khaldūn's, Abū Muslim (d. 449/1057-8) was a disciple of Majrīṭī (Qifṭī, *Tārīkh al-ḥukamā*, ed. J. Lippert, Leipzig, 1903, p. 243, & Q, 3: 99; T, 3). The most serious counter-argument to this view of the Khaldunian nature is presented by M. A. Al-'Ālim ('*Muqaddimat* Ibn Khaldūn–madkhal ibistimūlūjī', in *Al-Fikr al-'Arabī*, 1/6(1978), pp. 36-40), where the author reiterates the common identification in Khalduniana of necessity and the modern conception of nature as relational regularity and expressing it in a language less foreign to the Khaldunian language than is usually the case.

13 See Kraus, *Jābir*, vol. 2, pp. 168 ff, and S. Sambursky, *Physics of the Stoics* (London, 1971), pp. 2, 17, 22 ff. Like all educated (and not so educated) men of his time, Ibn Khaldūn had a good knowledge of medical theory, and he quotes Avicenna's didactic summary of his treatise (Q, 1: 152-3). The only study of Stoic presence in Arab-Islamic physics is in F. Jadaane, *L'lnfluence du stoicisme sur la pensée musulmane* (Beirut, 1968), ch. 2. The author, unfortunately, adopts too restrictive and classical a view of philosophy generally and of physics particularly, and does not bring out the medical and alchemical connection and connotation which is all important, and he limits himself, consciously (p. 137), to problems as defined and addressed by theologians.

14 Avicenna emphasizes the essentiality of these essential accidents rather than their accidental quality (GL, 422.2).

15 For the terms used here to denote priority (*qidam, sabaq*), see JT, 179-80; GL, 572; LA, s.v.

16 Cf. Jābirī, *'Aṣabīya,* p. 170.

17 M. Talbi in EI^2, 3: 829.

18 Ibn al-Khaṭīb, 'Mufakharāt Māliqa wa Salā' in *Mushāhadāt Lisān ad-Dīn Ibn al-Khaṭīb fī bilād al-Maghrib wal-Andalus,* ed. A. M. 'Ibādī (Alexandria, 1958), pp. 61-2.

19 One author has remarked that 'logic is the science of pure time, just as geometry is the science of pure space ... a form of thought is always condensed time' (C. Noica, 'The Time of Reality and the Time of the Logos', in *Diogenes,* 74(1971), p. 31).

20 The significance of this aspect of the organization of the *Muqaddima* has been noted by Mahdi, *Ibn Khaldūn's Philosophy,* p. 172n.

21 The terms are, in order of chapters, as follows: 1) *muqaddimāt,* 2) *uṣūl* and *tamhīdāt,* 3) *qawāi'id,* 4) *sawābiq,* 5) none, 6) *muqaddima.* Some chapters have a complement to this beginning: ch. 3 has *mutammimāt,* ch. 4 has *lawāḥiq,* as does ch. 6.

22 See the stimulating remarks of Al-'Ālim, 'Muqaddimat Ibn Khaldūn', p. 45.

23 See the count in M. Shatzmiller, *Les historiographes merinides du XIVe siècle et Ibn Khaldūn,* unpub. doctoral thesis, Aix-en-Provence, 1974, p. 160. Of these examples, 177 were extracted from the Maghrib, while 288 were of Mashriqī provenance.

24 The 'seventh', whose intended position is not clear, does not appear in any of the printed editions of the *Muqaddima.* It was first published and translated into French in Redjala, 'Un texte inédit', a reading and translation that was challenged on some points by A. Guellouz, 'À propos d'un texte inédit de la *Muqaddima*', in *Arabica,* 23(1976), pp. 308 f.

25 The technical Arabic term for this type of apodicticity is *sharṭ.* On this concept, and on analogies between it and notions of causality (*'illa* and *sabab*), see TK, 1: 106 and cf JL, s.v.

26 On first principles in the construction of a science, see Ibn Sīnā, *Najāt,* p. 158 and Ghazālī, *Maqāṣid al-falāsifa,* ed. S. Dunyā (Cairo, 1961), p. 125.

27 On this concept in Ibn Khaldūn and in Koranic exegesis, see the perfunctory account of A. Oumlil, *L'Histoire et son discours* (Rabat, 1979), pp. 196 ff.

28 See n. 22 above.

29 This is by virtue of the Avicennan conception of the soul. See S, 6-7.

30 'al-ghalaba wal-sulṭān wal-yadd al-qāhira'. On the animal soul, see Ibn Sīnā, *De Anima,* ed. F. Raamān (London, 1959), p. 41.

31 See LA, s.v. 'w-z-''; Ghazālī, *Mīzān al-'amal,* ed. S. Dunyā (Cairo, 1964), pp. 234-7; Ṭurṭūshī, *Sirāj,* pp. 41-42. See the comments of 'A. Zai'ūr, 'Madkhal ilā dirāsat al-fikr al-siyāsī li Ibn Sīnā', in *Al-Bāḥith,* I /2 (1978), pp. 50 ff.

32 This Ptolemaic geography existed alongside one in which the seven zones were represented as concentric circles, and Mas'ūdī subscribed to this school (*Tanbīh,* pp. 51-2). See the discussion and maps in Miquel, *Géographie*, vol. 2, pp. 56-60.

33 It is possible to conceive of the 'seventh' prolegomenon as an ancillary to this one.

34 See, for instance, Maqdisī, *Kitāb al-Bad' wat-tārīkh,* ed. by C. Huart and attributed to Al-Balkhī (Paris, 1899 ff.), vol. 4, p. 53.

35 Hegel, in line with a long geographical tradition, believed that nature excluded the frigid and torrid zones from history because they are incapable of producing world-historical peoples. See his *Philosophy of History,* tr. J. Sibree, (New York, 1956), pp. 80-81.

36 This was a common idea and had its place in medical compendia. See Ibn Sīnā, *Al-Urjūza fī al-ṭibb*, ed. H. Jahiers and A. Noureddine (Paris, 1956), 11. 66-7, 69. Ibn Khaldūn cites the *Urjūza* in this very context.

37 On these medical notions, See Ibn Sīnā, *Urjūza*, 11. 107 ff.

38 Mas'ūdi, *Murūj al-dhahab*, ed. C. Barbier de Meynard and Pavet de Courteille (Paris, 1861 ff.), vol. I. pp. 163-5.

39 See GL, 610.23 and Shahrastānī, *Al-Milal wal-niḥal*, ed. W. Cureton (London, 1846), pp. 252-3.

40 Cf the comments of F. Rahman, *Prophecy in Islam* (London, 1958), p. 107.

41 A. Lovejoy, *The Great Chain of Being*, Cambridge, Mass., 1956.

42 The fullest statement of this in Arab-Islamic culture is in Qazwīnī, *'Ajā'ib al-makhlūqāt was gharā'ib al-maujūdāt*, ed. F. Sa'd on the basis of the Wüstenfeld edition (Beirut, 1977).

43 Commentators have almost invariably mistaken this for a statement of Darwinist import, or at least resonance. The structure put forward by Ibn Khaldūn belies this perspective. He presents us with a cosmography of graduated being *in statu quo* where transition is a continuous possibility but never an actuality. On some aspects of Arab-Islamic cosmography, see S. H. Nasr, *Science and Civilization in Islam*, New York, 1968.

44 The only author to address this question is A. Lakhsassi, 'Ibn Khaldūn and the Classification of Science', in *The Maghreb Review*, 4/1 (1979), pp. 21 ff. The thrust of this interesting article is, unfortunately, narrowly confined to epistemology.

45 The literature on this matter is vast, and a convenient presentation is given by L. Gardet, 'Kalb', in EI1^2, 4: 486-8.

46 See above, ch. 1, p. 24 and n. 27-30.

47 This work was not, strictly speaking, written in response to this question, but to a related controversy. See Ṭanjī's preface to S, p. 'ṣ.ṭ'; M. Mahdi, 'The Book and the Master as Poles of Cultural Change in Islam', in S. Vryonis, *Islam and Cultural Change in the Middle Ages* (Wiesbaden, 1975), pp. 3 ff.

48 'fī anna suknā al-badū lā yakūn illā lil-qabā'il ahl al-'aṣabīya'.

49 This point has been noted by 'A. Ḥilū, *Ibn Khaldūn* (Beirut, 1969), p. 101.

50 Redistribution as term and concept characterizing a class of economic regimes was introduced by Polanyi and his associates in *Trade and Market in the Early Empires*, Chicago, 1971.

51 See the remarks of J. Caro Baroja, 'The City and the Country: Reflexions on some Ancient Commonplaces', in J. Pitt-Rivers (ed.), *Mediterranean Countrymen* (Paris-The Hague, 1963), pp. 27 ff

52 See, for instance, Ibn al-Muqaffa', *Al-Adab al-kabīr*, (Beirut n.d.), para. 11 and, in Ibn Khaldūn's time, Abū Ḥammū, *Wasīṭa*, pp. 23 ff.

53 See my Ibn Khaldūn in *Modern Scholarship*, pp. 76 ff.

54 Ghazālī, *Al-Iqtiṣād fil-i'tiqād*, ed. I. A. Çubuçku and H. Atay, (Ankara, 1962), pp. 234 ff. Ghazālī does, however, provide a rational demonstration.

55 A generation after Ibn Khaldūn, Qalqashandi produced the most comprehensive–and vastly underused–statement of the standard position (*Khilāfa, op. cit.*).

56 Ghazālī had canonically proscribed hostile reference to the Umayyads and other contemporaries of the Prophet and branded Traditions purponing to damn them as fabrications (*Iqtiṣād*, pp. 242-4). Most scholars, however, persisted in this hostile attitude, as

did Ibn Khaldūn's pupil Maqrīzī (*Nizā'*, pp. 28-9), although he adopts a realistic view of the matter. He says that the basis for Umayyad power was indeed laid by the Prophet himself who appointed Umayyads as governors to Najrān, Yemen, Bahrain, and elsewhere, and explicitly denies that the caliphate was the prerogative of the Hāshimites (*ibid.*, pp. 29-30, 43).

57 The Medinese regime was often regarded as miraculous. See, for instance, Ibn Ṭabāṭabā, *Fakhrī*, p. 60.

58 This seems to have been general knowledge. See Abū Ḥammū, *Wasīṭa*, p. 38.

59 'insiḥāb ḥukm al-khilāfa al-shar'īya fi al-milla al-islāmīya 'alā rutbat al-mulk wal-sulṭān'.

60 On the miasmic theory in Arab-Islamic medicine, see Ibn Sīnā, *Al-Qānūn fiṭ-ṭibb* (Būlāq, A. H. 1294), vol. I, pp. 91-3, and Dols, *The Black Death in the Middle East*, (Princeton, 1977), pp. 85 ff.

61 See G. Richter, *Zur Geschichte der älteren arabischen Fürstenspiegel* (Leipzig, 1932), pp. 80 ff.

62 Arabic literature on these subjects is vast, and a most convenient collection is in Ibn Kathīr, *Nihāyat al-bidāya wan-nihāya*, ed. M. F. Abū 'Ubayya, 2 vols., Riyadh, 1968. Sha'rānī's *Mukhtaṣar al-tadhkira al-Qurṭubīya* (Cairo, A. H. 1302) provides a summary of the mystical statement. I have taken up these matters in *Ibn Khaldūn*, ch. 4 and in 'Annalistics'.

63 By a certain Aḥmad Ibn al-Ṣiddīq, of whose identity nothing further is known, though stylistic elements in his criticism could date him in the nineteenth century. In *Ibrāz al-wahm al-maknūn min kalām Ibn Khaldūn* (Damascus, A. H. 1347), he dismisses Ibn Khaldūn as not being a Tradition scholar as such, chides him for attacking authorities such as Tirmidhī and Ibn Māja, and rejects the rigour with which Ibn Khaldūn dismisses all Traditions passed by traditionists he accuses of partisanship.

64 See the comments of Subkī, *Ṭabaqāt*, vol. 2, p. 9.

65 On the cyclic conception of sacred history, see my 'Annalistics'.

66 There are indications that at least some public works under the Zayyānids were undertaken by *'abīd al-makhzan*, the royal slaves: Dufourcq, *Espagne Catalane*, pp. 71 ff.

67 'tafāḍul ... fil-qilla wal-kathra'.

68 This can clearly be seen from a fairly early commercial primer, *Al-Ishāra ilā maḥāsin al-tijāra* by Dimashqī (Cairo, A. H. 1318), p. 4 (of which a German translation was published by H. Ritter in *Der Islam*, 1(1917)). It must be stressed in the face of common misinterpretation that there is no question here of a theory of scarcity: people share the common provisions of the world not because they are scarce and thus have to be divided, but because these cannot be properly valorized except collectively in accordance with the first chapter of the *Muqaddima*.

69 The conception of need (*ḥāja*), again like that of exchange, has nothing to do with modern economic theory but is really akin to the conception of 'rations' as the discrete items necessary to sustain the consumption of an individual. See my *Ibn Khaldūn*, pp. 167 f.

70 There was no uniform mode (or means) of expressing wealth in Ibn Khaldūn's time. It was dissolved into its visible components. Wealth is 'the name given to the plenty or mediocrity of belongings' and is of two kinds: the silent (*al-ṣāmit*–a category which Ibn Khaldūn himself utilizes in Q, 2: 91) and the vocal (*nāṭiq*). The former

comprises landed property, currency, jewels and other properties, and the latter comprises slaves, cattle, and other animals (Dimashqī, *Tijāra*, pp. 2–3).

71 A slight terminological uncertainty is presented by the text of Ibn Khaldūn, as the term *kasb* is also used to denote gainful activity as such with no regard to the theological connotations of the term.

72 Just as there was no conceptual medium through which wealth could be theoretically expressed in the time of Ibn Khaldūn, there was also no theoretical aniculation of currency. It is defined in terms of the intrinsic worth of individual items as 'the price of all things' (Dimashqī, *Tijāra*, pp. 4–5).

73 A report by a writer posterior to Ibn Khaldūn claims that treasure hunters in Fez possessed treabses on their an and suggests that they were organized in a corporation: Leo Africanus, *Description de l'Afrique*, tr. A. Epaulard (Paris, 1956), vol. 1, p. 226.

74 This seems a rather unrealistic picture. Ibn Khaldūn himself (Q, 2: 300) mentions a qāḍi of Fez who was asked by the Sultan Abū Sa'īd to choose a tax farm for his income and chose to farm the taxes on alcoholic beverages. But on the whole, Maghribi scholars seem to have generally been of modest circumstances. For Tunis, see Brunschvig, *La Berbérie orientale*, vol. 2, pp. 131–2, and for Fez, see Leo Africanus, *Description de l'Afrique*, vol. 1, p. 206.

75 See F. Rosenthal, *Ibn Khaldūn, the Muqaddimah* (Princeton, 1958), vol. 2, p. 411 n.

76 Cf. Ibn Sīnā, *De Anima*, pp. 207–8.

77 It is noteworthy in this connection that in his inaugural lecture as professor of Mālikī law at the Ṣarghatmushiyya College in Cairo, Ibn Khaldūn presented his hearers with his credentials in the form of the oral and written tradition through which he learnt the *Muwaṭṭa'* of Mālik, and which goes back to Mālik's Andalusian pupil Yaḥyā b. Yaḥyā al-Laithī, who died in 234/848 or 236/851. The text is in T, 305–10.

78 See Ch. Pellat, 'Fahrasa' in EI^2, 2: 743–4 and G. Vajda, 'Idjāza' in EI^2, 3: 1020–1.

79 The sciences of *ḥikma* are constantly identified exclusively with philosophy. They generically denote, however, all non-positive sciences, as Ibn Khaldūn makes clear. See A.-M. Goichon, 'Ḥikma' in EI^2, 3: 377–8 and JT, 96.

80 Even the most cursory glance at statements by scholars in one discipline towards other disciplines is testimony of the very clear and sharp demarcation of paradigms. Instances are too numerous to quote, and it will suffice here to cite the discussion of this matter by Subkī in *Mu'īd al-ni'am wa mubīd al-niqam*, ed. D. W. Myhrman (London, 1908), pp. 94, 115–7.

81 See Y. Eche, *Les bibliothèques arabes* (Damascus, 1967), p. 329.

82 For the context of this matter, see my *Ibn Khaldūn*, pp. 102 ff.

83 As, for instance, in Fārābī, *Iḥṣā' al-'ulūm*, ed. A. Gonzales Palencia (Madrid, 1932), pp. 7 and *passim*, where theology and jurisprudence are grouped together with morality and politics.

84 See JL, q.v. "ilm'.

85 On the Ash'arism of Mālikī scholars, see, for instance, Subki, *Ṭabaqāt*, vol. 3, pp. 352, 366–67, vol. 5, pp. 192–93, and L. Gardet, 'Quelques réflexions sur la place du *'Ilm al-kalām* dans les "sciences religieuses" musulmanes', in G. Makdidi (ed.), *Arabic and Islamic Studies in Honor of H. A. R. Gibb* (Leiden, 1965), pp. 266–67. There is considerable disagreement among scholars on the position of Ash'arism in Arab-Islamic culture: G. Makdisi ('Ash'ari and Ash'arites in Islamic Religious His-

tory' in *Studia Islamica*, 17 (1962), and 18 (1963) holds that its effect was negligible and was not a cultural force as such, while A. S. Nashshar (*Manāhij al-baḥth 'inda mufakkirī al-Islām*, Cairo, 1965) represents the opposite view. Makdisi's conception of Ash'arism is too restrictive and limited to the explicit evocation of Ash'ari (d. 324/935-6), as in Ibn Asākir (d. 571/1176) and Subkī (d. 771/1370), to have much force. Ghazālian Ash'arism seems to have been imported into the Maghrib by Ibn Tūmart (d. 523/1128) and the Almohad cultural hierarchy.

86 A formulation identical to Ibn Khaldūn's occurs in Ghazālī, *Iqtiṣād*, p. 4. Ibn Khaldūn's eastern contemporary Taftāzāni (d. 792/1390) detected the same trend in his *Sharḥ al-'āqa'id an-Nasafīya* (Cairo, A.H., 1335), p. 14. On this issue and the progressive systematization of theology, see L. Gardet and G. Anawati, *Introduction è la théologie musulmane* (Paris, 1970), pp. 157 ff. and L. Gardet, 'Ilm al-kalam', in EI^2, 3: 1146-7.

86a The term *quṭb* is usually rendered literally as 'pole'. I prefer 'primate' because it preserves the sense of *quṭb* as the highest point in a saintly hierarchy (involving the four *awtād* or *abdāl*, etc.) and because it is unlike 'pole' in not connoting the sense of an opposition, of polarity, with some other pole.

87 This manner of stating the relation is unusual. For one thing, philosophers are usually singled out and treated as a sect (Shahrastānī, *Milal, ad. loc.*) and the rational sciences are normally treated as disembodied from the histories of peoples. Indeed, it appears that the contention that the Arabs are inept at these sciences was fairly common, as was the opinion that each people excelled in certain sciences or arts. Ibn Ṭabāṭabā (*Fakhrī*, 16) claims that the Persians specialized in wisdom and history, the Arabs in linguistic sciences, poetry, and history, and the Mongols in politics and arithmetic for the administration of the state. Ibn Khaldūn (Q, 3: 270 ff.) uses Islam as a cultural-scientific unit, within which he sees a panicularly prominent role for the Persians, for the Arabs were busy with the affairs of state.

88 Valuable symbolic representations of Ibn Khaldūn's sketch of arithmetical procedures and formulae are given in the footnotes to the relevant passages in Rosenthal, *Ibn Khaldūn, the Muqaddimah*.

89 As in Ibn Sīnā, *Najāt*, p. 5.

90 Theoreticians of all sciences define knowledge as being either apprehension (*taṣawwur*), whether sensuous perception or apprehension, expressed in the form of a definition (*ḥadd*), or else as demonstration (*tasdīq*), expressed in the form of a syllogistic or analogical judgement. For theology, see Ibn Khaldūn's statement in L, 3, in addition to Ghazālī, *Maqāṣid*, pp. 33-5, Rāzī, *Muḥaṣṣal*, pp. 2-3; for jurisprudence, see Ibn al-Ḥajib, *Mukhtaṣar al-muntahā al-uṣūlī* (Cairo, A. H. 1326), p. 5 and Qarāfī, *Sharḥ tanqīḥ al-uṣūl fī al-uṣūl* (Cairo, A. H. 1306), p. 3; for philosophy, see Ibn Sīnā, *Najāt*, pp. 3-4.

91 I have studied Ibn Khaldūn's knowledge of Averroes in my *Ibn Khaldūn*, p. 90.

92 On the structuration of theological treatises from Ghazālī through Rāzī and Baiḍāwī (d. after 685/1286) down to Ījī and Ibn Khaldūn's contemporary Taftāzānī, see Gardet and Anawati, *Introduction*, pp. 157-69. The intermingling of topics in philosophy and theology was accepted procedure, although the boundaries of the sciences were recognized as such. Ibn Khaldūn was unique in seeing this. See, for instance, Subkī, *Mu'īd*, p. 112.

93 'ittiḥād al-maṭālib 'ind al-istidlāl'.

94 'al-ta'lil bil-dalīl ba'd an lam yakun ma'lūm'.

95 On the literature of these sciences, see M. Ullmann, *Die Natur- und Geheimwissenschaften im Islam,* Leiden, 1972 (Handbuch der Orientalistik, 1. Abt., Ergänzungsband vi, 2. Abschnitt).

96 See the account of Subkī, *Mu'īd,* pp. 166 ff., which enumerates some magical acts but does not reduce them to any form of order. Ibn Khaldūn (Q, 3: 127) states that scholars who denied the existence of magic were merely referring to prestidigitation, while those who affirmed it were referring to talismanic magic and to sorcery. The controversy between those who affirm and those who deny the existence of magic is therefore an imaginary one.

97 Rosenthal, *Ibn Khaldūn, the Muqaddimah,* contains valuable charts and tables along with the translations of the relevant passages on the *zā'irja.* Cf. above, ch. 1, n. 27-30. In the sixteenth century, Leo Africanus (*Description,* vol. 1, p. 219) reported that very few people knew this particular art, and Ibn Khaldūn was long considered in Europe, on the authority of Leo Africanus, exclusively as a master of the occult sciences. See my *Ibn Khaldūn,* p. 58, n. 1.

98 See my *Ibn Khaldūn,* ch. 3.

99 Ghazālī, *Tahāfut al-falāsifa,* ed. S. Dunyā (Cairo, 1955), pp. 249-50; Qifṭī, *Tārīkh al-ḥukamā',* ed. J. Lippert (Leipzig, 1903), pp. 51-3. These matters are: 1) denial of hell, 2) denial of God's knowledge of particulars, and 3) the assertion that the world is eternal.

100 Cf R. Arnaldez, 'Falsafa', in EI^2, 2: 764-7.

101 The most forceful, succinct, and radical formulation of this critique is the polemic of Ibn Taimīya (d. 728/1327) who is, oddly, never mentioned in the *Muqaddima.* More generally, see Nashshār, *Manāhij, passim.* On Ibn Khaldūn's epistemological Ash'arism, see the exaggerated and unnuanced statement in 'A. Makkī, *Al-Fikr al-falsafī 'inda Ibn Khaldūn,* Alexandria, 1970.

102 'dalīluh shuhūduh lā tilk al-barāhīn' (Q, 3: 214), and cf. the statements of Ibn Taimīya, *Naqḍ al-manṭiq,* ed. M. Hamza *et al.* (Cairo, A. H. 1370), pp. 191-2.

103 For the Platonic statement and the possible conduits it followed to reach Ibn Khaldūn, see Rosenthal, *Ibn Khaldūn, The Muqaddimah,* vol. 3, p. 252 n. 1029.

104 Comprehensive statements can be found in Ibn Ḥazm, *Al-Faṣl bayn al-milal wal-ahwā' wal-niḥal* (Cairo, A. H. 1317), vol. 5, pp. 38-9 and in Ibn Qayyim al-Jawzīya, *Miftāḥ dār al-sa'āda,* (Beirut, n.d., reimpression of the edition of Cairo, A. H. 1341), pp. 148 ff. For an overview, see C. A. Nallino, 'Sun, Moon, and Stars (Muḥammadan)', in *Encyclopedia of Religion and Ethics* (New York, 1951), vol. 12, pp. 91-3.

105 See Rosenthal, *Ibn Khaldūn, the Muqaddimah,* vol. 3, p. 284 n. 1123.

106 'Al-wujūd 'ain al-maujūd'.

107 See the discussion of N. Nassar, *La pensée réaliste d'Ibn Khaldūn* (Paris, 1967), pp. 66, 80, and, more generally, Nashshār, *Manāhij,* pp. 90 ff.

108 On performative statements, see TK, I: 4 ff., 1360; H. Fleischer, *Kleinere Schriften* (Leipzig, 1885 ff.), vol. 3, pp. 541-2; J. Van Ess, *Die Erkenntnislehre des 'Aḍudaddīn al-Īcī* (Wiesbaden, 1966), pp. 97-98.

109 'ikhbār 'an al-wāqi' '. It is interesting to note that, in the principles of jurisprudence, a transformation takes place of performative statements in such a way that they take on the guise of statements of fact. This is the only way in which a legal judgement can become realistic, for this process transforms pregiven value judgements into

variations on only one of two concepts: reward or punishment. It is reward or punishment which endows the juridical oracle, such as the Koran is, with the aspect of a statement of immediate relevance. See the discussion of 'A. Fākhūri, *Al-Risāla ar-ramzīya fī uṣūl al-fiqh* (Beirut, 1978), pp. 64-5.

110 Cf. Taftāzānī, *Sharḥ*, p. 16.

111 Baiḍawī, *Minhaj al-wuṣul ila 'ilm al-uṣūl* (Cairo, A. H. 1326), p. 18: 'dalalat al-lafẓ 'alā tamām musammāh'.

112 Bīrūnī, *Al-Āthār al-bāqiya min al-qurūn al-khāliya*, ed. E. Sachau (Leipzig, 1923), p. 5.

113 Ibn Ḥazm, *Manṭiq*, p. 202.

114 Sakhāwī, *I'lān*, p. 44.

115 Mas'ūdī, *Murūj*, vol. I, p. 151.

116 'khabar 'an al-ijtimā' al-insanī'.

117 Ibn Sīnā, *Najāt*, p. 17.

118 See, for instance, Taftāzānī, *Sharḥ*, pp. 31-5.

119 A general account is found in TK, 1 410-11. For definitions of philosophers, see GL, 206; of jurisprudence, see Ibn al-Ḥājib, *Mukhtaṣar*, p. 68; of lexicography, LA, s.v.; of Tradition, Baghdādī, *Al-Kifāya fī 'ilm al-riwāya* (Hyderabad. A. H. 1357), p. 16.

120 Pseudo-Qudāma, *Kitāb naqd an-nathr*, attributed to Qudāma b. Ja'far by the editors, T. Ḥusain and A. 'Ibādi (Cairo, 1933), p. 23.

121 Rāzī, text in F. Kholeif, *A Study of Fakhr ad-Dīn Rāzī and His Controversies in Transoxiania* (Beirut, 1966), para. 80 ff.

122 Rāzī, *Lubāb al-ishārāt* (Cairo, A. H. 1326), p. 9.

123 This characterization of *uṣūl al-fiqh* is suggested by J. Van Ess in his intervention in N. Shehaby, 'The Influence of Stoic Logic on Al-Jaṣṣaṣ's Legal Theory', in J. E. Murdoch & E. D. Sylla (eds)' *The Cultural Context of 'Medieval Learning* (Boston, 1973). p. 81.

124 Pseudo-Qudāma, *Naqd*, pp. 23-5.

125 Rāzī, quoted in Qārfi, *Sharḥ tanqiḥ al-uṣūl fil-uṣūl* (Cairo, A. H. 1306), p. 153.

126 '... inn wāfaq [al-khabar al-uṣūl] wa jarā 'alā muqtaḍāhā kāna ṣaḥiḥan wa illā zayyafuh [ṣāḥib fann at-tārīkh]'–Q. I: 44.

127 This point was made very frequently. See for instance Ibn Fārighūn, *Jawāmi'*, pp. 459-60 and Sakhāwī, *I'lām*, p. 63.

128 Van Ess, 'The Logical Structure of Islamic Theology'. in *Logic in Classical Islamic Culture*, ed. G. E. von Grunebaum (Wiesbaden, 1970), p. 34. The common Arabic terms are *waṣf*, *'alāma*, and *imāra*, all of which are subsumed under the generic term *'illa*. See Pseudo-Qudāma, *Naqd*, pp. 18-22; Rāzī, *Muḥaṣṣal*, p 32; Ibn Sīnā, *Kitāb al-Shifā': Al-Qiyās*, ed. S. Zāyid (Cairo, 1964), pp. 575-6.

129 See the discussion of Islamic theological logic in L. Gardet, 'La dialectique en morphologie et logique arabes', in J. Berque *et al.*, *L'Ambivalence dans la culture arabe* (Paris, 1967). p. 128.

130 J. Berque, *Essai sur la méthode juridique maghrébine* (Rabat, 1944), p. 22.

131 In an overstatement that is not totally inaccurate, one scholar states 'c'est par un abus de langage, en principe, que le *ḳiyās* a été conçu en tant que source de droit (*uṣul al-fiḳh*): il ne s'agit, essentiellement, que d'interpretation de la regle préexistante de droit'–E. Tyan, 'Methodologie et sources du droit en Islam', in *Studia Islamica*, 10(1959), p. 83.

132 'tabā'i' al -aḥwāl fil -'umrān'.

133 '[taḥkim] uṣūl al-'āda', 'radd ... ilā al-uṣūl'.

134 See, for instance, Ghazālī, *Maqāṣid*, pp. 66, 90 and Rāzī, *Lubāb*. p. 33.

135 'qiyās al-ghā'ib bil-shāhid wal-ḥādir bil-dhāhib'. See especially Qarāfī, *Tanqīḥ*, pp. 180-1. The very influential scholar Ṭurṭushī declared this specific type of analogy to be coterminous with the mind (*'aql*) itself: *Sirāj*, pp. 57-8.

136 JT (p. 90) states that, for *uṣūl* scholars, 'al-qiyās muẓhir lil-ḥukm lā muthbit'.

137 TK, 1: 71: Āmidī *Al-Iḥkām fī uṣūl al-fiqh al-aḥkām* (Cairo, 1914), vol. 1, p. 11.

138 See the statements of Baiḍāwi, *Minhāj*, pp. 3-4 and Āmidī, *Iḥkām*, vol. 1, pp. 7-8.

CHAPTER THREE

THE HISTORICITY OF *KITĀB AL-'IBAR*

It may be said of certain texts that they transcended their historical specificity and achieved a trans-historical significance. This can be said of certain holy and devotional books, of epic materials, of some philosophical and mathematical classics, and of a handful of others. The same cannot be said of *Kitāb al-'Ibar*. Unlike texts which have achieved different measures of transhistorism, Ibn Khaldūn's title to fame, the *Muqaddima*, is infirmed within its historical specificity, and shares only the limitations of history with the trans-historical texts. For the transhistorism of texts if not a pan-historism, but is rather the adoption of these texts by historical circumstances other than those in which they were originally conceived as texts, and this adoption is the result of a ceaseless effort of exegesis and the unearthing of different significations from the boundless plenty provided by the text which are consonant with the circumstances under which the exegetical effort is practised.[1] Exegetical work on *Kitāb al-'Ibar* has been, at best, either perfunctory, or else strictly circumscribed within the confines of very small circles. In both cases, and as I have shown elsewhere,[2] modern appropriations of the Khaldunic text have shown much less respect for its integrity than is normally expected of exegetical work. More germane to the purpose of this chapter is the fact that attention to and regard for *Kitāb al-'Ibar* by Ibn Khaldūn's contemporaries and by other thinkers in Arab-Islamic civilization was scanty and piecemeal. Only one person, Ibn al-Azraq, who was the last qāḍī of Granada before its conquest by the Crusaders, paid systematic attention to the *Muqaddima*.[3] There was no 'Khaldunic school' in Ottoman historiography,[4] if only because use of the Khaldunic text was in no wise systematic or otherwise respectful of the integrity of the Khaldunic text, but was rather by way of piecemeal adoption of sagely pronouncements. The reason for this is clear as well as distinct: that in terms of the sciences of his age (as well as of ours), Ibn Khaldūn produced no new science that bears any reference to paradigmatic shifts or epistemological breaks that would have given it an integrity and specificity of its own. His new science always referred back to its component sciences; it was the node of confluence of a number of sciences of his age which were not deprived of their original paradigmatic properties and which thus preserved the pristine solidity of the original. The *Muqaddima* is the textual space where these sciences coexisted, but did not blend. What happened in the *Muqaddima* was that a number of procedures and concepts derived from certain sciences were applied to thematic material to which their application was, in terms of the paradigmatic properties of both, very anomalous.

It must be stressed at the very outset that our concern here is not with influences on Ibn Khaldūn by sciences of his age, but with the presence and configuration of these sciences within his work. There is no issue of the influence of a certain thinker or group of thinkers on the psychological unit 'Ibn Khaldūn', whereby this psychological unit becomes a sort of depository for an ahistorical influence. This sort of procedure cannot lead to any measure of adequate certainty, as I have shown elsewhere.[5] More importantly, *ad hominem* considerations of this kind evade the central issue in any study of cultural and scientific continuity: that the issue is not one of reduction to an ulteriority, but of the specification of a particular instantiation–what Hegel would have termed an individuality–of the sciences in question. It is the instantiation in its specificity and individuality that is of interest here, not in its archaeological bearing, in the sense imparted to the term by M. Foucault. In short, the procedure adopted here consists of treating the sciences present in Ibn Khaldūn's work as distinct from the psychological individuality and concreteness of the author, and as the concatenation of concepts and thematic elements which were of wide currency in our author's culture and which met in a specific fashion in his work.

The *Muqaddima* treats a great profusion of topics. But it would be derisory to call the *Muqaddima* 'encyclopedic', as is so often done. The book has far too much verve and too much style for an appellation as stodgily definitive as an encyclopedia aspires to be. The multiplicity of sciences and thematic elements in the *Muqaddima* (and in *Kitāb al-'Ibar*) as a whole, moreover, is not subject to an arrangement which is as contingently arbitrary as the abecederian order of the encyclopedia. We have seen that the thematic and paradigmatic material from geography, from history, from natural science, from philosophy, from occult sciences, from *uṣūl al-fiqh*, and from other domains of the scientific armoury of Ibn Khaldūn's age, is related according to multiple criteria of order: order of textual sequence, order of conceptualization, and order of thematic association (see figure one). The textual order regulates the relation between the various parts of *Kitāb al-'Ibar*, both as the relation between its various books and within each of the books. The order of conceptualization regulates the choice of thematic material to be treated in the chain of textual sequence and dictates the technical sense and association of the units that make up the textual sequence and which also represent its metatextual, conceptual sequence. Finally, the order of thematic association is that which regulates the expansion of the thematic material beyond that which is necessary to provide the bare bones of the Khaldunic argument.

There are two great classes into which the scientific material of *Kitāb al-'Ibar* falls: the paradigmatic and the topical. The latter contains the thematic material utilized, and the former designates the conceptual apparatus whereby the thematic components are utilized, and hence the conceptual physiognomy adopted by this thematic material. Ibn Khaldūn himself was aware of this. He is careful to distinguish his new science from established ones and, at the same time, brings out the thematic similarity between his new science and others from which it differs paradigmatically. He notes that the *Fürstenspiegel* of Ṭurṭūshī (d. 520/1126), *Sirāj al-Mulūk*, has divisions topically similar to his own. But Ṭurṭūshī, he adds, neither delved deep enough into the topics at hand, nor did he undertake to make a demonstration of his statements. He merely posited the theme and presented under its title sundry traditions, illustrious happenings, and sagely Persian sayings. Ṭurṭūshī's is, therefore, not a scientific discourse, lacking in natural demonstrations, and is but pure traditional transmission of statements akin to sermonizing (Q, 1: 66). Other authors and other sciences similarly present a thematic similarity to the thematic content of the *Muqaddima*. The need for a custodial authority (*wāzi'*) can be encountered in demonstrations of the need for prophecy; the need for people to cooperate is encountered in *uṣūl al-fiqh*, where that science proves the necessity for language as an offshoot of the necessity for cooperation; the direct relation between tyranny and the atrophy of civilization is met with in the jurisprudential discourse of divine intent and its concomitant exhortation to justice (Q, 1: 63–4).

So far, Ibn Khaldūn accounts for a very substantial proportion of the material used in the *Muqaddima*. He accounts for most of what has been read as politological material, and indeed for most of the topics under which the study of the fully-formed state is organized and for material on the prelude to the formation of the state and the unfolding of civilization (prophecy, the custodial authority, and the need for aggregation). Ibn

Khaldūn also adduces the examples of Bakrī and Mas'ūdī, as we have seen, in his sketch of the geography and ethnography of the world as he knew it, and we have seen how this material was mingled with elements from Arab-Islamic medicine in discussions of the effect of climate, terrain, and diet, on the form of habitation and the character of its inhabitants. Discussions of prophecy and divination, as we have seen, contain elements from the Avicennan conception of the soul as well as a context derived from the cosmography of the chain of being and associated hermetic ideas of the emanation of benign and satanic forces and their sympathies in the elemental world. The transformation of headship into kingship and the vicissitudes of the latter until it atrophies is thematically accounted for by material from *Kitāb al-'Ibar* and by historical and political material generally. Notions such as *badāwa*, *ḥaḍāra*, and *'aṣabīya*, as already mentioned, do not separately and in themselves present a great mystery, and cannot be considered as such great innovations as to require explanation. They are vernacular notions which would have been understood in Ibn Khaldūn's time by all and sundry, both as to their signification and to their reference and content, and can be understood today by any person living in a situation where *badū* and *ḥadar* dwell in proximity, such as throughout the Arabian Peninsula. Indeed, a casual conversation with a contemporary Yemeni or Qatari would be enough to dispel the mysteries of the 'sociological categories' that Ibn Khaldūn is supposed to have discovered. The mystery lies elsewhere: that these vernacular notions were endowed with the respectability of being mentioned in a work of scholarship and, moreover, of being given the discursive role of metaphysical and other categories. The state, as we have seen in detail, is derivable from the notion of the state that orders Arab-Islamic historical writing and political thinking. As for the largely ethical discussion of economic activity, Ibn Khaldūn's topics are derived again from sagely literature, from historical fact, from legal reasoning, and from dogmatics. There is no problem as regards the sciences, for their origins are clear. The only problem is rather similar to that presented by the vernacular concepts of the political order: why and how unofficial (yet highly developed) sciences such as magic found their way so systematically into a work which, though not official, is yet exoteric and public.

So much for the topical components, which we have studied in detail earlier on in their own right as well as in their relation to the pool of scientific concepts and topics of Ibn Khaldūn's age. The discourse upon the topics *badāwa*, *ḥaḍāra*, *'aṣabīya*, and their cognates is a fulfilment of the requirements for the formation of a science, the new science of civilization, which should actuate in a realistic fashion the craft of historiographic criticism and the judgement upon the veracity or falsity of narratives about the past. But it is a fulfilment of the project in terms of that which is readily accessible to Ibn Khaldūn's field of vision: the vernacular notions of political action of his time, which, as we saw in the first chapter, structures the unit of historical narrative. In effect, this is the result of a robust stance of realism. This is a realism that is peculiar neither to Ibn Khaldūn nor to his culture, but is the realism of the politician that Ibn Khaldūn was for a long while. It is not, however, a reflective, philosophical realism; for Ibn Khaldūn, philosophy is provided by the philosophical sciences that he used and not by this realism, and these were perfectly adequate to his purposes. It is, rather, a vernacular realism, an everyday common sensical realism, one which does little more than register things as they appear to happen. Hence the elevation of vernacular realities such as *badāwa* to the status of concepts. It is the realism that produces the simple causal arguments contained within the *Muqaddima* which have given occasion to numerous latter day commentators to read a 'sociology' in Ibn Khaldūn. It is, equally, the realism that does not and cannot but admit magic and its cognate scientific and hermetic concepts to the fore, and this is reflected in Ibn Khaldūn's contention which we have met above that most critics and students of magic have evaded the real issues. And it is this very same realism which, as we have seen, refutes the claims to knowledge by philosophers, astrologers, magicians, and alchemists because their claims go beyond that which is possible for human knowledge.

But the very sobriety of this realism is that which incapacitates it. It is a receptive realism, one that registers what it sees without delving unaided into that which lies behind it. It is a sort of phenomenological realism, a phenomenology of history which registers its apparition but not its more essential descriptions. It is a pessimistic realism which discourses on the *fait accompli*, a realism that is retrospective and which, thus, does not bear the comparison, often made by commentators, with Machiavelli's prescriptive realism. Ibn Khaldūn's descriptive realism recapitulates what it sees as reality in a manner consonant with the sensualist nominalism that is professed at more than one point in the course of the *Muqaddima*—an epistemological preference which is itself eminently realistic in the sense being argued here.

It is Ibn Khaldūn's retrospective realism that accounts for the form of his recapitulation of Maghribi history. His 'abstract analysis of a historical sequence'[6] has no explicative value–it is the statement of the historical sequence in the form that it presented itself in historical writing. Maghribi history is that of the various chronological classes of the main peoples that populate the Maghrib and of the antagonism between beduinism and sedentary life as quintessentially expressed in the myth of the Hilālī invasion.[7] Ibn Khaldūn, in the *Muqaddima*, as well as in the rest of *Kitāb al-'Ibar*, adopts the politically operational and historiographically ideological realities of his age concerning genealogy, kinship, and the polity of the clan, and transforms them into a pattern which latter-day commentators have taken for a theory of history. The ideological unit of political action in state formation having been the clan, this is taken as a genealogical group whose very genealogy somehow transforms it into a political group capable of founding a state. He imports wholesale into his genealogical discussions, for instance, the incoherence and telescoping of Lumtūna genealogies,[8] and affirms that the Ṣanhāja and the Kutāma are of Semitic not of Berber origin, as we have seen, although he was very well aware that virtually all Berber peoples were claiming some form of Arab descent (BD, 6: 192 and *passim*).[9] He sees as axiomatic the assertion that entities such as Zanāta do exist, although he does state that they dwell not only in the Ghadames oasis, but in the Tripolitanian hills, in the Aures, in the central Maghrib, and elsewhere in North Africa, living under very different ecological, social, and political circumstances (BD, 7: 3–4) which makes it absurd to think of them as a unit. Yet not only are the broader strokes of historical writing in Ibn Khaldūn ordered around these names, but even the account of detailed historical episodes is narrated in terms of such names, as I have shown elsewhere with respect to one such episode, the rebellion of Abū Yazīd Sahīb al-Ḥimār against the Fatimid regime in the tenth century of the Christian era.[10] Ibn Khaldūn, thus, continues the practice of writing history in terms of names which signify little beyond themselves and which can only be considered as mythological and classificatory qualifiers whose precise significance is as yet unclear but which merits a serious anthropological study. Moreover, he continues to regard the formation of the state as a process impelled by some sort of force inherent in genealogy which forms a genealogical group and a force whose incipience is activated by the conjunctions of the heavenly bodies. But in reality there are factors which Ibn Khaldūn could very well observe but could not place in relation to the formation of states and the political activation of clans on the edge of the Sahara and elsewhere in the Maghrib, namely, the gold trade which fed the economies of Egypt, the Levant, Spain, and much of Europe before the discovery and plunder of South America.[11] All that Ibn Khaldūn can see in the formation of a state is the militarily expanding tribal core. The Hilālīs are seen as a horde which attacked North Africa like a plague of locusts (BD, 7: 31), although his lengthy account of the Hilālīs in the seventh volume of *Kitāb al-ʿIbar* provides enough material for the reconstruction of the very orderly progress of their movements and settlements.

Like every other robust realism, that of Ibn Khaldūn is bounded by a field of vision described by constraints which are both vernacular and scientific (i.e., paradigmatic). Limits are thus set not only to the field of vision of which realism is capable, but also of the modes of such vision. It is not only topics that are visible, but specific cadences of these topics. The fundamental topic of the science of civilization brought in its train other subsidiary and auxiliary topics which we have identified both as to their theme and to semantic and paradigmatic fields from whence they hail. Considerations on the vernacular and historiographic state and on *badāwa* and associated notions, which form the object of Ibn Khaldūn's investigations, necessitated discourses on a variety of other topics. But the textual entities which were vernacular or merely thematic and topical (taken over as topics from various sciences and genres), became scientific when transformed into concepts that formed part of a line of sequential argumentation, be that logical or otherwise. And the scientification of the vernacular as well as the topical thematic in the *Muqaddima* was undertaken by means of natural philosophy, of metaphysics, and of logic. For Ibn Khaldūn's stance was not only realistic. The *Muqaddima* is also informed by a truly systematic and philosophical bent which scientificates the vernacular and retrospectively realistic. But this philosophical bent is not a vernacular bent, a mere uncultured speculative proclivity. For whatever proclivity to systematize there may have been, it was articulated in scholarly form: it was scientifically stylized, articulated in terms of concepts active in the sciences of the age.

We have seen that the sequential flow of the historical narratives contained in the second and third books of *Kitāb al-ʿIbar* is structured by the concomitant movements of branching and consecution. The flow of the first book, the *Muqaddima*, is far more complex, as Diagram One shows. In the *Muqaddima*, natural philosophy with its medical and hermetic conception of nature and of generation and decay provided the fundamental categories in terms of which the topics of the science of civilization were formulated and, consequently, scientificated. The teleological structure of the medieval 'nature' also provided a criterion of order and of movement between these categories: form became substance, and substance became form: *badāwa* became the state which generated *ḥaḍāra* which naturally atrophied. A relation of modal entailment is thus generated. This is paralleled by a temporal, sometimes causal, succession, as well as by a process of logical entailment which links the seven prolegomena to the first book of *Kitāb al-'Ibar* with the first chapter until the establishment of the state. Order is thus imposed upon the topics of the *Muqaddima* by natural philosophy, by logic, and by straightforward temporal causality, the vernacular causality of precedence.

We are left with the relations between the major textual components of *Kitāb al-'Ibar*, namely, between the *Muqaddima* and the historical narratives that succeed it in the second and third books. We have shown in the last section of the second chapter above that it was *uṣūl al-fiqh* that provides the history, the aetiology, of the connection between historical narrative and the criteria of the veracity of these narratives, for the science that is charged with relating a particularity to a generality in the medium of narrative, *khabar*, can be none other than jurisprudential methodology. The *Muqaddima* in this light constitutes a sort of *uṣūl at-tārīkh*. The relationship between the narrative and its *archē* is that between a *far'* and its *aṣl*, which is not a deduction of the former from the latter, as we have had occasion to see, but a reduction and assimilation (*ilḥāq*), the instantiation of conditions of plausibility which are the statements of the new science. This is the sense of Ibn Khaldūn's statement that *Kitāb al-'Ibar* proceeds from conditions and requisites (*asbāb*) in their generality to narratives in their particularity, so that the work endows events that take place under the aegis of the state with the generality derived from their causes (*'ilal*) (Q, 1: 7)–and causes can only be general when they are the derivatives of generalized test case in such a way that the particularity is embedded in this generality, and this is precisely the function performed by the term *'illa*, which is both material cause, and the cause of a judgement.[12] The *'illa* is the cause of the judgement in that it acts as a connective which serves to subsume the particularity under a generality which is decreed a normative paradigm.

I will digress briefly and justify further the choice of *uṣūl al-fiqh* as the fundamental repository of conceptual and methodological armature from which Ibn Khaldūn derived his model for the testing of historical narrative. This seems to be in order because the science of *uṣūl al-fiqh* is almost totally ignored in modern scholarship in spite of the central role it played in forming and providing the logical tools not only of jurisprudence, but of dogmatics (*kalām*) as well.[13] I have shown elsewhere the central role it played in the culture of North Africa in the Middle Ages and the associations it had with logic and grammar.[14] It appears that these sciences were cultivated more at the Merinid court in Fez than in more easterly parts of the Maghrib, or, indeed, in the formal educational system of Fez. For there does appear to have been opposition in the Qarawīyīn to the study of *uṣūl al-fiqh* according to the logical and systematic methods developed by the 'moderns' and principally by Rāzī.[15] The more rationalist orientation was doubtless enhanced by the presence of Ibn Khaldūn's most revered teacher al-Ābilī[16] who instructed Ibn Khaldūn in *uṣūl al-fiqh* (T, 22) and of Al-Sharif al-Tilimsānī (d. 771/1369–70).[17]

As for Ibn Khaldūn, he had very definite preferences among the arcane complexities of the science. His own teaching of *usūl al-fiqh* was modelled upon Ghazālī and Rāzī and he was said to have been very hostile to post-Razean *uṣūl*, especially developments in the East contemporary with him, in which he saw an excessive formalism and verbosity.[18] Moreover, he was much more in favour of Ḥanafi *uṣūl*, especially the treatises of Bazdawī (d. 482/1089) and Sā'ātī (d. after 690/1291), than he was of Ibn al-Ḥājib's (d. 646/1248) compendium which was the normal textbook used using his time.[19] In his hostility to the fellow Mālikī Ibn al-Ḥājib he was at one with his Mālikī near-contemporaries Qabbāb, Ibn al-Ḥafid, and the great Ibrāhīm b. Mūsā al-Shāṭibī (d. 790/1388).[20] Ibn Khaldūn's praise for Hanafī *uṣūl* is praise for the rationalism of their procedures (Q, 3: 21, 25)–they marry, in the words of Bazdawī, Tradition with ratiocination and never use the one without the other,[21] and this seems to have been the reason for the strictness almost bordering on hostility with which Abū Ḥanīfa (d. 150/767), unlike some of his later successors, treated the transmission of traditions (Q, 2: 405–6). Such strictness, which reminds us of Ibn Khaldūn's account of eschatological narratives, naturally militates in favour of ratiocination and of the rationalism which Ibn Khaldūn praised, and which indeed was seen by others as a certain exactitude with which *furū'* are based upon their *uṣūl*.[22]

Uṣūl al-fiqh cannot be brought into the system of relations among sciences that exist in *Kitāb al-'Ibar* because it is a master science, a scale, a gauge which *ipso facto* remains external to the others. Just like this gauge, the other sciences encountered in *Kitāb al-'Ibar* are fully constituted, so that in the *Muqaddima* especially we encounter the confluence of a number of distinct sciences, each with its well-defined topics, concepts, and procedures–in short, each with an integral paradigmatic constitution–although the topics are sometimes held in common by more than one of the sciences in question. And the integrity of each of these sciences is left unassailed upon entry into the discursive body of the *Muqaddima*, each being discursively active at one or more of the three layers of logic, nature, and time, according to which it unfolds. It will be assumed that the three layers are reducible to two, a deductive layer (formally and modally) which encompasses the first two, and a temporally serial layer.

The same vernacular and politological empirical material is active along both the deductive and the serial layers. *Badāwa*, *ḥaḍāra*, and *daula*, the main components of this flow, are textual units which are at one and the same time empirical and vernacular units with specific and visible *denotata*, and concepts in chains of modal and formal entailment. The sensuously nominal, the vernacular, palpable units are not, sadly, made to dissolve into the conceptual moulds that are meant to scientificate them. As purely empirical units, they have no immanent connection with each other beside the fact of succession, which is sometimes (but by no means always) accompanied by a causal link–and this in itself is just another observable which does not transcend the level of sensuous perception. As components in deductive chains, they point to their empirical and vernacular bearings without taking them over and absorbing them into their conceptual being if they were to truly integrate them within this conceptual being. We have seen how matter and form change personae in the process of state formation: the state and civilization take on both metaphysical functions, they both perform as both matter and form in relation to each other. The particular function performed by the two vernacular entities and textual groups 'state' and 'civilization' is dependent, as we saw, on the empirical unscientificated unfolding of civilization, on the temporal stage reached in the movement between *badāwa* and *ḥaḍāra*. The same empirical entity takes on more than one conceptual colouration, and this is the way in which the exigencies of deductivism which were so paramount in the foundation of Ibn Khaldūn's new science adapt to the equally exigent nominalism that is the vernacular custodian of truth according to Ibn Khaldūn. There is, therefore, no real conceptualization of the vernacular realities in the rigorous sense of the term; they flow in their givenness as their conceptualization tries to account for them. For if they were to be fully and rigorously conceptualized, then their empirical appearance would take place only in keeping with the exigencies of the conceptualization, and this would have produced very severe limitations on the topical freedom, the freedom of thematic association, which the main textual components of the *Muqaddima* enjoy, as we have seen.

There is a constant attempt by the vernacular entities of reality to transform themselves into conceptual entities, in aid of the deductive intent of the architecture of the *Muqaddima*, as there is, conversely, an attempt by conceptual entities to behave as do their empirical apparitions.

The topic *badāwa* is both an identifiable group of characteristics visible to Ibn Khaldūn as well as a metaphysical entity in the realm of nature and a point in the logical unfolding of the text of the *Muqaddima*. But none of the three avatars of this topic completely becomes another. They tend towards each other, but never blend. So much so, indeed, that if the metaphysical and logical cover were taken away from the *Muqaddima*, we would only be left with what a very perceptive student of Ibn Khaldūn's has called a 'topographic sketch' of certain political and other historical and contemporary events.[23] We are left with a landscape of empirical descriptions organized under the aegis of topical divisions and connected, sometimes, by simple causality, and otherwise by thematic sympathy. Indeed, this is precisely what happened when the metaphysical umbrella was removed by Ibn al-Azraq (d. 896/1491) in his rendition of the *Muqaddima*. Ibn al-Azraq produced a text which looks far tidier than its predecessor: it is exhaustively and painstakingly divided and subdivided into thematic sections which completely deprive the original of its coherence. Ibn al-Azraq's treatise on kingship starts with a *muqaddima* professing to be a disquisition on the rational propedeutics for the investigation of kingship, and this turns out to be an enumeration of a number of Khaldunian topics without any attempt at linking them together in any manner other than their appurtenance to the thematic class carried in the title of the *muqaddima*.[24] This procedure does not change throughout the work which is thus far poorer than those chapters of the *Muqaddima* that treat kingship and the state, in spite of the clearer thematic division given by Ibn al-Azraq and of the keys he provides as to the literature on the subject from which he quotes so extensively–so extensively, indeed, that if one were interested in tracing all the textual antecedents of Ibn Khaldūn's pronouncements from the fields of dogmatics, jurisprudence, *Fürstenspiegel*, and others, a combing of Ibn al-Azraq's text would be an invaluable guide and key. Conversely, if we were to remove from the *Muqaddima* the historical and other topical material that constitutes its substance, we would be left with a skeletal structure consisting of two termini, a beginning and an end, the connection between which is punctuated by points that denote matter, form, and *telos*, each of which would take its due from the names 'civilization', 'beduinity', and 'state', without its connection to civilization, beduinity, or the state being of any significance, let alone necessity, or of historicity.

We thus have in the *Muqaddima* discursive layers which remain unintegrated and.which are essentially intransitive with respect to one another. The vernacular and topical realism we have encountered is not properly theorized or properly conceptualized. Neither is the opposite movement realized: the topical elements subjected to vernacular realism are not fully absorbed into the conceptual anatomy of the *Muqaddima* but are merely associated with it in their capacity as topical elements whose constitution is totally independent of the conceptual processes that structure the work. There is, therefore, no movement that achieves integrative coherence within the text of the *Muqaddima*. But neither is there in the work any evidence of a dissonance between these layers. There is a coexistence between deductivism and seriality which articulates itself in the form of parallelism: we have a serial movement between textual units, between which also and simultaneously exists a deductive movement and connection. The layers of the *Muqaddima* are juxtaposed, with the layer structured by deductive connection giving metaphysical cover to realism, and endowing the whole work with a systematic allure that hides the impassivity with which each of its layers, in reality, regards the other.

In terms of the sciences of Ibn Khaldūn's age, this coexistence of layers presents us with a very interesting situation. For we are faced with a situation where there is an attempt which, regardless of the extent of its success, tried to bring into a unitary purview concepts and topics from sciences the relationship between which was nonexistent and the boundaries between which were very sharp and very real. The topics provided by history, by *Fürstenspiegel*, and by pietistic and legal texts about the states and the body politic, were liable and subject to valorization in terms of the paradigmatic requirements of these sciences and genres: to chronological and genealogical organization, to sagely commentary, and to disquisitions in terms of public law. They were not, however, liable to valorization in terms of the modal deductivism of the concept of nature, even though such a marriage of the idea of nature with the state marching towards its inevitable doom was a common vernacular–i.e. oral and not scholarly–notion. Neither was the nature of the state liable to a discussion in terms of logic; the transition from *badāwa* to *ḥaḍāra* and the relationship between them was never a topic discoursed upon in terms of nature or in terms of metaphysics. Nor were the sciences ever the subject of such a conceptualization, let alone being considered as crafts among others by the learned–for whom Ibn Khaldūn wrote, and who must necessarily have considered it preposterous to be compared to masons, for instance, notwithstanding the honour conferred upon their professions by Ibn Khaldūn. The historical merit of Ibn al-Azraq lies in his having stripped away the incongruous and paradigmatically impossible garb with which political subjects were clothed in the *Muqaddima*.

Moreover, it must have appeared pretty outlandish for Ibn Khaldūn's contemporaries that he brought into a unitary perspective the sciences of geography and prophecy, and that he made these into the preconditions of a theory of the state. The positing of a science of civilization which should stand in a systematic relation to the narratives of history must also have seemed exceedingly odd, for, after all, history is the business of the state and civilization, and the concern of the state is really fiscal administration, which falls within the province of the art of governance, *siyāsa*, and not of systematic science. Even the idea that a science can be constructed with such a self-evident object as civilization must have seemed strange by virtue of this same selfevidence. And lastly, the transference of concepts and methods of narrative criticism as those in use in *uṣūl al-fiqh* to textual domains whose nature is not only profane, but largely theoretical (as opposed to ethically and legally practical), domains which are, moreover, subject to a radically different type of criticism (that of authorities)–such a transference must have seemed one that did violence to both the methods of *uṣūl al-fiqh* and to the integrity of historiography–with the proviso that violence done to historiography is not displayed in the naïve rationalist rejection of stories because of clear implausibility, for such rejection was not very rare, but rather in the attempt to construct a systematic science for validating implausibilities.

No science exists without a scientific institution which watches over its integrity and polices innovation and deviation. This paradigmatic police reacts most vigorously when there is disruptive dislocation, when there is an attempt to alienate part of the scientific patrimony–concepts and topics–which a paradigm regards as its own, and to transfer it to alien territory. After all, this is the function of the paradigm within the institution of a science. It is, therefore, quite natural that the web of paradigmatic torsions effected by Ibn Khaldūn in the *Muqaddima* should have met with what is historically a devastating rejection in the forms of silence, derision, and occasional grudging admiration. And it is equally natural that any admiring or not so admiring use of material developed in the *Muqaddima* should relate to such topics and concepts in such a way that the effect of the systematic paradigmatic torsion that the *Muqaddima* would have liked to produce is not displayed.

Like most works, the *Muqaddima* has had its share of a certain inane largesse of praise.[25] More to the point is the praise by his contemporary in Fez, Ibn al-Aḥmar, for Ibn Khaldūn's eminence in the rational sciences.[26] But much more usual was the statement by his rival in Cairo, Rakrākī, that Ibn Khaldūn had a solid but mediocre knowledge of the rational sciences but no knowledge of jurisprudence.[27] Ibn Ḥajar, a one-time pupil of Ibn Khaldūn's,[28] contended that his erstwhile teacher was of such eloquence that he had lent himself to mystification and to being overpraised.[29] Even as an historian he is not rated exceptionally by Ibn Ḥajar, who considered his knowledge of eastern Muslim history to be defective.[30] What is strange is that it is to Ibn Ḥajar that the tradition, according to which Ibn Khaldūn's text is certified and ratified, goes, even in parts of the Maghrib,[31] and it is equally odd that both the *Muqaddima* and the rest of *Kitāb al-'Ibar* were not directly known in Tunis in the seventeenth and first half of the eighteenth centuries.[32]

That which was noted and appreciated was put to use in a far less systematic and much more perfunctory manner than even the procedure of Ibn al-Azraq that we have already encountered. A certain Ibn al-Sakkāk, a contemporary of Ibn al-Azraq, used Ibn Khaldūn's ideas on luxury in a book of political wisdom, but failed to mention Ibn Khaldūn's name.[33] In the eighteenth century, one Ṣaghīr b. Yusūf of Tunis tried to complete Ibn Khaldūn's history of the Berbers, while a contemporary of Ṣaghīr, Ḥammūda b. 'Abd al-'Azīz, made use of our author's ideas on the grandeur and decadence of dynasties in an account of the Hafṣids,[34] During Ibn Khaldūn's time, he was quoted on such things as his considerations on the corruption of genealogies,[35] and of why the earliest Muslim conquerors refused to take to sea.[36] Later on, the bibliographer Ḥajjī Khalifa (d. 1067/1657) said that the *Muqaddima* was meritorious in unique ways, without further qualification.[37]

It is thus that Ibn Khaldūn was received and understood: as a writer on topics that belong to sciences such as genealogy and political wisdom, as a sort of compiler whose merit resided in bringing forth the elements of the compilation with particular skill and perceptiveness. That there was something beyond this passed, at best, unnoticed. And the scientificated vernacular was ignored. It was probably attributed to a certain eccentricity, for, according to a contemporary, Ibn Khaldūn 'liked to be different in all things'.[38] Even the great and perceptive historian Maqrīzī, one of the few persons truly to admire Ibn Khaldūn and to have studied the *Muqaddima* under him, does not show any evidence of having appreciated the genius for eclecticism displayed by Ibn Khaldūn. Like Ibn al-Azraq, Hajji Khalīfa, Qalqashandī, and others who made use of the *Muqaddima*, they made use of topical material therefrom, of 'topographic detail', without the cover provided by metaphysics, by logic, or by nature.

Such a capricious approach to the *Muqaddima* was not entirely due to the obtuse conservatism of its recipients and of its public. Nor was the hostility towards Ibn Khaldūn evinced by 'jurists' simply due to his call to throw away *taqlīd*[39]–indeed, we have seen that he did not make a call as unqualified as this. The failure to appreciate the eclectic dimensions of the *Muqaddima* was because, as we have seen, these extra-textual dimensions were preserved in the form of their extra-textual presence. The conceptual and topical elements derived from various sciences and fields of vernacular vision, and inserted within the levels and layers along which the *Muqaddima* is structured, are synthesized in direct proportion to the degree to which the layers are synthesized. They are, therefore, not at all fused. The marriage of logic and nature and their joint association with historical and political topics, in terms of Arab-Islamic culture, could only have produced an historical freak. And this is a freak which preserves the solidity of its original components in their original form: had they been fused, the resultant would have created a compulsion of its own. The *Muqaddima*, despite the eclecticism which is so thoroughly and vigorously sustained as almost to produce a systematic synthesis of its elements, did not have the potency of conception to produce a paradigmatic omnipotence which could make it claim the topics discussed as its own and exclusively its own within an integral, autonomous, and well-defined conceptual articulation. The amalgam of paradigmatic elements *in statu quo* which Ibn Khaldūn lodged within the *Muqaddima* is thus a very artificial construct, one that allows us to contend that the unity of the *Muqaddima* is really the physical unity of print, paper, and binding, and not the paradigmatic unity of a coherent discourse. Had it been a real unit of novel constitution, it would not have been possible for Ibn Khaldūn's contemporaries to take over whatever elements they wished without regard to the conceptual profile under whose regime these elements are present in the *Muqaddima* and are constituted by it. For the novel and unified conceptual constitution would have created a situation where the adoption (or at the very least, the recognition) of an element would have entailed the adoption of certain of its conceptual features, and not solely the sagely, or the realistic physiognomy with which it is adopted, and which constituted its original topical properties.

The physical unity of the *Muqaddima* is therefore the artificial unity of a cluster of discourses. As such, it has no centre, no internal agency of integration and of unified articulation. The criterion of this physical unity thus can only lie *hors de texte*. It can only provide disparate and independent elements of a topical and conceptual nature, without the presence of a central constitutive principle which would select the elements according to criteria of relevance internal to the text of the *Muqaddima*.

Having no centre, the *Muqaddima* does not provide us with an explanation, or even with clues to the explanation of its existence. Had it been coherent, its principle of coherence would have been its clue. Under the circumstances, however, we can only *register* the amalgam of sciences, stances, and events that make up the *Muqaddima.* We can find or deduce no explanation for it, for it does not possess a compelling force either textually or historically which would make such an explanation at all possible: it is the unintegrated amalgam of its topical and conceptual elements, which thus retain their original physiognomies, and therefore recover their explanation in their original existence. The *Muqaddima* adds no elixiric element that transforms them and transmutes them to different paradigmatic and discursive orders. In Hegelian terms, the *Muqaddima* is not an individuality, but a cluster of particularities. All that one can register is the original project informing *Kitāb al-'Ibar* as Ibn Khaldūn states it in the preface to the work: the question of historical narrative led to the construction of a science which would assure the veracity of historical writing. But we can detect no 'crisis' in historical writing or in the exigencies and conditions of historical writing which would have occasioned a transformation in its paradigmatic acceptation. Indeed, historical writing was particularly flourishing in the Mamlūk era and dynastic history was prospering monotonously in the Maghrib. And of the many personal and intellectual 'crises' that commentators have declared they detected in Ibn Khaldūn's life, none would account for the configuration of elements and the order in which they are clustered in the *Muqaddima.* We are therefore left with only a project whose execution used elements readily available in the deep sediments of Ibn Khaldūn's cultural universe but whose mode of combination is itself just another one of those elements readily available. The exigencies of the project executed by Ibn Khaldūn in *Kitāb al-'Ibar* are internal to Ibn Khaldūn's intentionality which, sadly but inevitably, is totally inaccessible to us.

NOTES

1 See the recent interesting statement on the inexhaustibility of the text with reference to the New Testament by F. Kermode, *The Genesis of Secrecy,* Chicago, 1979.

2 *Ibn Khaldūn in Modern Scholarship, passim.*

3 Aḥmad Bāba al-Tinbuktī, *Nayl al-ibtihāj bi-taṭrīz ad-dibāj,* on the margin of Ibn Farḥūn, *Ād-Dībāj al-mudhahhab fī ma'rifat a'yān 'ulamā al-madhhab* (Cairo, A. H. 1351), p. 324.

4 On this, see J. von Hammer, *Geschichte des Osmanischen Reiches* (Prest, 1825 ff.),

vol. 1 p. 301, vol. 3 p. 765; F. Babinger, *Die Geschichtsschreiber der Osmanen und ihre Werke* (Leipzig, 1927), pp. 212, 282, 369, 379; F. Z. Fahri, 'Turkiyede Ibn Haldunizm', in *Fuad Köprülü Armagani* (Istanbul, 1953), pp. 153 ff.

5 *Ibn Khaldūn*, pp. 122 ff.

6 A. Laroui, *History of the Maghrib*, p. 219.

7 I have discussed this matter in detail in *Ibn Khaldūn*, ch. 6.

8 H. T. Norris, *Saharan Myth and Saga* (Oxford, 1972), pp. 58 ff.

9 See R. Basset, 'Les genéalogistes berbères', in *Les Archives Berbères*, 1/2(1915), pp. 3-4.

10 *Ibn Khaldūn*, pp. 215 ff.

11 On Saharan trade in relation to the Almoravids, the Almohads, the Ḥafṣids, the Merinids, and the Zayyānids, see J. Devisse, 'Routes de commerce et échanges en Afrique occidentale en relation avec la Méditerranée: Un essai sur le commerce africain mediéval du XIe and XVIe siècle', in *Rev. d'Histoire Economique et Sociale*, 1(1972). See also R. A. Messier, 'The Almoravids: West African Gold and Gold Currency of the Mediterranean Basin', in *Journal of the Economic and Social History of the Orient*, 17(1974) pp. 31 ff. and, more generally, Laroui, *History, passim*, F. Braudel, 'Monnaies et civilizations', in *Annales*, 1(1946) pp. 12 ff.; *idem.*, *The Mediterranean* (London, 1972 f.), vol. 1, pp. 467 f.

12 Ibn Khaldūn was not the lone scholar who endeavoured to make such a review of historical material. A Shams ad-Dīn b. Shihāb ad-Dīn al-Ījī, in a *Fürstenspiegel* dated A.D. 1397 and entitled *Tuḥfat al-faqīr ilā ṣāḥib as-sarīr*, included a chapter on the principles of history and on the criticism of historical narratives subdivided into the following sections: 1) the definition *of khabar*, 2) proofs of its veracity, 3) reasons for believing or rejecting a narrative 4) contradictions among narratives and the contradiction between transmission of narratives and ratiocination, 5) reasons that lead the historian to produce a positive or negative judgement upon a narrative, 6) the reasons for preferring one narrative of an event over another, 7) the value of transmission in theology, 8) the value of reason in the material world, 9) principles of narrative criticism, 10) a study of Bīrūnī's (d. 440/1048) opinions on the lifespan of humans, 11) the value of the contention that in the deepest past men had thick bones, and 12) the sources for the foregoing discussion. (Z. V. Togan, in *Proceedings of the 22nd Congress of Orientalists*, Istanbul, 1953, p. 82). I have unfortunately been unsuccessful in obtaining a microfilm of Ījī's manuscript which appears to be more systematic than Ibn Khaldūn's historical criticism.

13 See the comments on the relation between theology and *uṣūl al-fiqh* among the Mālikī's in L. Gardet, 'Quelques réflexions', p. 267.

14 *Ibn Khaldūn*, pp. 102 ff.

15 Ghubrīnī, *'Unwān ad-dirāya fī-man 'urifa min al-'ulamā fil-mā'a as-sābi'a bi-Bijāya*, ed. A. Nuwaihiḍ (Beirut, 1969), pp. 109-110. There was considerable tension between the Merinid court and the scholarly and religious circles in Fez: see for instance M. Shatzmiller, 'Les premiers Merinides et le milieu religieux de Fés: l'introduction des Medersas', in *Studia Islamica*, 43(1976), pp. 112 ff.

16 Al-Ābilī was known as 'shaikh al-ma'qūl bil-Maghrib' (Sakhāwī, *Ḍau'*, vol. 4, p. 145). On him, see T, 21 f, 33 ff., and Ibn Maryam, *Al-Bustān fī dhikr al-awliyā wal-'ulamā bi-Tilimsān*, ed. M. Bencheneb, (Algiers, A. H. 1326), pp. 214 ff.

17 Aḥmad Bāba, *Nayl*, pp. 256-8 and see Ibn Maryam, *Bustān*, pp. 164-6.

18 Sakhāwī, *Ḍau'*, vol. 4, pp. 148–9. Ibn al-Ḥājib's compendium (along with that of practical jurisprudence) were introduced to the Maghrib about a generation before Ibn Khaldūn's birth (Q, 3: 13–14). A casual count shows that there were no less than twenty commentaries on it in the seventh century of the Hijra (Ibn al-'Imād, *Shadharāt adh-dhahab fī khabar man dhahab,* Cairo A. H. 1351, vol. 6, *passim*), and his commentators included figures of such stature as Baiḍāwī, Taftāzānī, and Subkī (Ḥajjī Khalīfa, *Kashf aẓ-ẓunūn*, ed. G. Flügel, Leipzig, 1865 ff., vol. 2, pp. 1853 ff.), and there were also works specifically devoted to his terminology and the logical introduction to his compendium (Aḥmad Bāba, *Nayl*, pp. 32, 51, 305). On Ibn al-Ḥājib, see Ibn Khallikān, *Wafayāt al-a'yān*, ed. I. 'Abbās, Beirut, 1970, vol. 3, pp. 248 ff.

19 Sakhāwī, *Ḍau'*, vol. 4, pp. 148–9.

20 Aḥmad Bāba, *Nayl*, p. 73; Ibn Ḥajar, *Durar*, vol. 2, p. 343. Ibn al-Ḥājib was accused of having confounded the fine points of Mālikism by the importation into his textbooks of material inadmissible by the *madhhab.* Ibn Khaldūn charges that Ibn al-Ḥājib was a mere autodidact (Sakhāwī, *Ḍau'*, vol. 4, p. 149 and cf Q, 3: 12) and regards his compendium as paradigmatically indiscriminate (Q, 3: 13–14), a fact which he regarded as confusing for the learner to whom it should properly be directed (Q, 3: 250). It thus seems that hostility to Ibn al-Ḥājib is a defence of juridicial integrity as well as of the integrity of the legal hierarchy. It may be interesting to note that hostility to Ibn al-Ḥājib is not evinced except by Maghribis, and it would be instructive to link this with Ibn Khaldūn's strictures upon the laxity of scientific transmission in the Maghrib and with the sorrowful remarks by a contemporary of Ibn Khaldūn's on how the mantle of jurisprudence was being adopted by unqualified persons ('Uqbānī, *Tuḥfat an-nāẓir wa ghunyat adh-dhākir fī ḥifẓ al-sha'ā'ir wa taghyīr al-manākir*, ed. 'A. Shanūfī, [Damascus?], n.d., para. 62.

21 Bazdawī, *Kanz al-wuṣūl*, on the margin of 'Abad al-'Azīz al-Bukhārī, *Kashf al-asrār*, n.p. [1889], vol. 1, p. 17.

22 Sakhāwī, *Ḍau'*, vol. 2, p. 97.

23 Jābirī, *Al-'Aṣabīya wad-daula*, p. 161.

24 *Badā'i'*, vol. i, pp. 46 ff. The propedeutics are the following: 1) the necessity of aggregation, 2) the concomitant characteristics of aggregation (it is significant that Ibn al-Azraq uses the term *'awāriḍ* rather than the Khaldunic *a'rāḍ dhātīya* to refer to the same things, namely, beduinity, domination, cities, city life, and livelihood–p. 47), 3) the division of habitation into beduin and sedentary, 4) the precedence of beduinity, 5) the closeness of beduinity to goodness, 6) the closeness of beduinity to courage ... 9) *'aṣabīya* and genealogy, 10) *'aṣabīya* and leadership ... 20) that the Arabs are a natural people.

25 For instance, by a certain Buqqīnī, the author of an epitome of Ibn al-Khaṭīb's *Iḥāṭa*, quoted in Aḥmad Bābā, *Nayl*, p. 169.

26 Ibn al-Aḥmar, *Mustauda' al-'alāma*, p. 64.

27 Sakhāwī, *Ḍau'*, vol. 4, p. 147.

28 The text of Ibn Khaldūn's *ijāza* to Ibn Ḥajar is reproduced in facsimile in H. Ritter, 'Autographs in Turkish Libraries', in *Oriens*, 6(1953), p. 83.

29 Ibn Ḥajar, *Raf' al-'iṣr 'an quḍāt Miṣr*, vol. 2, p. 347, and cf. the praise of Ibn 'Ammār quoted in Sakhāwī, *Ḍau'*, vol. 4, p. 149.

30 Ibn Ḥajar, *Inbā' al-ghumr bi-abnā' al-'umr*, vol. 2, p. 340.

31 M. Bencheneb, 'Étude sur les personnages mentionnés dans l'Idjaza du Cheikh 'Abd El Qādir El Fāsī', in *Proceedings of the 14th Congress of Orientalists* (Algiers-Paris, 1908), vol. 3, p. 38.
32 A. Abdesselem, *Les historiens Tunisiens des XVIIe, XVIIIe, et XIXe siècles* (Paris, 1973), p. 464.
33 Benchekroun, *La vie intellectuelle marocaine sous les Merinides* pp. 356-7.
34 Abdesselem, *Les historiens Tunisiens*, pp. 249, 263.
35 Qalqashandī, *Khilāfa*, vol. 2, pp. 255-6.
36 Maqrīzī, *Al-Mawā'iẓ wal-i'tibār bi-dhikr al-khiṭaṭ wal-āthār*, (Būlāq, A. H. 1270), vol. 2, p. 1 90.
37 *Kashf aẓ-ẓunūn* (Istanbul, 1943), vol. 2, p. 1124.
38 Sakhāwī, *Ḍau'*, vol. 4, p. 146.
39 Nassar, *La pensée réaliste d'Ibn Khaldūn*, p. 224.

BIBLIOGRAPHICAL ORIENTATIONS

A full bibliographical guide to the study of Ibn Khaldūn is virtually coextensive with a bibliography of Arab-Islamic culture and history, a very great many of whose motifs, instants, sciences, and episodes are very present in the work of Ibn Khaldūn. This cannot be provided by the present bibliographical notes, which will concentrate on Ibn Khaldūn's text and on studies devoted specifically to this text.

There is one full critical study of the literature on Ibn Khaldūn, including the translations of his work, which is my *Ibn Khaldūn in Modern Scholarship: A Study in Orientalism* (London, 1980). This contains a reasoned bibliography as part 4 of the book which cites over 850 items and which was intended to have been exhaustive up till the middle of 1979 as an Ibn Khaldūn bibliography could ever be. Part VI.A of the bibliography contains items about the cultural and political contexts of Ibn Khaldūn studies. The bibliography was printed in a slightly different form in *The Maghreb Review*, 5/2(1980).

There are two basic editions of the *Muqaddima*, that of Quatremère (3 vols., Paris, 1858), and that of Hūrīnī as the first volume of *Kitāb al-'Ibar* (7 vols., Būlāq A. H. 1284). Neither of these is a truly scientific edition of the work, and the edition produced in four volumes by 'A. Wāfī (Cairo, 1956 ff.) is a collation of the two above editions with the addition of punctuation. Most editions on the market are pirated versions of the Hūrīnī text, including the very common and very commonly pirated vocalized edition of Beirut, 1900.

The basic edition of *Kitāb al-'Ibar* as a whole is that of Hūrīnī cited above. The edition of Y. A. Dāghir (7 vols., Beirut, 1956 ff.) is really the Būlāq edition, which was very hastily but very amply provided with division into paragraphs, with punctuation, and with misprints. The most valuable asset of Dāghir's effort, however, is the provision of indexes of subject, proper names, places, books mentioned or quoted, verses of the Koran, and (very arbitrarily) terminology.

Ibn Khaldūn's autobiography is very often printed along with editions of the *Muqaddima* and invariably at the conclusion of *Kitāb al-'Ibar*. There is one scientific edition by M. b. Tāwīt aṭ-Ṭanjī, *At-Ta'rīf bi Ibn Khaldūn wa riḥlatuhu gharban wa sharqan* (Cairo, 1370/1951). This same scholar also produced an edition of Ibn Khaldūn's tract on sūfism, *Shifā' as-sā'il li tahdhīb al-masā'il* (Istanbul,

1958). Another edition of the same work was published in Beirut in the same year (1958) by I. A. Khalifé. Ibn Khaldūn's youthful epitome of Rāzī's theological tract has been edited by L. Rubio: *Lubāb al-muḥaṣṣal fī uṣūl* ad-din (Tetouan, 1952). The other works of our author no longer seem to be extant.

The best translation of the *Muqaddima* is still that of W. M. de Slane, *Les Prolégomènes d'Ibn Khaldoun* (3 vols., Paris, 1863), which shows remarkable sensitivity to Ibn Khaldūn's style, to his metaphor, and to his terminology. Not so sensitive or reliable are the more recent French translation of V. Monteil (3 vols., Paris, 1967), and the English translation of F. Rosenthal (3 vols., Princeton, 1958). Both evince a systematic misreading of Ibn Khaldūn's text and hence constitute systematic distortions of his terminology and of his arguments in what appears a literalist translation devoid of 'subjectivity'. The saving grace of the Rosenthal translation is that it is provided with an excellent index along with copious notes to the text on persons mentioned, books quoted, and the like. There is an abridgment of Rosenthal's translation by N. J. Dawood (London, 1967), and translations of the integral text of the *Muqaddima* into Turkish, Farsi, Hebrew, Hindi, Portuguese, Urdu, Hungarian and Russian.

There are numerous anthologies in various languages of Ibn Khaldūn texts. The most balanced in Arabic is H. Pérès, *Ibn Khaldoun. Extraits choisis de la 'Muqaddima' et du 'Kitab al-'Ibar'* (Algiers, 1947). Perhaps more accessible is the anthology of texts from the *Muqaddima* alone by D. B. Macdonald, *A Selection from the Prolegomena of Ibn Khaldūn* (Leiden, 1905, 1948), which is provided with notes and a glossary. One selection of texts exists in English, although the translation is tendentious: C. Issawi, *An Arab Philosophy of History* (London, 1950). Better anthologies are two more recent French collections: G. Labica & J.-E. Bencheikh, *Le Rationalisme d'Ibn Khaldoun* (Paris, 1965), and A. Lahbabi, *Ibn Khaldūn* (Paris,1968). An anthology in German translation exists: A. Schimmel, Ibn Chaldun, *Ausgewählte Abschnitte aus der Muqaddima* (Tubingen, 1951).

There are various translations of passages and sections from Ibn Khaldūn's historical narrative, and these are all cited in my Bibliography. Two pieces of work are noteworthy in the context of the text of Ibn Khaldūn: A. Jones of the Oriental Institute, Oxford, has produced a computer concordance of the second chapter of the *Muqaddima* (unpublished), and the late Father M. Allard of the Université St. Joseph in Beirut meted the punch card treatment to the *Muqaddima* as he had done to the Koran.

There are numerous general works on Ibn Khaldūn, in the form both of books and of articles. The best general introduction to Ibn Khaldūn's life and work in English is still N. Schmidt, *Ibn Khaldūn: Historian, Sociologist and Philosopher* (New York, 1930, 1967). The best Arabic introductions are 'A. Ḥilū, *Ibn Khaldūn: Mu'assis 'ilm al-ijtimā'* (Beirut, 1969) and M. 'A. 'Inān, *Ibn Khaldūn: Hayātuhu wa turāthuhu al-fikrī* (Cairo, 1932 and many subsequent editions). There is an English translation of 'Inān's book as *Ibn Khaldūn: His Life and*

Work (Lahore, 1941 and subsequent editions). One book in Russian and with an Arabic translation is also noteworthy in this context: S. Batsieva, *Istorikosotsiologlicheski traktat Ibn Khaldūna 'Muqaddima'* (Moscow, 1965), Arabic tr. by R. Ibrāhīm as *Al-'Umrān al-basharī fī muqaddimat Ibn Khaldūn* (Tunis-Libya, 1978).

There are three synthetic works on Ibn Khaldūn which are of outstanding value and do not simply reproduce the commonplace wisdom on the author. They are: M. K. Ayad, *Die Geschichts- und Gesellschaftslehre Ibn Ḫaldūns* (Stuttgart-Berlin, 1930), N. Nassar, *La pensée réaliste d'Ibn Khaldūn* (Paris, 1967), and M. 'A. Al-Jabirī, *Al-'Aṣabīya wad-daula: Ma'ālim naẓarīya khaldūnīya fit-tārīkh al-Islāmī* (Casablanca, 1971). The last mentioned work has this advantage over the two others (and, indeed, over the great bulk of Ibn Khaldūniana): that it treats Ibn Khaldūn's thought as something whose bearings are to be found in Arab-Islamic culture rather than in a 'universal' intellectual history comprising mankind. There are also two articles of very particular interest: W. Sharāra, 'Al-Muqaddima, at-tārīkh, wa jasad as-sulṭān al-mumtali', in *Dirasat 'Arabīya,* 13/3 (1977), pp. 126 ff., and M. A. Al-'Ālim, 'Muqaddimat Ibn Khaldūn Madkhal ibistimūlūji', in *Al-Fikr Al-'Arabī,* 1/6(1978), pp. 35 ff.

All these works deal almost exclusively with the *Muqaddima* and there is no integrative study of Ibn Khaldūn's historical narrative. A. Oumil's *L'Histoire et son discours* (Rabat, 1979) makes a move in this direction, while P. von Sivers' *Khalifat, Königtum, und Verfall* (Munich, 1968) attempts an identification of the main historical units in *Kitāb al-'Ibar* but has the merit of intention rather than success, adopting too facile a view of the manner in which Ibn Khaldūn read his age. A closer study of the notion of 'people' in Ibn Khaldūn is that of N. Nassar in *Mafhūm al-umma bain ad-dīn wat-tārīkh* (Beirut, 1978), pp. 107 ff. W. J. Fischel's *Ibn Khaldūn in Egypt* (Berkeley-Los Angeles, 1967) attempts to study the sources of Ibn Khaldūn's treatment of non-Islamic peoples.

The *Muqaddima* has been regarded by some commentators as constituting a philosophy of history. The classical statement of this position is A. von Kremer, 'Ibn Chaldun und seine Culturgeschichte der islamischen Reiche', in *Sitzungsberichte der Kaiserlichen Akademie der Wissenschaften - Philosophisch-historische Klasse* (Vienna), 43(1879), pp. 581 ff., with an English translation by S. Khuda Bukhsh printed in *Islamic Culture,* 1(1927), pp. 567 ff., and in Kremer, *Contributions to the History of Islamic Civilization* (Calcutta, 1929 ff.), vol. 2, pp. 201 ff. There are two other noteworthy contributions in the same vein, the first being a comprehensive statement of the standard position on the matter: A. Bombaci, 'La dottrina storiografica di Ibn Ḫaldūn', in *Annali della scuola normale superiore di Pisa,* 15/ 3-4(1946), pp. 150 ff., and M. Talbi, *Ibn Khaldūn et l'histoire* (Tunis, 1973).

With regard to the study of Ibn Khaldūn in relation to his culture, the two main interpretive strands attach him to one of the poles of the opposition imagined by orientalists between Reason and Belief in Arab-Islamic culture. In the case of Reason, he is regarded as a Philosopher, in that of Belief, as a Jurist. The classical statement of the former tendency is M. Mahdī, *Ibn Khaldūn's Philosophy of History. A Study in the Philosophical Foundations of the Science of Culture* (London and Chicago, 1957). The equally classical statement of the second position is that of H. A. R. Gibb, 'The Islamic Background of Ibn Khaldūn's Political Theory', in *Bulletin of the School of Oriental and African Studies*, 7(1933–5), pp. 23 ff., reprinted in *idem., Studies in the Civilization of Islam* (London, 1962), pp. 166 ff. Both produced a numerous progeny. Of particular note is the fertile but totally misdirected discussion in M. Hodgson, *The Venture of Islam* (Chicago, 1974), vol. 2, pp. 478 ff.

Of the relation between Ibn Khaldūn and philosophy, two articles are worthy of note 'A. Badawī, 'Ibn Khaldūn wa Arisṭū', in *A'māl mahrajān Ibn Khaldūn* (Cairo, 1962), pp. 152 ff., and S. Batsieva, 'Uchenie o "dvoistvennoi istine" Averroesa-Ibn Khalduna' in *Palestinskii Sbornik*, 19/82(1969), pp. 149 ff. (with a German summary on p. 158, and an Arabic translation in *idem., Naẓarīyāt Ibn Khaldūn*, tr. R. Ibrāhīm (Tunis, 1974), pp. 57 ff.). With regard to the 'classification of sciences', there is the interesting study of A. Lakhssassi, 'Ibn Khaldūn and the Classification of Sciences', in *The Maghreb Review*, 4/1(1979), pp. 21 ff. Also worthy of mention here is S. van den Bergh, *Umriss der mohammedanischen Wissenschaften nach Ibn Khaldūn*, (Leiden, 1912).

On Ibn Khaldūn and ṣūfī thought, see the old study of H. Frank, *Beitrag zur Erkenntnis des Sufismus nach Ibn Ḫaldūn* (Leipzig, 1884), as well as the following: M. Syrier, 'Ibn Khaldūn and Islamic Mysticism', in *Islamic Culture*, 21(1947), pp. 264 ff., S. Batsieva, 'Shifā' as-sā'il: traktat Ibn Halduna o sufizm', in *Sbornik v tshest J. P. Petrushevskogo* (Moscow, 1968), pp. 40 ff. (Arabic translation in *Naẓarīyāt Ibn Khaldūn*, pp. 95 ff.), and M. Mahdi, 'The Book and the Master as Poles of Cultural Change in Islam', in S. Vyronis (ed.), *Islam and Cultural Change in the Middle Ages* (Wiesbaden, 1975), pp. 3 ff. As for Ibn Khaldūn's religious thought, one book can be consulted: I. Saade, *El pensamiento religioso de Ibn Jaldūn* (Madrid, 1973). One can also read, with much profit, G. Labica's *Politique et religion chez Ibn Khaldun*, Algiers, n.d. [1968].

The bulk of Ibn Khaldūniana has, unfortunately, been devoted to a 'universalist' conception of Ibn Khaldūn as a thinker whose importance resides in having been the 'father of sociology', the 'father of economics', and similar spurious historical (and conceptual) constructions. The classic representatives of the sociologization of Ibn Khaldūn are G. Bouthoul, *Ibn Khaldoun, sa philosophie sociale* (Paris, 1930) and R. Maunier, *Mélanges de sociologie nord-Africaine* (Paris, 1930). On economics, see S. Mahmassani, *Les idées économiques d'Ibn Khaldoun* (Lyon, 1932), and J. Spengler, 'Economic Thought in Islam: Ibn Khaldūn', in *Comparative Studies in Society and History*, 6(1963–4), pp. 268 ff. In a more properly historical context, Ibn Khaldūn's ideas on the economy are taken up in G.-H. Bousquet, 'L'économie politique non Europeano-Chrétienne: l'exemple de Dimachqī', in *Rev. d'histoire économique et sociale*, 35(1957), pp.

8 ff. As for the tendency which sees in Ibn Khaldūn's observations on the contemporary Maghreb a sociology and political economy of medieval North Africa, the classical and most integrative statement is in Y. Lacoste, *Ibn Khaldoun; Naissance de l'histoire passée du tiers-monde* (Paris, 1966).

Representative articles of newer trends in Ibn Khaldūn studies are published among the papers of the Ibn Khaldūn conference held in Tunis in February 1980, printed as a special issue of *Al-Ḥayat al-thaqāfiya*, 5/9 (May–June, 1980). This special issue also contains a bibliography of works on Ibn Khaldūn since 1956, which includes 339 items in the alphabetical order of authors.

ADDENDUM TO THE 2003 IMPRESSION

It is perhaps inevitable that much has been written about Ibn Khaldūn in the twenty years that have elapsed since the publication of this book, and there is indeed a case that bibliography of its predecerror, *Ibn Khaldūn in Modern Scholarship* (1981), should be supplemented and also completed by the inclusion of writings that I had not noted and registered at the time of writing. Such work is beyond my capacities at present. I have opted to take note, in the spirit of this "bibliographic orientation", of what I consider to have been particularly important for the analytical and historical study of our author, it being my judgement that the study of Ibn Khaldūn in the spirit advocated in this book still falls short of constituting a critical mass that might place Khaldunian studies on a firm footing, wary of anachronism.

First, to textual matters. An ethical and pietistic manual for the guidance of qadis, *Muzīl al-malām ʿan ḥukkām al-anām*, has been plausibly attributed to Ibn Khaldūn, and is thought to have been composed in Cairo during one of the periods in which he had been stripped of the qadiship. This work was discovered at the Süleymaniye library in Istanbul and edited by Fu'ād ʿAbd al-Munʿim Aḥmad, and published in Riyad, A. H. 1417 [1996–97].

We owe some important translations to Abdesselam Cheddadi, who rendered creditably Ibn Khaldūn's *Autobiography* into French (*Le voyage d'Occident et d'Orient*, Paris, 1980), and made a fresh French translation of extracts from the *History* (*Peuples et nations du monde: Extraits des ʿIbar*, Paris, 1986, 1998). A full new French translation, very promising in the light of precedent, of the *Muqaddima* by A. Cheddadi is forthcoming in the Pléiade edition, in addition to comprehensive notes and an apparatus criticus which are also intended to form the basis for the first scientific edition of the Arabic text, also by A. Cheddadi.

As for commentary and analysis, Cheddadi has over the two decades of engagement with Ibn Khaldūn written a number of essays that are worthy of note, some of which have been published together as *Ibn Khaldūn revisité* (Rabat, 1999). The major new contribution to the study of Ibn Khaldūn is undoubtedly that of ʿAbd Allāh al-ʿArwī (Abdallah Laroui), in his *Mafhūm al-ʿaql* (Casablanca and Beirut, 1996), ch. 4–8 inclusive, in which Ibn Khaldūn's manner of thinking is approached through a minute study of chapters in the *Muqaddima* treating of the economy. A number of other writings call upon the attention of the Ibn Khaldūn scholar: C. Fleischer, 'Royal Authority, Dynastic Cyclism, and "Ibn Khaldūnism" in Sixteenth-Century Ottoman Letters", in B. Lawrence (ed.), *Ibn Khaldūn and Islamic Ideology,* Leiden, 1984, pp. 46–68, F. Ghazoul, 'The metaphors of Historiography: A Study of Ibn Khaldūn's Historical imagination', in A. H. Green (ed.), *In Quest of an islamic Humanism. Arabic and Islamic Studies in Memory of Mohamed al-Nowaihy,* Cairo, 1984, pp. 48–61, and studies assembled in *Ibn Khaldūn and the Medieval Maghreb,* ed. M. Brett, London, 1998.

INDEX

Abbasids, 12, 17, 20, 21, 22, 23, 65, 69, 72, 76
'Abd Manāf, 20
'Abd ar-Raḥmān ad-Dākhil, 79
'Abd al-Wādids - see Zayyānids
'Abd al-Wāḥid, 1
Al-Ābilī, 3, 6, 41, 137, 145
Abū 'Abd Allāh, 3
Abū Bakr (Ḥafṣid caliph), 1
Abū Bakr Ibn 'Arabī, 106
Abū Bakr as-Ṣiddīq, 20
Abū Dāwūd, 80
Abū Ḥafṣ, 1
Abū Ḥammū, 3, 27, 41 n. 36, 42 n. 42, 122, 123
Abū 'Inān, 2, 3
Abū Sālim (Merinid monarch), 2
Abū Yazīd Ṣāḥib al-Ḥimār, 38, 134
Abū Zakarīya (Ḥafṣid caliph), 1
Abūl-'Abbās (Ḥafṣid caliph), 4
'Ād, 15
'Adnān, 17, 20, 37
Aghlabids, 34, 38, 64
Agriculture, science of, 98
Al-Aḥkām as-sulṭānīya, 77
Aḥmad Ibn al-Ṣiddīq, 123
Alchemy, 47, 59-60, 101-102, 104
Alexander of Aphrodisias, 97
Alexandrians, 18
'Alids, 21, 116
Almohads, 30, 31, 32, 39
Almoravids, 30, 39, 72, 145
'Amāliqa, 16
Analogy - *see qiyās*
Andalusians, 57, 58, 72, 75, 80
Anūshirwān, 13
Arabia, 17, 112
Arabic, 3, 4, 84, 89
Arabic, sciences of, 106-107, 119
Arabs, 4, 9, 10, 13-20, 24, 36-40, 61, 63, 64, 67, 69, 72, 77, 82, 88, 89, 97, 107, 125, 146
archē - see aṣl
Aristotle, 97, 98, 103, 105, 106, 109, 114
'Aṣabīya
as army, 42 n. 42
in the city, 65-66
composition of, 30, 31, 63, 64
grand, 65, 116
and lineage, 31
in the *Muqaddima*, 52
as power group, 26-27
and prophecy, 60, 69, 75-76
in the state, 32, 34-35, 46-47
(*see also badāwa, daula*, genealogy)
Ash'arism (and Ash'arites), 94, 105, 124 n. 85, 125
Asia, 17, 21
Aṣl, 45, 113-114, 117, 118
Astral spheres, 100-101
Astrology, 41 n. 29, n. 30, 81, 104, 122 n. 43
Augustus, 17, 19
Aus, 17
Averroes, 97, 98

Fiqh, 92
Al-Firghānī, 95
Fortune tellers, 60
Foucault, M. 130
Franks, 15, 19, 57
Fürstenspiegel, 27, 74, 131, 139, 140
Furū', 137

Galen, 58, 98
Gemeinschaft, 29
Genealogy, 14, 17-18, 19-20, 28-29, 32, 116
  of Arabs, 20, 37 n. 8, 116
  of Berbers, 36, 115, 134
  and historical succession, 23-24, 35
  and *naskh*, 110
  of Persians, 38 n. 11
  of tribes, 36
  of Turks, 40 n. 25
Ghāya, 48 (*see* teleology)
Ghazālī, 75, 92, 94, 95, 98, 102, 122 n. 56, 137
Gog and Magog, 15
Golan, 17
Gold trade, 134
Goliath, 116
Granadans, 66
Great Chain of Being, 59
Great lunar year, 33, 34
Greeks, 57, 74, 97

Ḥaḍāra, 26, 132-133, 138
  definition of, 51
  as telos of *'umrān*, 48-49
  and urban life, 48-49, 63, 68, 82-84
  (*see daula, 'umrān*)
Ḥadd, 125 n. 91
Ḥadīth, 80
Ḥafṣids, 1, 2, 3, 31
Ḥajjī Khalīfa, 142
Al-Ḥallāj, 96
Ḥām, 14, 109, 110
Ḥamdānids, 20
Ḥanafīs, 93
Hārūn al-Rashīd, 13
Hāshimids, 21
Hegel, 52, 57, 92, 121 n. 35, 130
Ḥisba, 77
Historical narrative - *see Khabar*
Historical writing
  and chronology, 18
  criteria of significance for, 9-10, 16, 19-20
  definition of, 9-10, 12, 15, 18, 22
  Ibn Khaldūn's criticism of, 108
  as narrative, 111-113
  object of, 9-10, 12-13
  subject-matter of, 9, 23-24, 26, 27, 111-113
  units of, 33-34, 36
Historiography, 11, 12, 20, 21, 25, 27, 28, 34, 108, 114, 129, 141, 156
History
  of Arabs,12-13
  of Berbers, 35, 36, 116
  of prophets, 114
  names, 134
  (*see also daula*, historical writing)
  of the world, 14, 15
Ḥijāb (of states), 78
Hijra, 18
Ḥikma, 124 n. 79
Ḥimyarites, 17
Holy fools, 60
Hume, D., 105

Ibn al-Aḥmar, 6, 141
Ibn 'Arabī, 4, 80, 95, 101
Ibn 'Arafa, 4
Ibn al-Athīr, 22
Ibn al-Azraq, 129, 139, 140, 142
Ibn Bishrūn, 47, 101
Ibn al-Ḥafīd, 137
Ibn Ḥajar, 6, 7, 142
Ibn al-Ḥājib, 137, 145-146 n. 18, 146 n. 20
Ibn al-Ḥakīm (Ibn Khaldūn's father-in-law), 1